# IVAN THE TERRIBLE
## Sergei Eisenstein

*Illustrations by Ivor Montagu
and Herbert Marshall*

*faber and faber*
LONDON · BOSTON

First published in French in 1965
as *Ivan le Terrible*
by l'Avant-Scène du Cinéma
First published in English translation in 1970
by Lorrimer Publishing Limited
This edition first published in 1985
Reissued in 1989
by Faber and Faber Limited
3 Queen Square London WC1N 3AU

Printed in Great Britain by
Richard Clay Ltd Bungay Suffolk
All rights reserved

Original French language edition © l'Avant-Scène
du Cinéma, 1965
English translation and description of the
action copyright © 1970
by Lorrimer Publishing Limited
This edition of the screenplay copyright © 1985
by Lorrimer Publishing Limited
Reissue © Faber and Faber Limited, 1989

*British Library Cataloguing in Publication Data
is available*

ISBN 0-571-12586-7

# CONTENTS

# A NOTE ON THIS EDITION

The script of *Ivan the Terrible* went through three different stages: first the scenario, that is Eisenstein's original concept of the film, which has already been published in English in a translation by Ivor Montagu and Herbert Marshall; secondly the shooting script, which in this case contains several important divergences from the scenario, notably in the placing of the scenes from Ivan's childhood (which in the scenario came right at the beginning) and the first scene at the Polish court (which came between Anastasia's poisoning and the scene beside her coffin in the cathedral); and thirdly a transcript of the actual film which was prepared from the final edited version. The present publication is based on a version published in French by *L'Avant-Scène du Cinéma*. Parts I and II of this were taken from a copy of the shooting script obtained from Moscow, which was then adapted to conform to the final version of the film. The English translation of this version, by A. E. Ellis, has once again been carefully revised and checked with a print of the film obtained from the British distributor, in order to make it as accurate a rendering as possible of the film which the English or American spectator will see on the screen. Part III is a translation of the scenario; as mentioned in the note on page 225, Eisenstein died before the shooting script for this part was completed.

Acknowledgments and thanks are due to *L'Avant-Scène du Cinéma* for providing stills, and to Contemporary Films Ltd, for providing stills and a print of the film.

# FROM HISTORY TO THE FILM*
## Rostislav Yurenyev

It was in 1940 that Eisenstein conceived the idea of making a film about Ivan IV. Eisenstein was fascinated by the historical film, as evidenced by his resoundingly successful *Alexander Nevsky*. In this genre, he could satisfy his passion for research, for the study of documents, for the analysis of facts. It was a field on which he could bring to bear his colossal erudition, his refined taste, his inexhaustible inventiveness. The basic essentials of the scenario were completed in the spring of 1941. In April, articles by Eisenstein appeared in *Izvestia, Vecherniaya Moskva* and the *Mosfilm* journal, giving the broad outlines of the projected film. In these articles, Eisenstein spoke out strongly against the particular image which artistic tradition has given to Ivan the Terrible, whether in sculpture, painting or literature.

'The things which have stuck in our memory are Ivan's seven wives with their bizarre names: Nagaya, Sobakina, etc.† . . . and also the memorable tales about the cruelty of this tsar, who as a child amused himself by throwing kittens down the long staircase in the Kremlin. It has been forgotten that, apart from his childhood and old age, this tsar also knew the height of his powers; that at the age of seventeen, of his own volition, he had himself crowned tsar and autocrat; that at twenty-two he took Kazan and forever set a limit to the domination of the Tartars. . . . I am studying very closely the contemporary accounts, historical works, popular songs and stories about Ivan the Terrible. The problem which I am faced with is to re-

---

* Rostislav Yurenyev is Professor of the History of Cinema at the Moscow Film Institute. This important study, from which the following extracts have been taken, appeared in the annual publication of the Soviet Academy of Sciences, *Voprossy Kinoiskusstva,* Moscow, 1961.

† Nagaya = 'naked', Sobakina = 'canine'. These names indicate that their bearers were hardly of noble origin, but it was the practice of the Russian tsars, up to the 18th century, to choose their wives for beauty alone, without worrying about where they came from.

create in the film the features of this 16th century "poet of the idea of a State" . . .' (Published in *Izvestia,* April 30th, 1941.)

Besides this problem of a general nature, which he defined so clearly and decisively, Eisenstein also had to face the more complex and subtle problems involved in bringing to life the hero and his period in a work of art. The director was consciously striving to take a new step forward, to reach a higher level than that of the film *Alexander Nevsky.* . . . The scenario, written in a stylised representation of old Russian, in a rhythmic prose which is near to blank verse, is a remarkable work in itself which has still not been sufficiently studied, nor its merits truly appreciated. We may legitimately criticise the language, which is sometimes pretentious, and also the composition as being overloaded, too rich in incident (a fact which was to have fatal consequences later). But the admirable qualities of the scenario are revealed in the physical detail; in the visual impact of the characters; in the tense and dramatic qualities of the dialogue in which each line is striking and significant, expressing a thought, a state of mind, an idea, a character; and finally in the unfailing continuity of the whole, through which the central figure of the tsar is displayed, in conjunction with the collective image of the people aspiring to the unity and strength of a State.

Eisenstein used the style of high tragedy to represent the historic struggle which Ivan waged, without stopping to count the cost, against the reactionary boyars and the fragmentation of his country, and to create an intensely personal hymn to the idea of the State, of a strong, centralised power enabling the people to achieve national independence and progress.

The character of Ivan, portrayed by Cherkasov in a noble, formalised and solemn style, was undoubtedly modernised to a certain extent. In utilising passionate polemics in the tradition of Russian pre-revolutionary art . . . which treated Ivan as a 'manifestation of divine wrath', Eisenstein, who was convinced (together with a number of Soviet writers and scholars) of the progressive aspects of his hero's actions, toned down the historical contradictions, passed silently over the catastrophic situation of the peasantry, and Ivan's unsuccessful wars, and tried to justify his suspiciousness, his vindictiveness and his cruelty. But, as a creative genius, Eisen-

stein understood perfectly that it was impossible to lend verisimili-
tude to this complicated character without showing his interior
conflict, the struggles of his conscience. And, in composing his hymn
to the 'idea of a State', the director also showed the tragedy of
power. In the film, the central drama lies in the struggle between
Ivan and Euphrosyne Staritsky. It is not only the fact that Ivan
is struggling for the unity of Russia while Euphrosyne defends the
fragmentation of feudalism. No, the crucial point is that for her,
power is an end in itself, the fulfilment of all aspirations and the
subject of a morbid passion; for Ivan the Terrible, on the other
hand, power is only a means to an end. His aim lies higher, in the
creation of a 'great and powerful State', while power itself is no
more than a 'heavy load'. Ivan understands that only power —
firm and absolute power — will lead him to victory. But he also
understands that if he raises the heavy sword of power he will be
forced to let it fall again . . . and that in falling this sword will
wipe out friendship, his nearest and dearest, and his personal
happiness. It is this which is the tragedy of Ivan the Terrible. And
as all true tragedy brings catharsis, so Ivan will find his purification
in the accomplishment of an historic act : the creation of a powerful
state and Russia's breakthrough to the Baltic Sea.

Such, in its broad outlines, is the basic idea of the tragedy *Ivan
the Terrible*, an idea which Eisenstein pursued clearly and consis-
tently throughout his scenario. However, in the course of shooting,
this original conception was to undergo some important changes. . . .

The first part of *Ivan the Terrible* was given its first showing at
the beginning of 1945. . . . The admirable artistic qualities of the
film were highly appreciated. . . . And on January 27th, 1946, the
Stalin Prize, first class, was awarded to Eisenstein, Cherkasov,
Birman, Moskvin, Tisse and Prokofiev.

By this time, Eisenstein had already finished the second part,
which he had begun in mid-February 1945. The film was submitted
to the artistic Council of the Ministry of Cinematography, and
approved by them. . . . On September 4th, 1946, the Central
Committee of the Party published its decision 'Concerning the
film *A Great Life*'.* Starting from the principles of socialist realism,

---

* *A Great Life*: a film by Leonid Lukov (1910-1963). The decision concerned
the second part of the film, the first part of which had appeared in 1940.
The second, which was made in 1946, was not shown publicly until 1958.

underlining the problems of the educative role which was incumbent on the cinematic art, the Central Committee's decision gave a searching criticism of the weaknesses of the Soviet cinema. But at the same time certain specific criticisms were made of the films and their authors, reflecting subjective opinions and typical of the period of the cult of personality.

The report included, for instance, the following statement : ' In the second part of the film *Ivan the Terrible*, the director Eisenstein displayed his ignorance of historic fact by showing Ivan the Terrible's progressive army of oprichniks as a band of degenerates in the style of the American Ku-Klux-Klan; and Ivan the Terrible, a man of great willpower and strong character, as a weak and feeble being, a sort of Hamlet.'

There are in fact a number of debatable points in Eisenstein's historical conception; his film does not give a complete and accurate image of the period of Ivan IV; it expresses above all Eisenstein's point of view, as an artist, about this period. But the tendency to see the character of Ivan the Terrible purified of all contradictions and stripped of all doubts, the unreservedly positive appreciation of his activities and, above all, of those of the oprichniks, could have led to a modernisation of the character, to a partial selection of facts. . . . In his article ' Concerning the film *Ivan the Terrible* ' (a letter to the editors of the journal *Kultura i Zhizn*), Eisenstein wrote :

> ' We all know that Ivan the Terrible was a man of great willpower and strong character. But does this exclude the presence of certain doubts in particular cases? It is hard to believe that this man, who was carrying out actions which were unheard of and unprecedented in his time, never reflected on his choice of means, never hesitated over the question of how to act in a particular instance. . . . Is it in these hesitations and doubts, or rather in the fact that he surmounted them without compromise, in the implacable continuity of his actions, that we find the essence of this powerful figure of the 16th century? ' (October 1946.)

Both the scenario and the second part of the film prove incontrovertibly that Eisenstein had never harboured the intention of making Ivan's doubts and hesitations the essential theme of his

12

film. By 'Shakespearising' his hero, by making him pass through the crucible of suffering and psychological duality, he intended to underline further his strength of character and his inflexibility. It would have been both inaccurate and artistically unconvincing to show Ivan the Terrible meting out justice to the boyars and to his friends and relations without a shadow of hesitation. Eisenstein very rightly saw the grandeur of Ivan's character, not in the absence of any hesitations, but in his ability to overcome them. . . .

With all the sincerity and compassion that he was capable of, Eisenstein tried to re-examine the contradictions in his film, and became more and more imbued with the necessity of bringing his work to a conclusion. But it was not an easy task to correct, re-arrange and re-edit the film. Eisenstein obstinately sought for a composition which would enable him to show the conspiracy of the boyars, their links with the reactionary expatriot prince, Kurb-sky, and through him with the king of Poland, Sigismund Augustus; then the collapse of Russia's internal enemies and the victory over her external ones, with the breakthrough to the Baltic Sea.

Such a harmonious composition, conforming to the contemporary view of history, could only be achieved at the expense of certain sacrifices : the rejection of the scenes of Ivan's childhood, the extensive editing of a series of scenes which had already been shot, and finally the abandoning of the scenes envisaged for part three and not yet shot — the Novgorod cycle and the episode at Windsor Castle. Eisenstein was very fond of the childhood scenes and the Novgorod episodes, which were interesting in their conception and had the tension and passion of a real tragedy. In spite of this, he was prepared to abandon them for the sake of the whole, for the sake of the film's future.

There was only one thing that he could not sacrifice — the desire to create the character of Ivan the Terrible through the techniques of high tragedy, to reveal the contradictions in his make-up between the personal and the general, between will and duty, cruelty and humanity. . . .

Again and again, Eisenstein immersed himself in contemporary accounts, returned to historians, writers, art and folklore. He listened with concentrated attention to the opinions of anyone who was bold enough to give him advice. . . .

He died during the night of February 11th, 1948. His friends and

13

pupils were preparing to celebrate his fiftieth birthday. Instead of having a party, they had to attend his funeral. And there can have been few amongst those gathered round Eisenstein's coffin who were not thinking of the supreme duty of the living towards the dead — the duty of Soviet cineastes to complete his film and show it to the world.

But what the author himself had not succeeded in doing, his friends were unable to accomplish either. In 1958, the Soviet government made the wise decision to release the film as Eisenstein had made it, with all its contradictions and its remarkable achievements. This decision was an enormous contribution to the development of the art of cinema, both in the U.S.S.R. and throughout the world.

The complex and contradictory personality of Ivan the Terrible will be the subject of studies, historical researches and artistic discussions for a long time to come. Eisenstein's interpretation of it may be considered debatable and incomplete. The criticism of not having sufficiently brought out the progressive aspect of Ivan's achievements may be replaced by its opposite — that of having tried to modernise and embellish the picture of Ivan too much. Historians will no doubt find it fertile ground for discussion. But for all of us, without exception and without doubt, one thing will remain obvious, and that is the immense artistic value of Eisenstein's work and his incomparable mastery. . . .

One remarkable feature of the second part of *Ivan the Terrible* is that it contains a scene which is unique in Eisenstein's work, filmed in colour — the banquet scene.

Inevitably, this scene is also the subject of studies and commentaries. When he was working on his last article ' Colour film ', Eisenstein intended to dwell upon it at length and in detail. The manuscript bears the mark of his illness where a heart attack halted him in the middle of a line. Regaining control of himself, Eisenstein pencilled round the passage and continued his work. He never finished it. The article ends with the sentence : ' I shall now briefly explain the process by which the coloured episode of the film *Ivan the Terrible* is constructed. . . .' These words were written on February 10th, 1948. But what Eisenstein the theoretician did not have time to explain, Eisenstein the creator had already accomplished. . . .

The second part of the film is also a rich source of material for studying the techniques which Eisenstein used in working with his actors. He had long since abandoned the theory and practice of type-casting, but had been able to retain those things which derived from it — the science of expressiveness, the art of discovering a physique which was capable of expressing the state, the character, even the social class of a man. . . . In *Ivan the Terrible* (and in the second part in particular), Eisenstein moves far beyond the direct, outwardly imposed style of the actors in *Alexander Nevsky*. Cherkasov is discontented with his performance in the role of Ivan, he is rather reticent in speaking about it and one can even detect a hint of irritation in what he writes. Personally I think he is splendid. . . . Generally speaking, in the second part of the film, the quality of the acting reaches a very high level. The individuality of each actor is revealed in an entirely new fashion, with extraordinary expressive force. The style of acting — slightly heightened, emphatic, at times outwardly conventional — in no way detracts from its psychological depth, from the delicacy of the nuances or from the logical development of the characters. Eisenstein's chosen genre, that of high tragedy, demanded precisely this style. . . .

Let us repeat once more : Eisenstein's historical conception is contradictory; it can and should provoke discussion and critical examination. But the enormous talent of this classic master of the Soviet cinema is displayed in this film with such force and brilliance that its influence will remain beneficent and irresistible.

*The following are two eyewitness accounts, one by Mikhail Romm
(director of* Nine Days of One Year*), who was a member of the
artistic Council which judged the second part of Eisenstein's film,
the other by Nikolai Cherkasov, who was the principal actor. The
facts which they relate are strictly identical, yet seen from totally
different points of view. Where one sees a masterpiece, the other
can only find an ' accumulation of errors '. There is a difference in
tastes here, perhaps, but it is the difference in dates which is significant. Mikhail Romm's article was published in 1957; Cherkasov's
account is taken from his book,* Notes of a Soviet Actor, *which
appeared in 1953, shortly after the death of Stalin. Better than
any commentary, the juxtaposition of these two pieces underlines
the force of the unmentionable ' malaise ' which Romm speaks
about.*

## THE SECOND SUMMIT
### Mikhail Romm

Yesterday I saw again the second part of *Ivan the Terrible*, the
last film of Sergei Mikhailovich Eisenstein.

I have seen this film several times. Many years ago, Sergei Mikhailovich showed me the sequences of the splendid scene where
Ivan passes through the cathedral with the oprichniks. It was an
endless procession. Sergei Mikhailovich had used the montage
method, shooting the scene from scores of different angles, taking
scores of different shots. The viewing lasted almost an hour. For
almost an hour, sombre silhouettes passed between the pillars; the
assassin ran from one pillar to another, hiding; Kadochnikov
glanced anxiously around him and the sombre silhouettes continued to file past, heightening the anguish of the crime to come.

Then I saw the rushes, and afterwards the already finished
film when it was viewed by the artistic Council.

The film was banned.

Three years ago I saw it again. It was almost immediately after
the death of Stalin, and it was only then that I understood that the

second part of *Ivan the Terrible* is the second summit of the achievement of our master, S. Eisenstein. The first summit is known to everyone. It is *The Battleship Potemkin*. . . .

Ivan the Terrible. . . . Eisenstein was fascinated by the character. Having himself known all the bitterness of disgrace, he felt strongly attracted by Ivan's personality — capricious, hysterical, cruel, inconsistent and neurotically suspicious. The tyrant's character hypnotically obsessed his thoughts. Everyone knows of the unbelievable scrupulousness with which the production was prepared. . . . Everything had been studied, composed, calculated in advance as precisely as possible. And in spite of this, the first part is no more than a sort of trial run, preceding the immense step forward of the second part. . . .

What distinguishes the first part from the second is neither the orchestral perfection of production techniques, nor the admirable completeness of each episode, nor the overwhelming expressiveness of the action, nor the editing, nor the frenetic rhythm, nor the counterpoint between image and sound — though all these aspects are more perfect in the second part. The two films differ in their internal theme. In the second part, at a time when Stalin's personality cult was at its most oppressive, Eisenstein dared to raise his hand against that cult.

The second part of *Ivan the Terrible* is a film about the tragedy of tyranny. It does not contain any open historical parallels, but the whole construction of the film suggests them, they form the context of practically every scene. Expressive to the point of being almost physically tangible, the atmosphere of murders, executions, disorders, anguish, cruelty, suspicion, trickery and treachery filled the first spectators of the film with a malaise bordering on panic, and one whose meaning they did not dare to put into words.

When the film was almost finished, a group of directors were called to the Ministry. ' Go and see Eisenstein's film,' we were told. ' There's going to be trouble. Help us to decide what to do.'

We saw it. And we felt the same dull anguish in the face of those alarming allusions. But Eisenstein affected an attitude of impertinent gaiety. He asked us : ' Well, what's the matter? What's wrong? What's troubling you? Tell me frankly.' But no one dared to tell him frankly that Ivan was a direct allusion to Stalin, Malyuta Skuratov to Beria, and the oprichniks to his acolytes. And

17

there were many other things which we felt but did not dare to express.

Eisenstein's impertinent air, the twinkle in his eye, his sceptical and defiant smile, showed us that he knew exactly what he was doing, that he had decided to stick his neck out. It was frightening.

The film was submitted to the artistic Council. Some were silent, others raised meaningless objections, half-heartedly voting against it. Then a member of the Council, a director, spoke up. With a charming, innocent smile he said: 'We also criticised the first part, and that has just received the Stalin Prize. Sergei Mikhailovich knows better than we do what he is doing; it is not for us to judge his work. I propose that the film be accepted.' The film was accepted.

A few days later there was a celebration at Cinema House, when the prizes of the previous year were presented, including that awarded to the first part of *Ivan the Terrible*. During the evening, Eisenstein was informed that the second part had been sent to the Kremlin. Half-an-hour later he was taken to hospital with a haemorrhage. It was there that he learned that his film had been banned. He received the news with unexpected calmness; he had foreseen it, he knew that it could not be otherwise.

This third and last blow was too much for Eisenstein's heart. He died a few days before his fiftieth birthday. Two days beforehand (he had already returned home), one of his friends telephoned him about organising the party which had been arranged for the occasion. He replied: 'Let us wait, otherwise things may turn out badly. It would never do if the hero of the occasion pegged out in the middle of it.'

He knew that he was going to die, and shortly before his death he discussed with Eduard Tisse the question of who could finish *Ivan*, who could shoot the third part of the film from his drawings and notes. But no one dared to embark upon that task.

Now, the second part has been released to the public. I see in it the second summit of Eisenstein's work. . . . Today, now that the era of the cult of personality is fading into history, the film no longer arouses the continuous flood of associations which it did formerly. One can watch it with a more objective eye. But it remains a great film.

Thus, at the end of his life, Eisenstein founded the bases of his

18

future biography. Formerly he used to say: 'I've missed my chance, I didn't die at the right time. What a monument you would have raised in my memory if I had died straight after *The Battleship Potemkin*! I've made a mess of my own biography. . . .'

(First published in 1957, reprinted in *Bessedy o Kino*, by M. I. Romm, Moscow, 1964.)


## INTERVIEW WITH STALIN
### Nikolai Cherkasov

This time, S. M. Eisenstein assumed the functions of scriptwriter, director, and to a certain extent designer. . . . Absorbed by his problems as director and designer, he was led to sacrifice the development of the subject, as everyone knows; as a scriptwriter, he proved unequal to the magnitude of his task.

Amongst ourselves, we recognised the faults (of the first part) of the film. . . . While working on the second part, S. M. Eisenstein accumulated more errors. . . . These errors were violently aggravated by the historically inaccurate picture of the progressive army of the oprichniks and by the distortion of the character of Ivan IV himself. . . . All these failings of the second part were justly criticised in principle in the historic decision of the C. C. of the C. P. of the U.S.S.R.,* which played an important role in the subsequent development of the Soviet cinema.

When the C.C.'s decision was published in the autumn of 1946, and its severe criticism of our work on the second part of *Ivan the Terrible* was known, I myself, as an actor, although in no way accused, accepted equal responsibility with the director. S. M. Eisenstein and myself wrote a letter to the Party concerning the errors which had been committed, and asking its help in correcting them.

Comrade Stalin decided that it would be possible to receive us. We were then given full opportunity to correct the second part of *Ivan the Terrible* . . . without any limits as to time or expense. S. M. Eisenstein was positively overjoyed at the prospect, and thought about it unceasingly. . . . His premature death prevented

---

* September 4th, 1946.

him from undertaking the task.

However, we wanted to finish the work, with the help of some director who was capable and worthy of the task, so as not to leave millions of spectators in ignorance as to the completion of the theme which had so felicitously been started in the first part. Some time later — in fact three years after the end of the shooting of the second part — I saw the film once more at the Ministry of the Cinema, in company with V. Petrov* whom I hoped would accept the task of finishing the film.

As we entered the viewing room, I thought that in spite of everything the material which we had filmed would move me, touch me, make me want to set to work again. But I experienced nothing of the sort. I watched the screen with a critical eye, and the errors of the film became more and more obvious to me. When the lights went up I looked at V. Petrov; our eyes met and we understood each other immediately : there could be no question of correcting the material we had just seen, we would have to re-shoot the whole of the second part.

*(The following account of the meeting with Stalin occurs in another chapter of the book.)*

[Our] meeting with J. V. Stalin took place on February 24th, 1947, when Josef Vissarionovich invited S. M. Eisenstein and myself to talk about the second part of the film *Ivan the Terrible*. We were due at the Kremlin at 11 o'clock (in the evening), but we were already in the waiting room half-an-hour beforehand. . . . Comrade J. V. Stalin was in his study together with Comrades V. M. Molotov and A. A. Zhdanov. . . . Josef Vissarionovich invited us to sit down at a long table; V. M. Molotov and A. A. Zhdanov sat on his right, myself with S. M. Eisenstein on his left.

' I received your letter,' J. V. began in a strictly official tone. ' I received it in November, but had to put off our meeting until now for lack of time. Admittedly, it would have been possible to reply by letter, but I considered that a personal conversation would be preferable. Well now, what do you intend to do with the film?'

We replied that as far as we could see our basic error had been to make the second part too long and then cut it into two distinct

---

* V. Petrov, director of *Peter the Great* and, later, *The Battle of Stalingrad*.

20

episodes (the second and third parts). In this way, the Livonian war, the defeat of the Livonian knights, the victorious breakthrough to the sea, that is to say the events for which the film had been conceived, could not be included in the second part. . . . Thus episodes which should have been secondary were given exaggerated emphasis. We added that we thought it would be possible to do something about the film, but that it would be necessary to cut the material already filmed unmercifully and shoot the scenes of the Livonian war.

In reply to our questions, Comrade J. V. Stalin made a whole series of extraordinarily valuable and interesting remarks about the era of Ivan the Terrible and the principles of the artistic represen-tation of historical figures. 'These figures,' he emphasised, 'must be shown with truth and forcefulness, and it is essential to preserve the style of the historical period.' A number of problems concerning the Soviet cinema were discussed during the conversation, and we were able once again to appreciate the vigilant attention with which Josef Vissarionovich had considered the problems of the cinematic art.

We mentioned the question of the time it would take to complete our film. J. V. said that in this field excessive haste was useless, and the essential thing was to make a film in the style of the period, one which conformed to historic truth. Only flawless films, he said, should be released. Our spectators had grown up, they had become more demanding and we should only show them works of art of the highest quality.

At the end of our conversation, J. V. asked how we intended to finish the film. I replied that, as in the original scenario, the film should end with the Livonian war and Ivan IV's victorious arrival at the sea: 'We have reached the sea, and here we will stay!' Comrade Stalin smiled and exclaimed cheerfully: 'Well . . . that is just what happened, and it was even better than that!' He ended the interview by wishing us complete success.

After leaving the Kremlin, we walked up and down Red Square for a long time, exchanging our impressions of this unforgettable meeting.

(*Zapiski sovetskogo aktera*, N. K. Cherkasov, Moscow, 1953; pp. 135, 138, 139 and 379-81.)

## CREDITS:

| | |
|---|---|
| Scenario and dialogue by | Sergei M. Eisenstein |
| Produced and directed by | Sergei M. Eisenstein |
| Associate director | V. Sveshnikov |
| Director of photography | Eduard Tisse (exteriors) |
| | Andrei Moskvin (interiors) |
| Music | Sergei Prokofiev |
| Lyrics | Vladimir Lugovsky |
| Conductor | A. Stasyevich |
| Assistants to the director | L. Indenbom, V. Kuznetsova, |
| | I. Bir, B. Bunayev |
| Cameraman | V. Dombrovsky |
| Assistant cameraman | F. Soluyanov |
| Sound recordists | V. Bogdankevitch, V. Volsky |
| Editor | Sergei M. Eisenstein |
| Assistants to the editor | E. Tobak, L. Indenbom |
| Décor | Y. Spinel (from sketches by |
| | Sergei M. Eisenstein) |
| Costume designer | Leonid Naumova (from |
| | sketches by Sergei M. |
| | Eisenstein) |
| Costume assistant | N. Buzina |
| Wardrobe | I. Raizman, M. Safonova |
| Make-up | V. Goryunov |
| Make-up assistant | E. Chakon |
| Props | V. Lomov |
| Production directors | A. Eidus, I. Soluyanov, I. Zakar |
| Floor secretary | L. Chedin |
| Supervisor of set-building | Y. Shakhporonov |
| Religious and historical consultant | Archpriest P. Tsvetkov |
| Choreographer (Part II) | R. Zakharin |

| | |
|---|---|
| PART I | |
| Produced in 1944 by | Alma-Ata Film Studio |
| Shooting begun | February 1st, 1943 |
| Length | 2,745 metres |
| Running time | 99 minutes |
| Process | Black and white |

| First shown | December 30th, 1944 at the Bolshoi Theatre in Moscow |
|---|---|
| General release in Russia | January 1945 |
| General release outside Russia | 1946 |

PART II

| Produced in 1946 by | Mosfilm Studio |
|---|---|
| Shot during | 1943–46 |
| Length | 2,737.7 metres |
| Running time | 90 minutes |
| Process | Black and white and Agfacolor |
| General release in Russia | September 1958 |
| General release outside Russia | 1959–60 |

*CAST:*

PART I

| Ivan the Terrible | Nikolai Cherkasov |
|---|---|
| Anastasia Romanovna, the Tsarina | Ludmila Tselikovskaya |
| Euphrosyne Staritsky, the Tsar's aunt | Serafima Birman |
| Vladimir Staritsky, her son | Pavel Kadochnikov |
| Prince Andrew Kurbsky | Mikhail Nazvanov |
| Boyar Fyodor Kolychev, subsequently Philip, Metropolitan of Moscow | Andrei Abrikosov |
| Pimen, Archbishop of Novgorod, sometime Metropolitan of Moscow | Alexander Mgebrov |
| Peter Volynets, his acolyte | Vladimir Balachov |
| Malyuta Skuratov | Mikhail Zharov |
| Alexey Basmanov | Amvrosy Buchma |
| Fyodor Basmanov, his son | Mikhail Kusnetzov |
| Kaspar von Oldenbock, Ambassador of the Livonian Order | S. Timoshenko |
| Nikola, a beggar simpleton | Vsevolod Pudovkin |
| The Archdeacon | Maxim Mikhailov |
| A Foreigner | A. Rumnev |

*Other speaking parts for which no actor's names are available:*
Demyan Teshata, a Staritsky bondsman
Osip Nepeya, the Tsar's ambassador to
  the English court

ADDITIONAL TO PART II
The young Ivan                            Eric Pyriev
King Sigismund of Poland                  Pavel Massalsky
*Other speaking parts for which no actor's names are available:*
Helena Glinskaya, Ivan's mother
Boyar Shuisky
Boyar Byelsky
Peninsky, an old Staritsky boyar
*Non-speaking parts for which no actor's names are available:*
Ambassador of the Hanseatic league
Engineer Rasmussen

ADDITIONAL TO PART III
Eustace, Ivan's confessor
Heinrich Staden, a German mercenary
Queen Elizabeth I of England
The German Ambassador and Jester at
  King Sigismund's court
Ambrosio, Kurbsky's scribe
Foma and Yeroma Chokhov, Russian
  gunners

# IVAN THE TERRIBLE

## Part I

### Ivan the Terrible

*Shot 1. The credits unfold against a background of black clouds driven before an approaching storm whilst a* Choir *sings, off.*

Choir *off* : ' A black cloud is forming
A bloody dawn approaching.
The boyars have hatched a treacherous plot
Against the Tsar's authority
Which they are now unleashing.'

*At the end of the credits the following title flashes across the screen :*

Title : This film tells the story of the man who was the first to unite our country four hundred years ago : the Archduke of Moscow who welded greedy, warring and divided principalities into a single, powerful State . . . a military leader who made the glory of Russian arms resound in the East as in the West . . . a sovereign who resolved his country's cruel dilemmas by having himself crowned the first Tsar of all the Russias.*

*Shot 2. The sound of the* Choir *fades out. Interior of the Dormition Cathedral.† High angle medium close-up of the Monomakh crown as all the cathedral bells ring out. This sound continues throughout most of the scene. (Still on page 1)*

*Shot 3. Medium close-up of the* Tsar's *regalia: the sceptre and orb.*

*Shot 4. Long shot of the cathedral: the coronation is in pro-*

---

* Ivan IV (1530-1584) known as the Terrible (or more exactly the Formidable). The Russian word, *grozny*, means respectable, respected, or formidable.
† This is the Uspensky Sobor, a cathedral in the Kremlin. This coronation scene took place on January 16th, 1547. The crown was that of Vladimir II, known as the Monomakh (1053-1126).

*gress.* PIMEN, *Metropolitan Archbishop of Moscow, enters through the monumental Holy Door. Like those attending on him he wears full ceremonial robes. He halts and raises his arms to bless the congregation as he advances towards camera.* [*Shot 5. Close-up of him.*]*

PIMEN : In the name of . . .

*Shot 6. Long shot of the congregation in the cathedral, which bows and crosses itself.*

PIMEN *continues off* : . . . the Father, the Son and the Holy Ghost . . .

*Shot 7. Long shot, slightly high angle, of the congregation standing, seen between the columns of the Sanctuary.*

PIMEN *continues off* : . . . the Archduke and Sovereign Ivan Vassilievich . . .

*Shot 8. Medium close-up of* PIMEN.

PIMEN *continues* : . . . is crowned Tsar of Moscow.

*Shot 9. A group of* FOREIGN AMBASSADORS *are seen in long shot, wearing impressive white ruffs. They follow the ceremony from a corner of the cathedral.*

[*Shot 10. Shot of a member of the congregation gazing at the scene through square-lensed spectacles.*] *

PIMEN *continues off* : . . . anointed of God . . .

*Shot 11. Long shot, slightly high angle, of the listening congregation.*

PIMEN *off* : . . . Tsar of Moscow . . .

*Shot 12. Resume on* PIMEN.

PIMEN : . . . absolute sovereign of all the Russias. *The bells stop ringing.*

*Shot 13. Medium shot of three of the* FOREIGN AMBASSADORS; *they exchange remarks. The* CHOIR *starts to sing quietly off.*

A FOREIGN AMBASSADOR *turning to his neighbour* : The Archduke of Moscow has no right to the title of Tsar !

*Shot 14. Medium close-up of another group of* FOREIGN AMBASSADORS.

A FOREIGN AMBASSADOR *murmuring to his neighbour* : Europe will never recognise him as Tsar. *(Still on page 1)*

*Shot 15. Medium close-up of the* LIVONIAN AMBASSADOR,

---

* This shot did not appear in the copy of the film obtained from the English distributor, but was mentioned in Eisenstein's original screenplay.

Kaspar von Oldenbock, *and his young* Secretary. *(Still on page 1) Hymns continue off.*

Livonian Ambassador : If he is powerful enough . . . she will recognise him.

A Foreign Ambassador *off* : They say . . .

*Shot 16. Another shot of the group of* Foreign Ambassadors.

Foreign Ambassador *continuing off* : . . . some of his own subjects aren't too pleased about the coronation.

Another Foreign Ambassador : It's not surprising certain lordly personages aren't delighted. *As he speaks, the* Second Foreign Ambassador *glances significantly at a corner of the cathedral.*

*Shot 17. He continues off, whilst the camera cuts to a medium low angle shot of* Euphrosyne Staritsky, *the* Tsar's *aunt, and her son* Vladimir Staritsky. *The latter is about twenty and looks retarded. The mother looks very sour. She is surrounded by bearded* Boyars.

Foreign Ambassador *off* : That's the Grand Duke's cousin, Vladimir Staritsky . . .

*Shot 18. Close-up of* Euphrosyne *with* Vladimir *looking over her shoulder. (Still on page 1)*

Foreign Ambassador *continuing off* : . . . with his mother. Ivan's coronation bars their road to the throne of Moscow.

*Shot 19. Close-up of* Vladimir, *who looks vacantly round.*

*Shot 20. Medium low angle shot of two enormous, luxuriantly bearded* Boyars : Zakharin *and* Glinsky.

Another Foreign Ambassador *off* : But it also seems . . .

*Shot 21. Medium close-up of one of the* Boyars.

Foreign Ambassador *continuing off* : . . . that Ivan is not without allies.

*Shot 22. Medium close-up of an old* Nurse *in charge of two very pretty young* Girls.

Foreign Ambassador *continuing after an interval, off* : Those are the relatives of the Archduke's fiancée.\*

*Shot 23. Medium shot of* Anastasia, *the fiancée, surrounded by her maids-in-waiting.*

---

\* In historic fact, the fiancée had not yet been chosen from the thousand selected virgins — daughters of boyars, merchants, peasants. It was after his coronation that Ivan IV decided on Anastasia Romanovna, who came from an ancient family of boyars, the Zakharin-Kochkin. She was very beautiful and the Tsar nicknamed her his ' little heifer '.

*Shot 24. Medium close-up of* ANASTASIA, *her eyes cast down.*
LIVONIAN AMBASSADOR *off* : Not the Archduke's . . .

*Shot 25. Close-up of* ANASTASIA *raising her eyes. (Still on page 1)*
LIVONIAN AMBASSADOR *continuing off* : . . . but the Tsar's. For he is now Tsar !

*Shot 26. Long shot from the altar of the procession of* PRIESTS, *headed by* PIMEN. *The music swells up as it makes its way down the central nave and comes to a halt round a dais at the end. Camera tilts up slightly as* PIMEN *climbs onto the dais and stops.* IVAN *advances towards him, back to camera, supported by the two princes,* ANDREW KURBSKY *and* FYODOR KOLYCHEV. *They come to a halt, bow to* IVAN, *then withdraw.*

*Shot 27. Low angle medium shot of* PIMEN *standing over* IVAN, *who is back to camera.* PIMEN *turns to the right to receive the Monomakh crown, which is brought to him ceremoniously on a cushion. He blesses it.*

*Shot 28. Close-up of* PIMEN's *hands blessing the crown, then raising it very cautiously.*

*Shot 29. Low angle medium close-up of* PIMEN, *raising his eyes to heaven and kissing the crown.*

*Shot 30. Medium shot of* PIMEN *holding the crown. He slowly makes the sign of the cross with it in front of the motionless* IVAN.

*Shot 31. Medium close-up of* EUPHROSYNE, *watching the ceremony warily, her arm round* VLADIMIR.

*Shot 32. Medium close-up of* IVAN *from behind. His arms rise into view holding the crown and he lowers it onto his head.*

*Shot 33. Medium close-up of* ANASTASIA, *her eyes shining.*

*Shot 34. Close-up of the Monomakh crown on* IVAN's *head.*

*Shot 35. Medium shot of* PIMEN *from the side, as he takes the sceptre from a cushion presented to him by two* PRIESTS *on the right. As he takes it he turns towards* IVAN, *off-screen. (Still on page 1)* IVAN's *hand comes into shot.*
PIMEN : O . . . Tsar, the Lord's anointed, accept from Him this sceptre . . .

*Shot 36. Medium close-up of* IVAN's *hand, each finger of which is beringed, and* PIMEN's *hands holding the sceptre.* IVAN's *hand takes the sceptre, while* PIMEN *continues.*

PIMEN *off* : . . . Accept it, my son.

> *Shot 37. New medium shot of* PIMEN. *He takes the orb from the two* PRIESTS *who have come round to stand on the left, and turns towards* IVAN.

PIMEN : Accept this orb from God.

> IVAN's *hand enters the frame to take the orb.*
>
> *Shot 38. Close-up of* PIMEN's *hands holding the orb.* IVAN's *hand receives the orb and takes it slowly out of frame to the left.*

PIMEN : Accept it, my son.

> *Shot 39. Close-up of the crown (as shot 34).* IVAN *bows his head slightly.*
>
> *Shot 40. Medium close-up of* PIMEN *raising his hands to bless* IVAN.

PIMEN *making the sign of the cross with both hands* : In the name of God . . . now and forever. Amen.

> *Shot 41. Medium close-up of an enormous, black-bearded* ARCHDEACON. *He intones in a deep bass voice, holding up a ceremonial scarf and making the sign of the cross.*

ARCHDEACON : To the Tsar, the Lord's anointed . . .

> *Shot 42. A closer shot of the* ARCHDEACON.

ARCHDEACON : Ivan Vassilievich . . .

> *Shot 43. Close-up of the* ARCHDEACON's *face as he continues to chant.*
>
> *Shot 44. Medium close-up of* IVAN *from behind,* PIMEN *facing him on the dais.* IVAN *turns abruptly towards the congregation and we see his face for the first time. He is very young, pale, tense, but his eyes flash like lightning.*\*
>
> *Shot 45. Long shot of* IVAN *facing the congregation,* PIMEN *on the dais behind him, a line of* PRIESTS *on either side. (Production still on page 1)*
>
> *Shot 46. Medium close-up of the* ARCHDEACON, *still chanting (as shot 42).*
>
> *Shot 47. A longer shot of the* ARCHDEACON, *still chanting (as shot 41).*

---

\* Contrary to Eisenstein's concept, the young seventeen-year-old Tsar was tall and strong, and his face was framed by a fine red beard. All historians testify to his great nervousness, intensified by debauchery and the abuse of alcohol.

*Shot 48. Long shot of* IVAN, *crowned, sceptre in one hand, orb in the other, dominating the congregation. His robes gleam brilliantly in the dim light of the cathedral.*

*Shot 49. High angle long shot of the congregation bowing.*

*Shot 50. A high shot of the end of the nave and choir.* KURBSKY *and* KOLYCHEV *come forward and stand behind* IVAN *on either side of the dais. Two* BOYARS *come forward and hand them cups filled with coins; they stand for a moment on the bottom step of the dais, holding up the cups. Then, as the chanting of the* ARCHDEACON *reaches a climax, they step in behind* IVAN *and raise the cups over his head.*

*Shot 51. Medium shot of* IVAN *from below as* KURBSKY *and* KOLYCHEV *empty the cups of coins over him. The* CHOIR *bursts in, followed by the congregation, and the loud chink of falling coins mingles with their singing. (Still on page 1)*

CHOIR *off, then the congregation*: Long life to the Tsar! . . . Long life to the Tsar! . . . Long life! . . .*

*Shot 52. Medium close-up of* IVAN, *motionless beneath the shower of coins, the two princes on either side of him.*

[*Shot 53. Medium shot of* KURBSKY *and* KOLYCHEV *continuing to empty the coins over* IVAN.]†

*Shot 54. High angle medium close-up of the bottom of* IVAN'S *robe and the coins raining down on the ground. The* CHOIR *continues, off.*

CHOIR *off*: Long life! . . . Long life! . . .

*Shot 55. Close-up of* KOLYCHEV *emptying his cup.*

*Shot 56. Close-up of* KURBSKY *doing likewise. They both have the same look of mingled admiration and envy.*

*Shot 57. High angle medium close-up of the coins raining down on* IVAN'S *crowned head, the noise they make growing louder.*

*Shot 58. Medium close-up of one of* ANASTASIA'S *maids-in-waiting; she beams with pleasure.*

ARCHDEACON *off*: Long . . .

---

* Historically the words of the choir, repeated by the congregation, are: 'Ispolacti despota! Ad multos annos!'—'May he live long! Long life to him!'

† This shot did not appear in the copy of the film obtained from the English distributor, but was mentioned in Eisenstein's original screenplay.

*Shot 59. Medium close-up of another* MAID-IN-WAITING *smiling.*
ARCHDEACON *off* : ...li-i-i...

*Shot 60. High angle medium close-up of the coins falling on* IVAN's *head (as shot 57).*
ARCHDEACON *off* : ...i...fe!

*Shot 61. Medium close-up of* ANASTASIA, *watching with an ecstatic expression, whilst the* CHOIR *comes in again with the* ARCHDEACON.
ARCHDEACON *off* : Long life! ...Long life! ...

*Shot 62. Another shot of the coins piling up around* IVAN's *feet.*

*Shot 63. Long shot of* IVAN. *The two princes empty the last coins over him and hand the cups back to the two* BOYARS *who have come forward to receive them. Then they retire backwards along the dais, heads slightly bowed. As they do so, the* CHOIR *ends on a high note and a bell begins to toll solemnly. Slowly,* IVAN *advances towards camera.\**

*Shot 64. The bell tolls once more. Medium shot of* IVAN *from below as he commences his address, dominating the now silent assembly.* KURBSKY *and* KOLYCHEV *are on either side, in the background.*

IVAN : Today, for the first time, the Archduke of Moscow wears the crown of Tsar of all the Russias. *He glances fiercely from side to side and continues loudly* : He thereby puts an end to the pernicious power of the boyars. *A pause, then resuming still louder* : From now on, all the Russias ...

*Shot 65. Shot of* EUPHROSYNE, *dumbfounded and furious, beside her son* VLADIMIR.

IVAN *off* : ...will form a single State.

EUPHROSYNE *muttering fiercely* : What? He dares attack the power of the boyars?

*Shot 66. Medium close-up of the* BOYAR KOLYCHEV THE UNCONQUERABLE, *whose face darkens with repressed fury.*

IVAN *off* : But to maintain Russia ...

*Shot 67. Medium close-up of* KOLYCHEV THE UNCONQUERABLE's *son.*

IVAN *off* : ...as a single State ...

---

\* End of the first reel. Each one is approximately 300 metres.

*Shot 68. Resume on* IVAN *in medium close-up . . .*
IVAN : . . . we have to be strong. *A pause.* That is why from today
I am founding a regular army—well equipped, militant, permanent.
*He glances fiercely to the left.*
*Shot 69. Close-up from below, of the* BOYAR TURUNTAY-
PRONSKY. *He gazes stonily at* IVAN.
*Shot 70. Similar shot of another* BOYAR. *His eyes glitter.*
*Shot 71. Close-up of a third* BOYAR. *He looks sideways up at*
IVAN.
IVAN *off* : And whoever . . .

*Shot 72. Resume on* IVAN.
IVAN : . . . doesn't fight in this regular army will contribute to its
upkeep. *He looks straight ahead, then glances to left and right.*
EUPHROSYNE *furiously, under her breath, off* : Pay to cut one's
own . . .
*Shot 73. Medium close-up of* EUPHROSYNE *and* VLADIMIR.
EUPHROSYNE *continuing* : . . . throat !
*Shot 74. Medium shot of* FYODOR KOLYCHEV *looking up at*
IVAN. *He lowers his gaze, then looks sideways at* IVAN *as he*
*starts to speak again.*
IVAN *off* : Similarly the holy monasteries . . .
*Shot 75. Shot of* KURBSKY, *also turned towards* IVAN.

32

IVAN *off* : . . . with all their wealth . . .

> *Shot 76. Medium shot of* PIMEN *pricking up his ears and advancing towards* IVAN.
>
> *Shot 77. Resume on* IVAN *in medium close-up.*

IVAN : . . . will make their contribution. For their funds pile up without any advantage to the Russian land.

> *Shot 78. Medium close-up of* PIMEN *recoiling, outraged by what he has just heard.*

IVAN *in a thunderous voice, off* : We shall need a strong and undivided State . . .

> *Shot 79. A closer shot of* IVAN, *speaking with violent emphasis.*

IVAN : . . . if we are going to crush those who oppose the unity . . .

> *Shot 80. Medium close-up of* EUPHROSYNE, *so indignant that she raises her staff in an angry and threatening gesture.*

IVAN *off* : . . . of the Russian land.

> KOLYCHEV THE UNCONQUERABLE *seizes her by the arm on the left while* VLADIMIR *cowers behind her on the right.*
>
> *Shot 81. Low angle medium close-up of two* BOYARS *exchanging conspiratorial and vengeful glances.*
>
> *Shot 82. Resume on* EUPHROSYNE *trying to control herself: she lowers her head and hides her face in her handkerchief.* VLADIMIR *clings to her nervously.*
>
> *Shot 83. Shot of two* FOREIGN AMBASSADORS *exchanging ironic glances.*

IVAN *off* : Only a State . . .

> *Shot 84. Resume on* IVAN *in medium close-up, his eyes sweeping fiercely across the congregation.*

IVAN : . . . strong and unified within its frontiers can defend itself beyond them.

> *The* CHOIR *begins to sing again softly.*
>
> *Shot 85. Medium close-up of the* NURSE *and the young* GIRLS *listening very attentively.*

IVAN *off* : Our native land . . .

> *Shot 86. Close-up of* IVAN. *He is speaking less harshly now, his voice heavy with emotion.*

IVAN : . . . is no more than a trunk whose limbs have been hacked off. The sources of our waterways and rivers—Volga, Dvina, Bolkhovo—are ours; but the ports at their mouths are under foreign control. Our ancestral lands . . .

*Shot 87. Medium close-up of* ANASTASIA. *She listens, fascinated, her eyes moist.*

IVAN *off* : . . . have been torn from us . . .

*Shot 88. Resume on* IVAN *in medium close-up. His voice thunders out again, his eyes sweeping to and fro.*

IVAN : That is why, this coronation day, we are going to set about retaking occupied Russian territory.

*Shot 89. Close-up of one of the* FOREIGN AMBASSADORS *in a white ruff. His smile freezes on his lips. The hymn fades away.*

*Shot 90. Resume on* IVAN.

IVAN : Two Romes have fallen. Moscow is the third. There will be no fourth, for I am absolute master of this third Rome, the Muscovite State. *A bell tolls.*

*Shot 91.*

A FOREIGNER *in medium close-up, outraged* : The Pope won't sanction it!

*Shot 92.*

ANOTHER FOREIGNER *in close-up* : The Emperor won't tolerate it!

*Shot 93.*

A THIRD FOREIGNER *in close-up* : Europe will not recognise it!

*Shot 94. Medium close-up of the* LIVONIAN AMBASSADOR *in profile.*

LIVONIAN AMBASSADOR : If he is powerful, everyone will bow down to him.

*The bell tolls again, as he speaks. A pause. He turns towards his* SECRETARY.

*Shot 95. Close-up of* IVAN's *face. He glances sideways.*

LIVONIAN AMBASSADOR *murmuring off* : He must not be allowed to become powerful!

*Shot 96. Medium close-up of* PIMEN *watching* IVAN *somewhat apprehensively. The* CHOIR *comes in again.*

EUPHROSYNE *off* : The marriage is fixed for St. Simon's Day.

*Shot 97. Medium close-up of* EUPHROSYNE *as the singing swells slightly.*

EUPHROSYNE *continuing grimly* : We'll arrange a fine wedding . . . for this dictator! *Fade out.*

*Shot 98. Fade in on a long shot of an empty courtyard outside the Kremlin. Hymn-singing is heard off. It is night. Two*

34

SENTINELS *slumber, leaning on their halberds.*
LIVONIAN AMBASSADOR *off*: Why such . . .
> Shot 99. *Medium shot of* KURBSKY *and the* LIVONIAN AMBAS-
> SADOR *in a vaulted corridor in the Kremlin.* KURBSKY *is facing
> camera, the* AMBASSADOR *behind him on the right, speaking
> over his shoulder.*

AMBASSADOR *continuing*: . . . privileges for Ivan? . . .
> Shot 100. *Medium close-up of the two men.* KURBSKY *looks
> towards camera, frowning slightly, listening in spite of himself
> to the words of the* AMBASSADOR. *Dressed in black, with
> square-lensed spectacles tilted on edge above his nose, the
> latter has an extremely sinister appearance.*

AMBASSADOR: Why is Prince Kurbsky his vassal?
> Shot 101. *A closer shot of both men. The* AMBASSADOR *leans
> confidentially towards* KURBSKY.

AMBASSADOR: Is not the Kurbsky's nobility equal to that of Ivan
the Muscovite?
> *A pause.* KURBSKY *looks thoughtful.*
> Shot 102. *Close-up of the* AMBASSADOR *leaning insinuatingly
> towards him.*

AMBASSADOR: Why is Ivan of Moscow master of Russia? . . .
> Shot 103. *Resume on medium close-up of the two men.*

AMBASSADOR *continuing*: . . . and not Prince Andrew Kurbsky
of Jaroslav?
> KURBSKY *turns nervously towards the* AMBASSADOR; *the latter
> grins at him hypocritically.* KURBSKY *turns away again.*
> Shot 104. *Medium shot of the two men as* KURBSKY *turns and
> walks off down the corridor away from camera. The* AMBAS-
> SADOR *gazes after him for a moment, then goes off to the
> right, his black robe trailing after him. (Still on page 2)*
> Shot 105. *Medium shot of the* AMBASSADOR *coming down
> some stairs; he turns round again to watch* KURBSKY'S *dis-
> appearing figure. Bells ring in the distance.*
> Shot 106. KURBSKY *comes into frame in medium shot, hurry-
> ing up some stairs. At the top he turns and looks back in the
> direction of the* AMBASSADOR, *then hurries on again and goes
> out of frame to the left. The bells continue their rhythmic
> tolling.*
> Shot 107. *Long shot, slightly high angle, of the immense*

banqueting hall in the Kremlin, under a great vaulted ceiling. Numerous guests are seated at tables ranged against the walls. In the background, seated somewhat apart at the table of honour, are TSAR IVAN and ANASTASIA. It is the wedding feast.* KURBSKY, seen from the back, comes into frame on the right and, casting a last nervous glance behind him, begins to descend the staircase into the banqueting hall. As he does so, the sound of lutes comes in over the ringing of the bells and a CHOIR strikes up a lilting madrigal.

CHOIR off : ' Aaaah . . .'

Shot 108. Reverse shot of KURBSKY coming down the great carpeted staircase into the banqueting hall, massive candelabra on either side, angels painted on the walls.

CHOIR off : ' Aaaah . . .'

Halfway down the staircase, KURBSKY stops and places a hand on a candelabra on the right.

Shot 109. From a medium close-up of a carving on the ceiling the camera tracks out, tilting down past a sideboard laden with precious goblets to show IVAN and ANASTASIA, in medium shot, frozen in a long embrace. During this movement, the CHOIR comes in again with the first verse of the song.

CHOIR off : ' The oak trees, the oaks !
          On their boughs, the turtle doves . . .'

Shot 110. Medium close-up of the two of them. After a pause, IVAN slowly detaches himself from ANASTASIA and they both smilingly acknowledge their guests, bowing low.

CHOIR off : ' . . . sit nestling there !
          Lullay, lullay, lullay.'

Shot 111. As the singing of the CHOIR continues, cut to a table of black-robed PRIESTS. PIMEN, in a white cowl, is smiling jovially at the head. They all raise their goblets and look towards the couple.

Shot 112. Resume on IVAN and ANASTASIA. Hand in hand, they bow deeply and slowly, first to the right, then to the left.

Shot 113. Medium shot of one of the tables, the guests in serried rows on either side, two bearded BOYARS in the foreground. They all raise their goblets and call out.

---

* The historians contradict each other as to the exact date of the wedding: some specify February 3rd, 1547, others February 13th or 20th, 1547.

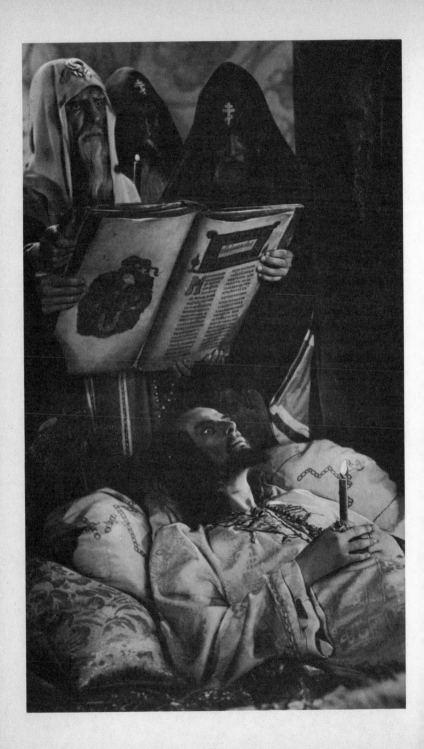

GUESTS : Kiss each other ! . . . Kiss !

> *A* SERVANT *carrying a pitcher hurries past in front of the camera.*
> *Shot 114. Medium shot of* IVAN *looking at* ANASTASIA. *The shouts of the guests continue, off. Bells ring out and the* CHOIR *continues its song.* IVAN *turns to face the guests.*

IVAN : Why are the bells of Moscow ringing so loudly ?

CHOIR *simultaneously, off* : ' Lullay, lullay, lullay.
> > > They are billing to each other . . .'

> IVAN *picks up a goblet and offers it to* ANASTASIA, *who smiles at him.*
> *Shot 115. Medium shot of* EUPHROSYNE *at the head of her table, leaning towards* VLADIMIR *on the left. As she speaks she glances slyly across the hall.\**

EUPHROSYNE *to* VLADIMIR : The citizens have gone wild with joy ! . . .

CHOIR *simultaneously, off* : ' Lullay, lullay, lullay . . .'

> *As the singing continues,* EUPHROSYNE *looks round in the direction of* PIMEN.
> *Shot 116. Medium close-up of* PIMEN *leaning forward as he catches her eye.*
> *Shot 117. Close-up of* EUPHROSYNE. *Having caught* PIMEN'S *attention, she nods significantly in the direction of* IVAN *and* ANASTASIA. *The bells ring out loudly over a lull in the singing.*
> *Shot 118. Medium close-up of* IVAN *raising the goblet to* ANASTASIA'S *lips. She smiles and looks up at him adoringly before she drinks.*

CHOIR *off* : ' They are cooing to each other . . .'

> *Shot 119. Close-up of* EUPHROSYNE *glancing slyly up at the couple. She raises her goblet and toasts them without conviction.*

EUPHROSYNE : Kiss each other !

CHOIR *off* : ' They sing in praise . . .'

> *Shot 120. Medium shot of* VLADIMIR *between two pairs of*

---

\* In historical fact, the marriage followed ancient Russian customs : Princess Euphrosyne Staritsky was godmother, Prince Vladimir Andreyevich godfather; the young Prince Yuri Glinsky prepared the bed of the newly-weds and accompanied the husband to the bath; throughout the night the Grand Equerry, Prince Michael Glinsky, patrolled with a naked sword beneath the windows of the nuptial chamber.

*candles. He raises his goblet and shouts inanely with his mouth full.*

VLADIMIR : Kiss each other ! Kiss each other !

CHOIR *simultaneously, off* : '. . . of joyous love . . .'

*Shot 121. Medium shot of the rows of guests at one of the tables; the two bearded* BOYARS *seen previously are in the foreground. They all wave their goblets in the air and shout.*

GUESTS : Kiss ! Kiss !

CHOIR *simultaneously, off* : ' Lullay, lullay, lullay . . .'

*Shot 122. Resume on medium close-up of the royal couple as they kiss.*

CRIES *off* : Kiss ! Kiss !

CHOIR *simultaneously, off* : ' Lullay, lullay, lullay . . .'

*Shot 123. Medium shot of* PIMEN'S *table, the* PRIESTS *on either side and* PIMEN *at the end, seen between two long rows of candles. As the chorus of the song ends, he raises his goblet and the* PRIESTS *follow suit. In time to the music of lutes, the goblets clink together between the two rows of candles, coming along the line towards camera.*

*Shot 124. Similar shot of* EUPHROSYNE'S *table,* EUPHROSYNE *at the end between two rows of candles. She raises her goblet and the other guests clink their goblets together along the line, in time to the music.*

*Shot 125. Medium close-up of* IVAN *kissing* ANASTASIA. *He draws away and looks down into her eyes. The* CHOIR *starts to sing again. (Production still on page 2)*

*Shot 126. Close-up of* EUPHROSYNE, *drinking, looking slyly across at* IVAN *over the top of her goblet. She sets down the goblet.*

*Shot 127. Medium close-up of* EUPHROSYNE. *We see her head at the bottom of frame, then she rises to her feet, filling the picture, and raises her goblet.*

EUPHROSYNE *shouting without conviction* : Kiss each other !

*Shot 128. Long shot of* EUPHROSYNE *standing at the head of her table, her goblet raised. The other guests all raise their goblets to the* TSAR *and* TSARINA, *who get up and embrace. As they do so,* EUPHROSYNE *parades down the hall between the tables, waving a handkerchief, coming towards camera on the right. She is followed by a procession of servants carrying pitchers. The* CHOIR *sings louder and louder and we hear the chime of bells over the music.*

*Shot 129. Another long shot of* EUPHROSYNE *coming down the hall between the tables, waving her handkerchief, her goblet raised. The bells ring out, the guests wave their goblets in the air.* EUPHROSYNE *goes out of frame to the right.*

*Shot 130. Medium shot of a small doorway at the top of some steps, leading out of the banqueting hall.* EUPHROSYNE *comes into frame on the left. She beckons a* SERVANT, *who appears from the right and helps her on with her cloak as she turns to take a last look at the* TSAR *and* TSARINA *at the end of the hall. Then she turns again and, with an angry toss of her head, goes out through the small doorway.*

*Shot 131. At the top of the dimly lit staircase outside the banqueting hall,* EUPHROSYNE *appears in long shot, glancing shiftily behind her. In the distance the* CHOIR *can still be heard, but it is partly drowned by the sound of bells.*

*Shot 132. Medium shot of* EUPHROSYNE *standing on the staircase. She looks off towards the left. Suddenly we hear the clanging of the alarm. She turns and leans over the edge of the staircase, listening. The singing and the bells stop. Only the strident and sinister clang of the alarm is heard.*

*Shot 133. Long shot of the guards drowsing on their halberds in the middle of one of the small courtyards of the Kremlin. The alarm rings out.*

*Shot 134. In the gilded banqueting hall, where the feast is still in progress,* FYODOR KOLYCHEV *is seen in medium shot leaning his head on his hand. Music.*

*Shot 135. Long shot in the direction of the* TSAR *and* TSARINA, *still at the table. Two* SERVANTS *appear from left and right, bearing pitchers of wine. The two princes,* KURBSKY *and* KOLYCHEV, *come up from behind the* TSAR *and* TSARINA *and take the pitchers.*

*Shot 136. Medium shot of the same scene. As the music continues,* KURBSKY, *who is on the right, leans forward and pours wine into* ANASTASIA'S *goblet. As he does so,* IVAN *turns to address him.*

IVAN : Why are my best friends . . .

*Shot 137. Medium close-up of* KURBSKY *pouring the wine.*

IVAN *continues off* : . . . so sad today?

   KURBSKY *looks abruptly round at* IVAN, *then turns away again and stops pouring. A pause.*

KURBSKY *starting to pour again*: Tsar, the people have a saying . . .

   *Shot 138. Medium close-up of* ANASTASIA. *She turns to look at* KURBSKY, *who continues off.*

KURBSKY *off* : . . . that marriage is the end of friendship.

   *Shot 139. A closer shot of* KURBSKY. *He turns and looks longingly down at* ANASTASIA.

   *Shot 140. Resume on* ANASTASIA *in medium close-up. She holds* KURBSKY'S *glance for a moment, then turns towards* IVAN.

   *Shot 141. Medium shot of the couple.* IVAN *looks down at* ANASTASIA, *then up at* KURBSKY *again and finally turns towards* KOLYCHEV.

   *Shot 142. The camera, following his glance, cuts to a medium close-up of* KOLYCHEV, *looking away.*

IVAN *off* : And what does Fyodor Kolychev say?

   *Shot 143. Medium shot of* KOLYCHEV *standing with the pitcher in his hand,* IVAN *facing him in three-quarter back view.*

KOLYCHEV *turning towards* IVAN : Tsar, you break with tradition.

   *Shot 144. Close-up of* KOLYCHEV.

KOLYCHEV *continuing* : I foresee trouble.

   *Shot 145. Close-up of* IVAN *in profile, turned towards* KOLYCHEV, *who continues off.* IVAN *turns away and stares straight in front of him for a moment, then looks at* KOLYCHEV *again.*

KOLYCHEV *off* : I don't dare go against my Tsar . . .

   *Shot 146. Medium shot of both of them.*

KOLYCHEV : . . . but I can't follow in his footsteps. *He drops to one knee before* IVAN. Let me take holy orders . . . *He bows his head.*

IVAN *putting out a hand and raising* KOLYCHEV'S *head:* You prefer the heavenly to the earthly king? KOLYCHEV *looks away;* IVAN *leans back on his throne.* Very well, I shall not stand between . . .

   *Shot 147. Medium close-up of* ANASTASIA.

IVAN *off* : . . . you and Him.

   *Shot 148. Resume on close-up of* IVAN. *(Still on page 3)*

IVAN : Go . . . *He raises his eyes to heaven* . . . and pray for us sinners . . . *He gets up.*

*Shot 149. Medium shot, reverse angle. Link on the motion as* IVAN *rises and places a hand on* KOLYCHEV'S *shoulder.* KOLYCHEV *looks up at* IVAN *as the latter towers over him.*

IVAN *continues*: I only ask one thing of you: do not abandon us if misfortune strikes.

*Shot 150. Medium close-up of* IVAN.

IVAN : If I need you, answer my call!

*Shot 151. Medium close-up of* KOLYCHEV, IVAN'S *hand on his shoulder. He bows his head.** 

*Shot 152. Rapid long shot of the small courtyard, empty except for the duty guard in the middle.*

*Shot 153. Medium shot of the staircase, where we find* EUPHROSYNE *still listening. Loud music. Alarm bells and general uproar can be heard, off.*

*Shot 154. Long shot of a passage; we see* EUPHROSYNE *on the staircase in the background.* DEMYAN *and two auxiliaries appear under an arch.* DEMYAN *bows and runs up the staircase towards* EUPHROSYNE.

*Shot 155. Medium shot of the top of the staircase.* EUPHRO-SYNE *appears from behind an archway as* DEMYAN *runs into frame from the right and speaks to her urgently. His words are drowned by the music.* EUPHROSYNE *glances down the staircase and pushes him backwards towards a dark alcove.*

*Shot 156. Medium shot of the two of them in the alcove.*

DEMYAN : The people are rising . . .

*Shot 157. Medium close-up of* DEMYAN *whispering urgently to* EUPHROSYNE.

DEMYAN *continuing*: . . . They are shouting against the Glinskys and the Zakharins, burning and pillaging and marching on the palace, demanding to see the Tsar!

EUPHROSYNE *pushes* DEMYAN *back through a small doorway.*

*Shot 158. Medium shot of the small doorway through which* EUPHROSYNE *left the banqueting hall. She reappears. Loud music and the sound of rioting continue off.*

*Shot 159. The loud music cuts out as the* CHOIR *strikes up a drinking song. Long shot of the top of the great staircase.*

---

* End of the second reel.

Servants come down in a majestic procession, carrying swans on great platters.

*Shot 160.* Medium shot of the procession of swans descending the staircase.

*Shot 161.* Reverse shot of the same scene, looking down the staircase towards IVAN and ANASTASIA at the far end of the hall. Carried on the heads of servants, the swans seem to float through the air. They are followed by other servants, carrying pitchers of wine. The CHOIR continues to sing off.

*Shot 162.* Medium shot of the dishes of swans passing in front of the tables. Seen from behind, the guests wave their goblets in time to the music.

*Shot 163.* Long shot down the hall as the procession approaches the TSAR's table.

*Shot 164.* A closer shot of the same scene. We see IVAN and ANASTASIA in medium long shot as the swans pass the camera from right to left, in medium close-up in the foreground. The servants circle round behind the couple and come forward again to form two equal rows on either side of the table. Then they turn, and the long, slender necks of the swans swing in to face each other on either side, a single swan facing camera over the heads of the TSAR and TSARINA in the background. IVAN and ANASTASIA look up, turning their heads to follow the procession.

*Shot 165.* Medium close-up of ANASTASIA. She smiles in wonderment, looking up at the swans, then shyly hides her face behind her sleeve.

*Shot 166.* Medium shot from below of the two rows of swans, their necks outstretched. IVAN and ANASTASIA exchange happy glances in the background. (Still on page 3)

*Shot 167.* Medium close-up of KURBSKY, his goblet in front of his face, drinking. Then, holding the goblet, he flings his arm in the air with a shout and gazes passionately down at ANASTASIA, off-screen.

KURBSKY *shouting*: Heigh!

*Shot 168.* Medium close-up of ANASTASIA who looks sideways up at him.

*Shot 169.* Reverse shot of KURBSKY in close-up, consuming her with his eyes. His look suddenly hardens as he registers *her indifference.*

*Shot 170. Medium close-up of* KURBSKY. *Behind him, the other guests raise their goblets as he flings his to the ground, in a fury.*

KURBSKY: Ha!

*As the goblet crashes to the ground, the singing of the* CHOIR *is replaced by the riot music heard previously.*

*Shot 171. Long shot of the Kremlin courtyard: armed with sticks, a crowd bursts in, headed by* MALYUTA. *Others follow behind, carrying torches. Riot music.*

*Shot 172. Close-up of the crowd from above. Heads and torches move rapidly past camera from right to left.*

*Shot 173. Medium long shot of* IVAN *and* ANASTASIA *in the banqueting hall, the swans on either side. The lights go out. The couple spring to their feet and the swans' necks waver grotesquely in the gloom as the servants turn and scatter in panic.* IVAN *and* ANASTASIA *are left standing at the table. Servants hurry out with candelabra in the background. Riot music and alarm bells off.*

*Shot 174. Medium shot of* MALYUTA *at the head of the rioters. Their way is barred by two* GUARDS *with crossed halberds. With a mighty heave,* MALYUTA *pushes the halberds up, and comes into medium close-up, his arms outstretched.*

*Shot 175. Close-up of* MALYUTA, *slightly from above.*

MALYUTA *shouting*: To the Tsar! . . .

*Shot 176. Medium shot of* MALYUTA; *he thrusts the halberds down again and aside and rushes off to the left. The crowd pour after him. (Still on page 4)*

*Shot 177. Long shot of the crowd in three-quarter back view, hurrying towards the left.*

*Shot 178. Close-up of the crowd from above. Shouting, bells and loud music continue.*

*Shot 179. Long shot of two windows under the vaulted ceiling at one end of the banqueting hall. A* BOYAR *hurries into shot from the right, back to camera. He bends down to look through the windows, then turns towards the guests, off-screen, and shouts above the uproar.*

BOYAR: Moscow is in flames! *He turns again and rushes towards the windows.*

47

*Shot 180. Medium shot of the windows, the flames flickering outside. Other* BOYARS *rush into shot from the right and bend down to look out through the windows. The bells ring out frantically.*

*Shot 181. Medium close-up of* VLADIMIR, *cowering beside the chair at the end of* EUPHROSYNE'S *table. He is clutching at his throat and staring off to the left. (Still on page 4) He ducks down behind the chair.*

*Shot 182. Long shot of the rioters bursting into the banqueting hall, carrying torches. They pour down the main staircase into the hall.*

*Shot 183. Medium close-up of the rioters, coming down the staircase towards camera.*

*Shot 184. High angle long shot of the banqueting hall. On the right, guards with halberds bar the crowd's way at the bottom of the staircase. On the left,* IVAN *comes forward accompanied by* KOLYCHEV *and* KURBSKY. *The two princes come in front of him to protect him from the crowd.*

*Shot 185. Medium shot of* IVAN *as he thrusts* KURBSKY *and* KOLYCHEV *aside and comes towards camera, raising his hand.*

IVAN : Let the people enter . . .

*Shot 186. Medium shot of* IVAN *dashing towards the guards and forcing back the halberds.*

*Shot 187.* MALYUTA *rushes out of the crowd towards camera, brandishing an enormous candlestick.*

*Shot 188. Close-up of* KOLYCHEV, IVAN *and* KURBSKY. *The latter passes in front of* IVAN *to protect him.*

*Shot 189. Close-up of* MALYUTA, *his face contorted with frenzy: he raises his arms to strike.*

*Shot 190. Extreme close-up of* MALYUTA'S *contorted face as he raises his head.*

*Shot 191. Medium close-up of* ANASTASIA *as she cries out, terrified.*

*Shot 192. Medium close-up of* KURBSKY *in front of* IVAN. *He raises his arm to catch the candlestick as* MALYUTA *hurtles into shot from the right.*

*Shot 193. Medium long shot as* KURBSKY *wrests the candlestick from* MALYUTA *and hurls it to the ground with a crash. At the same time,* KOLYCHEV *grabs* MALYUTA *from behind and the two princes force him to his knees in front of the* TSAR. *The crowd stands watching on the right. Alarm bells and loud music continue off.*

*Shot 194. Reverse shot of* MALYUTA *on his knees, facing camera, struggling to get free of* KURBSKY *and* KOLYCHEV. *They hold him still and gaze sternly down at him.*

*Shot 195. Close-up of* KOLYCHEV *glaring down at* MALYUTA.

*Shot 196. Close-up of* KURBSKY *doing likewise.*

*Shot 197. Close-up of* MALYUTA; *he gazes sullenly up, first at* KURBSKY, *then at* KOLYCHEV. *Then he catches sight of* IVAN *and his jaw drops.*

MALYUTA *in a whisper* : The Tsar ! . . .

*Shot 198. Close-up of* IVAN *looking down at* MALYUTA. *He raises his head to look at the crowd, his eyes blazing. The music gets louder and louder.*

*Shot 199. High angle medium shot of the crowd. They fall to their knees and remove their hats. Alarm bells.*

*Shot 200. Medium shot of* KOLYCHEV, MALYUTA *and* KURBSKY, *the crowd sinking to their knees in the background.* KOLYCHEV *and* KURBSKY *bend over* MALYUTA *as he kneels on the ground, looking up in awe at* IVAN. *The latter comes into frame from the left, in back view, obscuring our vision. The voice of* NIKOLA, THE SIMPLETON, *is heard off.*

SIMPLETON *shouting, off* : The Tsar is bewitched ! . . .

*Shot 201. Medium shot from below of the* SIMPLETON *at the top of the stairs. He shakes off several of the crowd who are holding him back and comes forward into medium close-up, pointing down at* IVAN.

SIMPLETON *still shouting* : . . . by the Tsarina's family . . .

*Shot 202. Close-up of the* SIMPLETON, *strongly lit from below.*

SIMPLETON : The Glinskys, the Zakharins have bewitched him !

*Shot 203. Close-up of* IVAN, *who turns towards the* SIMPLETON *as the latter continues off.*

SIMPLETON *off* : . . . bewitched him !

*Shot 204. Medium close-up of a* YOUNG MAN *with blond hair in the crowd as he cries out.*

YOUNG MAN : Justice against the Tsarina's family !

*Shot 205. Close-up of another* YOUTH, *shouting after him.*

YOUTH : Justice against the Glinskys and Zakharins !

*Shot 206. Medium shot of three* BOYARS *of the Glinsky and Zakharin families, who rise precipitately to their feet. Sound of bells, off.*

*Shot 207. Medium close-up of two of the* BOYARS *looking angry and uneasy.*

SIMPLETON *off* : They tear . . .

*Shot 208. Close-up of the* SIMPLETON. *As he speaks, he tears at the chain round his neck, then holds out his hand and makes sprinkling motions in front of him to illustrate his words.*

SIMPLETON *continuing* : . . . the hearts from the breasts of the people! They sprinkle our houses with human blood! The blood bursts into flame and burns the houses . . . *He raises a crooked arm and glares down at the assembly.*

*Shot 209. Medium close-up of* EUPHROSYNE *peering out from behind a candelabra.*

SIMPLETON *continuing off* : The houses burn! . . .

*Shot 210. Music. Medium close-up of* MALYUTA *kneeling,* KURBSKY *and* KOLYCHEV *bent over him.*

MALYUTA *looking up at* IVAN : Moscow is horribly bewitched! . . .

*Shot 211. Close-up of* MALYUTA. *He shakes free of* KOLYCHEV *and* KURBSKY *and raises an arm as he speaks.*

MALYUTA *continuing* : The bells are crashing down from the steeples!* *He gets up.*

*Shot 212. Close-up of* IVAN, *unmoved. He speaks with sinister calm.*

IVAN : Witchcraft, you say? . . . Bells falling without reason? . . .

*Half-sneering* : A head which believes in witchcraft is itself like a bell . . .

---

* In fact it was not until June 1547 that the fall of the Kremlin bells provoked this incident. Henry Valloton in his book on Ivan the Terrible relates: 'On June 3rd, 1547 a delegation of fifty leading members of the community had been sent to the Tsar by the town of Pskov to complain of the governor, Prince Turuntay-Pronsky; Ivan IV was on his Ostrovskaya estate near Moscow. Furious that they had dared to disturb him, he sprinkled their heads with burning alcohol, set fire to their long hair and beards and ordered that they should be stripped and laid out on the ground. At this moment a messenger, hot foot from Moscow, came to announce that the great bell of the Kremlin had fallen without apparent reason and that the arch was broken. The Tsar left at once for Moscow, forgetting the people of Pskov . . .' Ivan was frightened: this astonishing event appeared to him of very ill omen. It was followed by several other catastrophes in the city.

*Shot 213. Close-up of* IVAN's *hand tapping* MALYUTA's *head.*

IVAN : . . . empty !

*Shot 214. Close-up of the blond* YOUNG MAN *in the crowd who bursts out laughing.*

*Shot 215. Close-up of the other* YOUTH, *also laughing.*

*Shot 216. Close-up of two other* MEN *who laugh.*

*Shot 217. Close-up of* MALYUTA, *nonplussed.*

IVAN *off* : And can a head fall off . . . all by itself ?

*Shot 218. Close-up of* IVAN.

IVAN *continuing* : In order to fall, it has to be cut . . . *He makes a sudden chopping motion with his hand and glares up at the crowd.*

*Sinister music.*

*Shot 219. Close-up of the* SIMPLETON, *who gazes down at* IVAN, *then slips away out of shot.*

*Shot 220. Close-up of* MALYUTA, *who fingers his neck apprehensively, looking up at* IVAN. *The music gets louder.*

*Shot 221. Medium close-up of* IVAN, *standing next to* MALYUTA. *He puts a hand on the latter's shoulder and moves in front of him, towards the right.*

IVAN : It is just the same with bells. Those who, without the Tsar's orders . . .

*Shot 222. Medium shot of* IVAN, *the crowd on all sides of him. He steps up to a candelabra, places a hand on it, and looks round.*

IVAN *continuing* : . . . cut the ropes which support the bells . . .

*Shot 223. Medium close-up of* IVAN, *from below, standing by the candelabra.*

IVAN *continuing* : . . . will have their own heads cut off — this time on the Tsar's orders.

*Shot 224. Close-up of two* MEN *in the crowd.*

ONE OF THE MEN : The Tsar is pretty sharp.

*Shot 225. Close-up of another* MAN *in the crowd.*

MAN : There's no pulling the wool over his eyes.

*Shot 226. Medium close-up of* IVAN *speaking loudly and authoritatively.*

IVAN : We shall cut off heads ruthlessly . . .

*Shot 227. Close-up of* IVAN.

IVAN *continuing* : . . . to weed out the treason of the boyars . . .

*Shot 228. Close-up of* EUPHROSYNE, *looking sideways up at* IVAN.

IVAN *continuing off* : . . . to the very roots.

*Shot 229. Shot of two* YOUTHS *in the crowd, shouting in approbation.*

IVAN *off* : A Tsar can only rule if he holds the reins.

*Shot 230. Close-up of* KURBSKY, *as his head appears between the tops of the two thrones at the* TSAR'S *table. He looks across at* IVAN *as the latter continues off, then down at* ANASTASIA, *also off-screen.*

IVAN *off* : A State without reins is as uncontrollable as a horse without a bridle.

*Shot 231. Medium shot of* ANASTASIA, *crouched against the side of the throne on the left,* KURBSKY *looking down on her from above. He comes round from behind the throne and stands beside her, as she gazes intently across at* IVAN.

IVAN *continuing off* : But he who ranges himself at the side of the Tsar will be rewarded . . .

*Shot 232. Medium close-up of* ANASTASIA, *gazing ecstatically across at* IVAN. KURBSKY'S *sleeve is visible on the left. Suddenly, carried away by* IVAN'S *words, she grips* KURBSKY'S *sleeve. His other hand comes into shot, and enfolds hers and caresses it.* ANASTASIA *turns and looks down at* KURBSKY'S *hand, then up at him in surprise.*

IVAN *off* : . . . he will rejoice in the Tsar's bounty . . .

*Shot 233. Close-up of* KURBSKY, *gazing passionately down at* ANASTASIA.

IVAN *off* : . . . and the admiration of our soldiers.

*Shot 234. Resume on medium close-up of* ANASTASIA. *She withdraws her hand and looks sternly up at* KURBSKY.

ANASTASIA : Do not dare, Prince, even to dream . . . *She puts her hand to her breast* . . . I am dedicated to a high cause . . . *She gazes across at* IVAN *again* . . . A loyal slave of the Tsar of Moscow.

IVAN *off* : Our lands are vast and rich . . .

*Shot 235. Long shot of* IVAN *standing by the candelabra, surrounded by his people. His white robes stand out in the gloom.*

IVAN : . . . but disorder is everywhere.

*He walks away from camera, and raises an arm towards the*

back of the crowd. *Then he comes back to face camera again and throws both arms in the air.*

IVAN *continuing*: But we ourselves will set our house in order, without appealing to outside help.

THE PEOPLE *shouting*: We ourselves! . . . Ourselves!

*Shot 236. Reverse shot of* IVAN *in profile, standing in medium close-up by the candelabra. He makes a crushing motion with his arm to illustrate his words.*

IVAN: We will crush treachery!

THE PEOPLE *in unison*: We will crush it!

*Shot 237. A closer shot of* IVAN *in profile, by the candelabra. Torches flicker in the background.*

IVAN: And we will help the workers, the shopkeepers, the craftsmen! *He makes another sweeping motion with his arm.*

*Shot 238. Close-up of three* MEN *in the crowd, shouting.*

THE PEOPLE: We will help them!

*Shot 239. Medium close-up of* EUPHROSYNE. *A* SERVANT *comes into shot from the right and speaks in her ear.*

SERVANT: Three Tartar envoys from Kazan insist on seeing the Tsar.

EUPHROSYNE *gets up and looks across at the staircase, her eyes blazing.*

EUPHROSYNE: From Kazan? . . . *Roll of drums. Music.* Tell them to come in at once.

*Shot 240. Long shot of the entrance and main staircase of the banqueting hall from below. Guards come down and range themselves on either side. Then the* TARTAR ENVOY *appears at the top and comes down the steps, followed by his attendants. He advances towards camera, until we see the bottom of his robe in close-up. As he begins to speak, he draws aside his robe to show a pair of finely embroidered trousers.*

ENVOY: Kazan break off her friendship with Moscow.

*Shot 241. Long shot of* IVAN *by the candelabra. He swings round as the* ENVOY *speaks; the crowd rise to their feet and turn with him.*

ENVOY *off*: Kazan terminate her alliance.

*Shot 242. Medium close-up of* IVAN *from below, looking up at the* ENVOY. *At the latter's next words, he puts his hands on his hips, in an arrogant gesture.*

ENVOY *off*: We declare war on Moscow.

    *Shot 243. Close-up of the* ENVOY.

ENVOY: Kazan . . . great. *He holds up his thumb.* Moscow . . .
small. *He holds up his little finger.*

    *Shot 244. Medium close-up of the* ENVOY, *holding up his
thumb and little finger, looking down at* IVAN *from under
his wide-brimmed felt hat.*

ENVOY: Moscow hasn't a chance.

    *With the forefinger of his other hand, he pushes down his
little finger. At the same time, one of his assistants comes
round behind him from right to left, hands him a dagger and
then goes off again.*

ENVOY: Our great Khan send this present. *He holds up the dagger.*
Russian Tsar want no shame. *A pause.* Russian Tsar end his own
life.

    *He leans forward and smiles superciliously down at* IVAN,
*offering him the dagger.*

    *Shot 245. Roll of drums and loud music. Medium shot as* IVAN
*strides into frame from the left, goes up to the* ENVOY *and
grasps the hand holding the dagger. He forces it back, at the
same time turning to face the crowd so that the* ENVOY *is
behind him.*

IVAN: God is my witness that we did not want war. *He turns to
face the* ENVOY *again. The dagger is between them.* But the time
has passed . . .

    *Shot 246. Medium close-up of* IVAN, *three-quarters facing
camera, standing over the* ENVOY *whose richly embroidered
hat can be seen in the foreground.*

IVAN: . . . when insolent foreigners can invade Muscovite territory . . . *He forces the* ENVOY *to the ground.*

    *Shot 247. Close-up of* IVAN, *in profile, looking down at the*
ENVOY. *He turns to address the crowd.*

IVAN: . . . with impunity.

    *Shot 248. Close-up of the* ENVOY, *back to camera, holding the
dagger.* IVAN *seizes the dagger and puts a hand on his shoulder.*

    *Shot 249. Close-up of* IVAN *raising the dagger in the air.*

IVAN: And this dagger will strike down whoever raises his hand
against Moscow.

    *Shot 250. Medium shot of* IVAN, *standing, brandishing the dagger, the* ENVOY *at his feet on the right. He throws the dagger away from him and it crashes to the ground.*

IVAN : We will finish with Kazan once and for all.

*He rushes towards the camera, and stamps his foot on the dagger. The* ENVOY *follows him with his eyes.*

*Shot 251. Cut on the noise to close-up of* IVAN, *his head raised.*

IVAN : It is we who will go to Kazan.

*Shot 252. Close-up of* MALYUTA, *the crowd behind him. He raises an arm and yells enthusiastically.*

MALYUTA : To Kazan !

THE PEOPLE : To Kazan !

*Shot 253. Medium close-up of the* ENVOY *on the floor, dumbfounded. His attendants rejoin him.*

CRIES *off* : To Kazan !

*Shot 254. Resume on close-up of* MALYUTA. *The shouting rises to a crescendo and we hear the music of ' Ivan the Terrible '.*

MALYUTA : To Kazan ! *He turns and rushes into the crowd, away from camera.*

*Shot 255. Long shot from above of the crowd in the hall, wild with excitement. They wave their hats and torches, and continue to shout.*

THE PEOPLE *shouting* : To Kazan !

*Shot 256. Medium close-up of* MALYUTA *coming up to the* ENVOY.

MALYUTA : Listen, Khan !

*Shot 257. Close-up of* MALYUTA *and the* ENVOY.

MALYUTA : It is Kazan which is small . . . *He waggles his little finger at the* ENVOY . . . and Moscow . . . *He spits in his palm and waves his fist in the* ENVOY'S *face* . . . which is great ! . . . *He looks away.*

*Shot 258. Extreme close-up of* MALYUTA'S *face as he shouts excitedly.*

MALYUTA : To Kazan ! *He raises an arm in the air and turns back towards the* ENVOY.

*Shot 259. Medium close-up of the two of them. Link on the motion as* MALYUTA *brings his arm down and punches the* ENVOY *on the chest. Music. He hustles him away up the steps, followed by the crowd carrying sticks.*

*Shot 260. Long shot of the crowd pouring up the steps out of the banqueting hall.*

*Shot 261. Medium shot of* ANASTASIA *on the throne, looking on ecstatically. The music swells; she springs to her feet and, with an imperious gesture, holds out her arm to* KURBSKY, *without looking at him.* KURBSKY *hurries forward from his position beside the throne, takes her hand and looks sideways at her. She gives him a haughty glance and strides forward,* KURBSKY *trailing after.*

*Shot 262. Medium shot of* IVAN *with his arm around* ANASTASIA, *towering over* KURBSKY, *who is kneeling on the left.* IVAN *lays a hand on* KURBSKY'S *shoulder.*

IVAN : You will command the first regiment. KURBSKY *seizes his hand and kisses it with fervour.* IVAN *turns towards the crowd.* To Kazan!

*Shot 263. Medium shot of* EUPHROSYNE, *looking on sourly. The crowd continue their enthusiastic cries, off. We see the shadows of their waving arms on the wall behind her.*

*Shot 264. Long shot of* IVAN, ANASTASIA *and* KURBSKY, *seen over the heads of the crowd at the far end of the hall. The two men raise their arms.*

*Shot 265. Medium close-up of* IVAN, ANASTASIA *beside him. He raises his arm and shouts again fiercely, while* ANASTASIA *looks up at him and smiles.*

IVAN *still more loudly* : To Kazan!

*The cries of the crowd continue over loud music.*

THE PEOPLE : To Kazan!

IVAN : To Kaza-a-n!

*Shot 266. High angle shot of the crowd, then fade out.**

*Shot 267. Exterior shot of the countryside round Kazan. Some gunners are seen in medium shot, grunting and groaning as they heave away at an enormous and unwieldy gun.*

*Shot 268. Medium close-up of a great wheel as it rolls by. Music and the sound of wagons and marching troops.*

*Shot 269. Medium shot of the gunners, hauling several enormous guns up a sloping road.*

---

\* End of the third reel.

Shot 270. High angle long shot of the road. The Russian army advances; gunners haul along the heavy guns; the cavalry lines the flanks.

Shot 271. Another high angle long shot, looking towards Kazan, which can be seen on the horizon in the distance. The music grows louder. Black clouds pass across the sky. In the foreground, guns, and the cavalry with lances and banners. (Still on page 37)

Shot 272. High angle long shot of the road down which Russian troops are passing. Constant noise of troops, and music. An infantry detachment with long halberds passes the slower artillery. A cloud of dust rises. (Still on page 37)

Shot 273. Medium shot from above of the infantry passing a gun, a line of horses in the background.

Shot 274. High angle medium shot of gunners hauling on ropes fixed to an enormous gun. The breech is elaborately carved in the shape of an animal's head. The gun passes camera in medium close-up, from right to left. A detachment of infantry follow behind. The music gets louder above the noise of the troops.

Shot 275. Medium shot, slightly from below, of IVAN's richly ornamented tent standing out against the sky. Music: the rumbling of the guns dissolves into the tune 'The Tents of Ivan'. IVAN emerges and halts on the threshold, lit by the rays of the rising sun.* (Still on page 37)

Shot 276. Medium close-up of IVAN as he stands outside the tent, his arm across his breast.

Shot 277. A closer shot of IVAN, staring fixedly ahead.

Shot 278. Long shot of the town of Kazan on the horizon.

Shot 279. Resume on medium close-up of IVAN, who looks from right to left, then lowers his arm.

Shot 280. Medium shot as IVAN leaves the tent and goes out of frame to the left.

Shot 281. Low angle long shot of IVAN's tent perched on a hill, a line of banners slightly below it to the right. IVAN stops a few feet away from the tent on the left, scans the horizon

---

* It is October 2nd, 1552: Kazan is about to fall, after a seige of several months.

*and beckons to* RASMUSSEN, *a foreign engineer, who comes
up the hill and stands beside him.\**

*Shot 282. A longer, low angle shot of the hill with a line of
soldiers curving across it.* IVAN *and* RASMUSSEN *stand near
the tent, deep in discussion. Other tents are visible in the background, on the right. End of the music 'The Tents of Ivan'.*

*Shot 283. Medium shot of* IVAN, *from below.* RASMUSSEN,
*wearing a black helmet and carrying a roll of paper, comes
towards* IVAN *from the right. The latter puts his hand on*
RASMUSSEN'S *shoulder, and they both look downwards. Music
starts again with a different theme: a* CHOIR *begins to sing
'The Tartar Steppes'.*

CHOIR *off* : ' Misery . . .'

*Shot 284. Long shot from above of the army stretched out
like three serpents on the plain below.*

CHOIR *off* : ' Misery, sorrow,
       The Tartar Steppes . . .'

*Shot 285. A closer shot of the army, from above: two serpen-
tine lines of foot soldiers with halberds, marching slowly
forwards, and a third line of cavalry. The* CHOIR *goes on
singing.*

*Shot 286. Medium shot of a bearded* SOLDIER *in the foreground, holding a large metal dish filled with small coins.
As the armed soldiers march past, each throws in a coin. The
sound of the coins landing in the dish mingles with the*
CHOIR'S *song.*

*Shot 287. Medium close-up of* IVAN *and* RASMUSSEN *contemplating the men. The song fades slightly for a few seconds.*

IVAN : The unclaimed coins at the end of the battle will indicate
the number of our losses.

*Shot 288. Medium close-up of the soldiers throwing coins into
the dish.*

*Shot 289. Medium shot of the soldiers filing past the dish, a*

---

* Rasmussen was in fact a Danish engineer who had the idea of excavating a
series of tunnels under the walls of the town; he then sited there eleven
barrels of gunpowder which when exploded destroyed the only water
reservoir. Other explosions opened breaches in the fortifications through
which the Russians poured, shouting the Crusaders' war-cry: 'God is with
us! '

line of helmets and halberds stretching away into the background.

Shot 290. *Long shot of the troops from above (as shot 285). The* CHOIR *continues to sing quietly.*

Shot 291. *Long shot of the Russian camp, banners waving in the breeze, a pall of black smoke in the background, towards Kazan.* IVAN'S *tent is seen on the hill, on the left.*

Shot 292. *Medium shot of a row of guns, gunners at the ready beside them. Their elaborately carved barrels rear threateningly across the picture. (Still on page 37)*

Shot 293. *On the cut, the gunners'* CHOIR *strikes up a rousing song. Medium shot from above of feverish excavation in the earth. Sound of spades and pick-axes.*

Shot 294. *Another shot of the same scene. Shafts of sunlight light the tunnel from the outside. The gunners'* CHOIR *continues to sing lustily, off.*

Shot 295. *High angle medium shot of the interior of the tunnel where some men are trying unsuccessfully to drag along a wooden sledge, loaded with debris.* MALYUTA *appears in the background, grabs a pole and hurries forward to help them.*

Shot 296. *Close-up of* MALYUTA *from above.*

MALYUTA : One . . . two . . . heave !

Shot 297. *High angle medium shot of* MALYUTA *shoving at the back of the heavy sledge, which moves under the combined effort.*

Shot 298. *Medium shot of the men emerging into the sunlight, dragging the sledge after them,* MALYUTA *at the back. He stops and throws the pole onto the sledge.*

Shot 299. *Medium close-up of* MALYUTA *wiping the sweat from his eyes with his sleeve. He turns and looks up.*

Shot 300. *Long shot from below of the* TSAR *and* KURBSKY *standing at the edge of the trench. The gunners'* CHOIR *continues off.*

Shot 301. *Resume on medium close-up of* MALYUTA *looking up at them. He turns and goes off to the left.*

Shot 302. *Medium shot of* MALYUTA *from the back as he goes over and starts to climb up some steps carved in the side of the trench. As he does so, some men emerge from the tunnel, dragging more debris after them.*

*Shot 303. High shot of a column of men dragging debris out of the tunnel.* MALYUTA *climbs up the side of the trench in left foreground.*

*Shot 304. Another long shot of the same scene. The* TSAR *and* KURBSKY *are standing at the top of the trench as* MAL-YUTA *climbs up towards them.*

*Shot 305. Medium shot of* MALYUTA *as he arrives just below the* TSAR *and* KURBSKY. *He turns and points downwards.*

MALYUTA *satisfied*: The tunnel can now be packed with gunpowder.

IVAN: At last! . . . After a month of waiting! . . .

*Shot 306. Medium close-up of* IVAN *and* KURBSKY *from below. (Still on page 37)*

IVAN *continuing*: It's certainly time to start the attack!

KURBSKY *sceptically*: Tunnels and powder: the Tsar's own invention!

IVAN *suspiciously*: You don't think my gunpowder will work?

*Shot 307. Medium shot of* IVAN, KURBSKY *and* MALYUTA *from below. The gunners'* CHOIR *continues off.*

IVAN *scornfully*: Horsemanship . . .

*Shot 308. Medium shot of* KURBSKY *from below, soldiers and banners behind him.*

IVAN *continues off*: Parades . . . That's all you understand.

KURBSKY *turns away angrily and goes off to the right. The other soldiers watch him go.*

*Shot 309. Medium close-up of barrels of gunpowder being rolled into the tunnel.*

*Shot 310. Medium shot of the same scene,* IVAN *at the top in the background.*

*Shot 311. High angle shot of a long line of men rolling the barrels down the slope into the tunnel. A row of soldiers stand watching in the background.*

*Shot 312. A high shot of the same scene, from a different angle.* IVAN *stands on the right, waving the men on. The song of the gunners'* CHOIR *ends.*

*Shot 313. Long shot of* KURBSKY *coming towards camera past a row of guns, followed by a line of Tartar prisoners, who are stripped to the waist. He halts in medium shot and the prisoners file past him, going out of frame to the left. Then he moves on with them. Music: 'The Bringing-out of the Tartars'.*

*Shot 314. Medium shot of the palisade of wooden stakes in front of the Russian camp. Led by two guards, the Tartar prisoners file down the hill and round the front of the palisade, to the left. The barrels of the big guns rear over them on the hill above.* KURBSKY *stands watching on the right.*

*Shot 315. Another shot of the same scene.* KURBSKY *is now in medium close-up, looking bitterly across to Kazan, the row of prisoners behind him.*

*Shot 316. Long shot of Tartar soldiers appearing on the walls of Kazan and looking across at the Russians. (Production still on page 37)*

*Shot 317. A longer shot of the Tartars on the walls and battlements. The Tartar music continues.*

*Shot 318. Medium close-up of* KURBSKY *making a sign with his hand.*

*Shot 319. Medium close-up of a Russian* SOLDIER *tying a Tartar* PRISONER *to the palisade.*

*Shot 320. Medium close-up of another* SOLDIER *doing the same.*

*Shot 321. Medium close-up of* KURBSKY, *in profile, the walls of Kazan behind him. He turns to watch the prisoners, his face hard.*

*Shot 322. Medium shot from below, of a* PRISONER, *stripped to the waist, being lashed to the palisade.*

*Shot 323. Medium shot from below, of another* PRISONER, *his arms lashed behind him, looking across to Kazan; there is another* PRISONER *in similar pose behind him.*

*Shot 324. Low angle close-up of another* PRISONER, *a rope bound across his chest, a grotesquely contorted hand at the bottom of frame. (Still on page 37)*

*Shot 325. Close-up of another Tartar* PRISONER *in a patterned turban. (Still on page 37)*

*Shot 326. Long shot from the Russian camp: the prisoners bound to the palisade on the left;* KURBSKY, *in the centre, in medium long shot; and the walls of Kazan on the hill behind.* KURBSKY *walks towards the prisoners, coming into medium shot as he does so.*

*Shot 327. Low angle medium close-up of* KURBSKY, *looking across to Kazan. Tartar prisoners are bound to the palisade above and behind him, also looking across.* KURBSKY *gives the nearest one a blow on the side of the head with his fist.*

KURBSKY *to the* PRISONER : Shout, ' Surrender Kazan '.

*The* PRISONER *turns his head away and remains mute. The Tartar music continues.* KURBSKY *looks round at the other prisoners.*

*Shot 328. Close-up of a* PRISONER *from below (as shot 324). He lays his head on one side, in a gesture of mute defiance.*

*Shot 329. Close-up of another* PRISONER *(as shot 325). He does likewise.*

*Shot 330. Medium close-up of* KURBSKY. *He turns and brings his fist down hard.*

*Shot 331. Medium close-up of* KURBSKY's *fist landing on the back of another* PRISONER's *neck.*

PRISONER *looking up and howling* : Ooooh ! . . . Kazan !

*Shot 332. Long shot of the walls of Kazan, lined with Tartar soldiers. A* PRISONER *cries out in Tartar, off.*

*Shot 333. Long shot of an elderly white-robed* MUEZZIN *on top of the tower of Kazan. He cries out to the prisoners, raising his arms.*

MUEZZIN *shouting* : It is better that you die by our hands . . .

*Shot 334. Medium close-up of the* MUEZZIN *from below, his arms raised.*

MUEZZIN *continuing* : . . . than by those of the uncircumcised.

*Shot 335. Close-up of a* PRISONER *on the palisade, listening. He drops his head on his shoulder in weary resignation.*

*Shot 336. Resume on the* MUEZZIN, *giving a sign.*

*Shot 337. Medium close-up of two Tartar* SOLDIERS *bending their bows and firing their arrows.*

*Shot 338. Medium long shot of the Tartars firing down from the walls of Kazan. We hear the whistle of arrows over the music.*

*Shot 339. Close-up of a* PRISONER *from below. He flinches as an arrow strikes the palisade beside him.*

*Shot 340. Shot of the two Tartar* SOLDIERS *firing.*

*Shot 341. Music, the whistle of arrows and thuds as they pierce the palisade. Close-up of a* PRISONER *hanging at a grotesque angle from the palisade.*

*Shot 342. Close-up of two more dead* PRISONERS, *their bodies contorted. One of them has an arrow through his neck and blood trickles down across his chest.*

*Shot 343. Close-up of another* PRISONER, *his head lolling back, an arrow through his neck; two hands clutch at the palisade. Music and the whistle of arrows continue off.*

*Shot 344. Medium shot of* IVAN *hurrying past the guns towards camera. He stops under one of the barrels and gazes angrily across at the spectacle off-screen, then moves forward into medium close-up.**

*Shot 345. Medium shot of* KURBSKY *looking across to Kazan, dead prisoners hanging from the palisade behind him.* IVAN *comes up from behind and grabs him by the shoulder, swinging him round. The music ends.*

*Shot 346. Medium shot of the two men,* IVAN *standing over* KURBSKY *on the right, the dead prisoners just behind them.*

IVAN : Such bestiality is madness . . . It's stupid, revolting ! . . .

*Shot 347. Medium close-up of part of the palisade.* MALYUTA *comes into shot, looking anxiously across at* IVAN *and* KURBSKY.

IVAN *continues off* : Even an untrained beast . . .

*Shot 348. Medium close-up of* IVAN *standing over* KURBSKY, *his hand on his shoulder.*

IVAN : . . . has got more restraint.†

KURBSKY, *furious at being humiliated in front of his troops, loses his self-control and launches himself at* IVAN.

*Shot 349. Close-up of* IVAN *in profile as* KURBSKY'S *hand comes into shot and grabs him by the shoulder.* IVAN *stares at him.*

*Shot 350. Medium close-up of* MALYUTA *grabbing a stake from*

---

* If one discounts the opinion of one or two historians it appears that this scene has been invented by Eisenstein. In fact most historians agree about Ivan's passive role during the capture of Kazan. On the other hand, the role of Kurbsky, the future traitor prince, was crucial, since he alone directed the attack whilst Ivan refused to leave his tent all day on the pretext of praying ' against the infidel '.

† This scene also seems very improbable, considering the historical context. The fact is the cruel and bloody Kurbsky was a lamb compared to Ivan whose sadism, some claim, even outdid his ' terribleness '.

*the palisade, looking across at* IVAN *and* KURBSKY.

*Shot 351. Resume on close-up of* IVAN, *a dead* PRISONER *on either side in the background.*

MALYUTA *off*: He has dared to raise his hand against the Tsar!

*As* MALYUTA *speaks off,* IVAN *stares coldly down at* KURBSKY'S *hand gripping his shoulder, then back at* KURBSKY. *The hand is slowly removed.*

*Shot 352. Close-up of* KURBSKY *turning away with lowered head.*

*Shot 353. Medium close-up of arrows embedding themselves in the palisade with loud whistles.*

*Shot 354. Another similar shot of the arrows.*

*Shot 355. Medium shot of* KURBSKY *suddenly knocking* IVAN *aside and throwing himself in front of him, brandishing his shield. An arrow lands on his shield.*

KURBSKY: I wanted to protect you . . .

*Shot 356. Medium close-up of* MALYUTA *throwing down his stake and spitting.*

KURBSKY *continuing off*: . . . from the arrows.

*Shot 357. Resume on* IVAN *and* KURBSKY. IVAN *pulls the arrow out of the shield. (Still on page 38)*

IVAN: If that was your reason . . . thank you. *He points towards the left with the arrow and* KURBSKY *goes off.*

*Shot 358. Long shot of the cavalry, ready to go into action, waiting for the command. Link on the motion as* KURBSKY *comes into frame, confused and bitter, turns round, then strides up to his troops, away from camera.*

*Shot 359. Medium close-up of* KURBSKY, *beside his horse.*

KURBSKY *to himself*: The Baltic ambassador was right. Compared to him . . . I'll never be more than a cur! *He turns to mount his horse.*

*Shot 360. Shot of the guns as* IVAN *comes into frame from the left and stands under one of the barrels, in medium shot. He turns in the direction of* KURBSKY.

IVAN *to himself*: Some arrows arrive at just the right moment!

*Shot 361. Medium close-up of* ALEXEY BASMANOV, *standing by the breech of the gun.*

BASMANOV: Even deadlier than arrows . . . is the boyars' hatred.

*Shot 362. Resume on* IVAN *in medium shot. Hearing* BASMANOV's *words he turns and hurries towards the back of the gun.*

*Shot 363. Resume on* BASMANOV *in medium close-up.*

BASMANOV: Beware of boyars more than arrows.

*Shot 364. Medium close-up of* IVAN *standing under the gun barrel.*

IVAN: Your name?

BASMANOV *comes into frame on the right and approaches* IVAN. *We see the two of them standing in medium close-up under the gun barrel,* IVAN *in profile,* BASMANOV *three-quarters facing camera.*

BASMANOV: Alexey Basmanov, son of Daniel.

IVAN: I shall not forget the name of one who hates the boyars.

IVAN *turns, claps him on the shoulder and hurries off, away from camera. The gunners'* CHOIR *strikes up a rousing song.*

*Shot 365. Medium shot of* MALYUTA *going into the dark entrance of the trench.*

*Shot 366. Close-up from above of his hands fixing fuses round a candle in the trench.*

*Shot 367. Medium close-up of a* GUNNER *holding a lighted taper. He turns and looks anxiously at* MALYUTA, *then hands him the taper.*

*Shot 368. Link on the motion as* MALYUTA *takes the taper in medium close-up. The gunners'* CHOIR *starts to sing again.*

*Shot 369. Close-up of another* GUNNER. *He leans forward, watching* MALYUTA *intently.*

*Shot 370. Medium shot of* MALYUTA *from below, the two* GUNNERS *on either side of him. He raises his eyes to heaven and crosses himself, then bends down to bring the taper to the candle.*

*Shot 371. Close-up of* MALYUTA's *hands as he lights the candle connected to the fuses with the taper.*

*Shot 372. Resume on medium shot of the three men.* MALYUTA *blows out the taper and hands it to the* GUNNER *on the right. The three of them get up and retreat cautiously away from the burning candle.*

*Shot 373. Close-up of the candle burning slowly, the fuses leading away from it. The singing ends.**

*Shot 374. Music. Medium shot of the guns on a hill facing Kazan.*

*Shot 375. Long shot of the Russian camp from above. A banner waves in the breeze in the foreground. On a distant hillock, the* TSAR's *tent.*

*Shot 376. Long shot of* IVAN's *tent, standing on the hillock against the sky, a line of banners on the right.* IVAN *comes up the slope past the banners, passes the tent and stops to the left of it, looking across at Kazan. The music continues.*

*Shot 377. Medium shot of the breech of one of the guns, carved in the shape of an animal's head.* ALEXEY BASMANOV *appears (Still on page 38) and puts an arm round the shoulders of his son* FYODOR, *who appears from the bottom of the frame as he raises his head. We see the two of them in medium close-up. They gaze across at* IVAN.

BASMANOV : Look, Fyodor, look my son!

*Shot 378. Low angle medium shot of* IVAN *on the hillock, gazing across at Kazan.*

BASMANOV *off* : The Tsar of all the Russias . . .

*Shot 379. Close-up of* FYODOR. *He gazes across at* IVAN, *enraptured.*

FYODOR *murmuring* : The Tsar! . . .

---

* End of the fourth reel.

*Shot 380. A longer shot of* IVAN *in the same pose as before. His tent is now visible, above and behind him to the right.*

*Shot 381. Close-up from above of the candle in the trench, almost burnt down, the fuses snaking away from it out of frame. The music fades.*

*Shot 382. A longer shot of the candle. The fuses ignite with a roar and burst into flame.*

*Shot 383. Close-up of the flame reaching a cask of gunpowder.*

*Shot 384. Long shot of the walls of Kazan. There is a huge explosion and a column of earth and smoke shoots into the air.*

*Shot 385. High angle shot of another explosion.*

*Shot 386. Long shot as another section of the wall explodes.*

*Shot 387. Another similar long shot; another explosion.*

*Shot 388. Medium shot of three trumpeters in the Russian camp, backs to camera, sounding the advance. Explosions continue off.*

*Shot 389. Medium close-up of* KURBSKY *on horseback, drawing his sword and exhorting his men.*

KURBSKY *shouting* : To Kazan!

*KURBSKY spurs his horse forward, out of frame, followed by the cavalry. The music 'The Attack' begins, accompanied by explosions.*

*Shot 390. Long shot of the cavalry galloping towards camera. They stream past the camera in medium shot, slightly low angle. More explosions are heard, accompanied by the clatter of hooves.*

*Shot 391. Long shot of the advance, with Kazan on the hill in the background. In the middle of the shot a heavy assault tower stands motionless while the cavalry stream past it. Another assault tower moves ponderously across the screen in the foreground, pushed by foot soldiers.*

*Shot 392. Medium shot of the assault tower from below with soldiers perched on the top. As the tower moves out of frame to the right, the camera tilts down to show the other tower in the background, guns firing from the top of it. The cavalry stream across the shot from the left foreground, their cloaks flying in the wind.*

*Shot 393. Long shot of the assault tower, slightly from below, guns firing as foot-soldiers stream past with ladders in the foreground.*

*Shot 394. Another similar shot. The music continues. Some foot-soldiers carry a battering-ram past camera.*

*Shot 395. Long shot of the assault on the walls of Kazan, which can be seen on the hill in the background. The cavalry charges, the foot-soldiers run forward, away from the camera. Firing continues from the assault tower on the left.*

*Shot 396. Long shot of the gates of Kazan.* KURBSKY *rushes towards them bearing a banner. Foot-soldiers with halberds run into shot from the left, followed by the cavalry.*

*Shot 397. Another long shot of the stream of soldiers approaching the gates, Tartar soldiers massed on the battlements above. Foot-soldiers carrying assault ladders and spears hurry past camera in close-up.*

*Shot 398. Medium shot of two of the heavy guns.* IVAN *hurries towards camera and looks across at the assault.*

IVAN *shouting*: Support Kurbsky! *He gives the signal to fire.*

*Shot 399. Long shot of the guns going into action. They fire in turn. The music continues.*

*Shot 400. Resume on* IVAN *in medium shot admidst the guns, waving his arms as they fire. Clouds of smoke drift across, masking him.*

*Shot 401. Another medium shot of the guns firing.*

*Shot 402. Long shot of the assault. The music continues. A flaming projectile whizzes across the screen. Black clouds of smoke rise upwards. In the background, we see* KURBSKY *on the summit of the tower by the gateway of Kazan, holding aloft a banner.*

*Shot 403. Another long shot of the same scene. More projectiles whizz across; the smoke thickens.*

*Shot 404. Medium long shot of* KURBSKY *from below, standing on the tower. The defenders of the town lie dead about him. He spreads his arms wide and the white lining of his cloak gleams through the smoke, while above him the* TSAR's *banner flutters in the breeze beside the Tartar crescent.*

*Shot 405. Medium shot of* KURBSKY *from below, holding aloft the* TSAR's *banner. The Tartar crescent can be seen behind it. The music reaches a climax.*

*Shot 406. Shot of swirling clouds of smoke.*

IVAN *shouting off* : Now I am truly Tsar.

> Shot 407. *Low angle medium long shot of* IVAN, *standing by the guns. Black clouds of smoke pass behind him. He raises his arms in the air as he continues to shout.*

IVAN : The whole world will acknowledge the Tsar of Moscow . . .

> Shot 408. *Low angle medium close-up of* IVAN, *his arms outstretched.*

IVAN : . . . as the true ruler of all the Russias.

> Shot 409. *Another shot of swirling clouds of smoke. The music ends, a bell begins to toll. Fade out.*

> Shot 410. *A bell tolls loudly. Fade in on medium close-up of an icon in a courtyard in the Kremlin; lighted lamps hang in front of it.*

> Shot 411. *Medium shot of the* BOYARS SHCHENYATOV *and* KURLETOV; *they stand bare-headed and silent. Over a doorway behind them is the icon — a head of Christ. The bell continues to toll.*

> Shot 412. *Medium close-up of the* BOYAR KOLYCHEV THE UNCONQUERABLE, *leaning on his staff. We see* SHCHENYATOV *and* KURLETOV *in the background, beneath the head of Christ. The bell which punctuates this series of shots tolls again.*

> Shot 413. *Medium close-up of the* BOYAR KOLYCHEV THE WISE *and the son of* KOLYCHEV THE UNCONQUERABLE, *both wearing fur capes.*

> Shot 414. *Close-up of* ALEXEY BASMANOV *and his son. They are the first in this series of shots to look concerned.*

> Shot 415. *Medium shot of three* FOREIGN AMBASSADORS, *standing with heads bowed, wearing their chains of office. Another bell with a higher note starts to ring.*

> Shot 416. *Medium shot of two other* FOREIGN AMBASSADORS, *standing with heads bowed, the* BOYARS *behind them.*

> Shot 417. *Medium long shot: on the left the black-robed* LIVONIAN AMBASSADOR *stands on some steps, leaning on his staff. The two other* FOREIGN AMBASSADORS *seen in the previous shot are to the right of him. Bells continue to ring.* KURBSKY *comes into frame from the left and comes down the steps past the* LIVONIAN AMBASSADOR, *who turns to watch*

*him. One of the other* FOREIGN AMBASSADORS *comes forward to address* KURBSKY, *who glances back over his shoulder.*

FOREIGN AMBASSADOR : How is . . .

*Shot 418. Medium close-up of* KURBSKY, *looking back over his shoulder, and the* FOREIGN AMBASSADOR *in a white ruff, leaning forward to address him. His companion is behind him to the right.*

FOREIGN AMBASSADOR *continuing* : . . . the Tsar of Moscow's health?

*As the* FOREIGN AMBASSADOR *speaks,* KURBSKY *turns towards him.*

KURBSKY : The Tsar is very ill.

KURBSKY *goes past the* FOREIGN AMBASSADOR *and out of frame to the right. The* FOREIGN AMBASSADOR *turns to address his companion.* FYODOR BASMANOV *is standing behind them in the background.*

*Shot 419. Medium close-up of the two men.*

FOREIGN AMBASSADOR *to his companion* : The Tsar fell ill . . .

*Shot 420. Medium close-up of the* LIVONIAN AMBASSADOR, *turned towards them, listening with a sardonic expression.*

FOREIGN AMBASSADOR *continuing off* : . . . while still on the journey back from Kazan.

LIVONIAN AMBASSADOR : So now even you . . .

*Shot 421. Close-up of the* FOREIGN AMBASSADOR.

LIVONIAN AMBASSADOR *continuing off* : . . . acknowledge him as Tsar!

*The* FOREIGN AMBASSADOR *turns away, his nose in the air. The bells toll again.*

*Shot 422. Long shot of the courtyard, the head of Christ on the wall in the background.* EUPHROSYNE *and* VLADIMIR *come through a doorway and make their way through the throng, respectfully greeted by the* BOYARS. *We see the tall hat of a Tartar* ENVOY *amongst the crowd. Bells continue to ring off.* EUPHROSYNE *comes forward into medium shot, her hand on* VLADIMIR'S *shoulder, and stops, leaning on her staff. She raises her eyes to heaven and crosses herself as she speaks.*

EUPHROSYNE : God is just.

*Shot 423. Close-up of the two of them,* VLADIMIR *looking completely vacant.*

EUPHROSYNE *continuing*: This Muscovite prince wanted to set himself up above all other princes! . . . And now it's all over! . . .
> *She glances to the right, puts out an arm in front of* VLADIMIR, *and goes off.**
>
> *Shot 424. The bell tolls. Medium shot of* KURBSKY *standing deep in thought.*

EUPHROSYNE *going up to him*: Well, Prince, always second best?
> *Shot 425. Medium shot of them both.*

EUPHROSYNE *continuing*: You loved Anastasia. Ivan took her from you . . . *She pauses, then in a sly voice* . . . You fought the battle of Kazan . . .
> *Shot 426. Close-up of* EUPHROSYNE. *As she speaks, she raises her eyes, then bends towards* KURBSKY.

EUPHROSYNE: Yet it is Ivan who is the hero . . . and who has all the glory, whilst you . . .
> *Shot 427. Close-up of* KURBSKY, *listening reflectively.*

EUPHROSYNE *off*: Ah! Prince, your conquest of Kazan has only added to your misfortune as well as to that of the boyars.
> *Shot 428. Medium close-up of her. She looks off in the direction of* IVAN's *chamber.*

EUPHROSYNE: As for your head, that won't stay long on your shoulders.
> *Shot 429. Close-up of her from* KURBSKY's *point of view.*

EUPHROSYNE *continuing*: The Tsar won't forget the arrow at Kazan.
> *Shot 430. Close-up of* KURBSKY, *turning to look at her in alarm.*

EUPHROSYNE *continuing off*: And if he should forget . . .
> *Shot 431. Medium shot of the staircase. Bells continue to ring, off. A vast shadow comes slowly downwards, followed by its owner,* MALYUTA. *(Still on page 39)*

EUPHROSYNE *continues off*: . . . there will always be someone to remind him.
> *Shot 432. Medium close-up of* KURBSKY *and* EUPHROSYNE. *Hearing* MALYUTA's *approach, they turn towards the sound. A bell tolls again.*
>
> *Shot 433. Medium long shot of* MALYUTA *at the bottom of*

---

* End of the fifth reel.

the stairs. *He comes forward and stops, looking off towards camera.*

A VOICE *off* : The eye of the Tsar . . .

*Shot 434. Close-up of* MALYUTA's *face. He is staring suspiciously towards* KURBSKY *and* EUPHROSYNE.

VOICE *continuing off* : Malyuta !

*Shot 435. More bells. Medium close-up of* EUPHROSYNE *and* KURBSKY, *looking over their shoulders. They turn towards camera.* (*Still on page 39*)

EUPHROSYNE : As long as Ivan lives, Kurbsky will only vegetate.

KURBSKY *stares up at* EUPHROSYNE, *then turns away and looks straight in front of him.* EUPHROSYNE *looks round behind her as we hear the sound of hymn-singing.*

EUPHROSYNE : God is good ! . . .

*She turns back and taps* KURBSKY *on the shoulder. They both look round again, away from camera.*

*Shot 436. Long shot of a procession of* PRIESTS *advancing from the far end of the courtyard. The waiting dignitaries make a path for them, bowing. The lay brothers pass first, then* PIMEN, *bearing the Holy Sacrament. Behind him, the other* BISHOPS.

*Shot 437. Medium close-up of an archway.* MALYUTA *backs into it and stares suspiciously off.*

*Shot 438. Medium shot of* KURBSKY *and* EUPHROSYNE, *with her hand on his shoulder, as they bow, backs to camera. In the background, the procession goes up the steps. The hymn singing continues.*

*Shot 439. Medium shot of the procession climbing the staircase.*

*Shot 440. Medium close-up of the trains of the clerical robes as they glide along the floor in front of* VLADIMIR, *who is seated at the bottom of the staircase, staring in amazement.*

*Shot 441. Close-up of* VLADIMIR, *his eyes following the procession.*

*Shot 442. A high shot of the* PRIESTS, *all in black, carrying lighted candles, as they mount the staircase. They come past camera from right to left, in medium close-up, while* VLADIMIR *watches in the background.*

*Shot 443. The procession, still in medium shot, enters the royal*

*apartments. The* PRIESTS *duck as they pass through the low doorway. The hymn singing swells. The enormous studded door closes behind them.*

*Shot 444. Medium long shot of the* BISHOPS *in black, standing round a table holding candles.* PIMEN *in his white robe stands out amongst them. The* CHOIR *chants.*

*Shot 445. A closer shot of the same scene. Pan left from the group towards the enormous, sumptuously decorated bed on which* IVAN *is lying.\**

*Shot 446. Medium shot of the* BISHOPS *standing at the table, backs to camera. We see* PIMEN *in the centre, facing camera between their dark silhouettes. The chanting gets louder.* PIMEN *makes the sign of the cross then picks up a large gilded bible and holds it up in front of his face. He turns towards the left.*

*Shot 447. Medium close-up of a white-bearded* PRIEST, *who goes up to the bed and holds out a lighted candle. In the background, the procession can be seen, advancing slowly as they sing.*

*Shot 448. Close-up of the candle in the* PRIEST'S *hand.* IVAN'S *hand comes into shot and takes the candle.*

*Shot 449. Link on the motion as* IVAN *sinks slowly back onto his pillows in medium close-up, candle in hand.*

*Shot 450. A closer shot of* IVAN'S *face, wide-eyed and motionless.*

*Shot 451. Medium shot as* PIMEN, *now leading the procession, comes round to the head of the bed and holds the bible high above* IVAN'S *head.*

*Shot 452. Medium close-up of the elaborately gilded cover of the bible as* PIMEN *lowers it towards* IVAN. *The* CHOIR *continues to sing.*

*Shot 453. Medium shot as* PIMEN *holds the book while a white-bearded* BISHOP, *on the left, opens it to reveal the illuminated text. Another* BISHOP *steadies the book on the right. They*

---

\* This scene agrees, more or less, with all the historical accounts. It takes place in March 1553; Ivan was then twenty-three. It should be noted that the evening before Extreme Unction, Ivan had summoned his secretary, Mikhailov, in order to dictate his last wishes. The latter hastened to read them to the interested parties, thus putting an end to their hopes.

*tilt the book down towards* IVAN. *(Production still on page 40)*

*Shot 454. Medium close-up of the bible being lowered over* IVAN'S *head. He raises his head slightly, then sinks back.*

*Shot 455. Close-up of the spine of the bible as* PIMEN *withdraws his hands; the* BISHOPS *lay theirs on the book. The* CHOIR *sings.*

*Shot 456. Medium shot of* PIMEN *as he raises his eyes to heaven and makes the sign of the cross. On either side of him the* BISHOPS *gaze down at the Holy Book covering* IVAN'S *face. The singing fades out and the bell tolls again.*

IVAN *off* : Lord, have mercy on my soul.

*Shot 457. Slightly high angle close-up of* IVAN *almost hidden by the bible, holding the burning candle on his breast. The* BISHOPS *stand round him, candles in hand. The bell tolls again.* IVAN'S *lips move feebly.*

IVAN *murmuring* : Lord have mercy! Lord have mercy!

*Shot 458. Close-up of* IVAN.

IVAN : Lord have mercy!

*He struggles to raise his head from under the bible, glances round the room, then, exhausted, drops back on the pillow.*

*Shot 459. The bell tolls again. Medium close-up of an icon in the corridor outside, a black monk's robe lying beneath it.*

*Shot 460. Close-up of the robe.*

EUPHROSYNE *off* : To whom . . .

*Shot 461. Medium close-up of* EUPHROSYNE *and* KURBSKY *as we saw them previously.* EUPHROSYNE *is facing camera on the right,* KURBSKY *with his back to her in profile on the left.*

EUPHROSYNE : . . . will you swear an oath of allegiance?

KURBSKY : To Dimitri, the heir apparent. *He turns to face* EUPHROSYNE.

*Shot 462. Close-up of them both.*

KURBSKY *continuing* : To Ivan's son.*

---

* Ivan's children by the Tsarina Anastasia were as follows: Anna, born August 10th, 1548, died July 20th, 1550; Maria, born March 17th, 1551, date of death unknown; Dimitri, born October 6th, 1552, died June 26th, 1553. In the present scene Dimitri, the heir apparent, was only six months old. Later will come Ivan, born March 28th, 1554, murdered by his father on November 19th, 1582; Eudoxia; and Fyodor the First (who became

EUPHROSYNE *between clenched teeth*: And Anastasia! . . .
KURBSKY *turns away sullenly* . . . It's the widow's still-warm bed
which fills your thoughts . . . you want to make her your mistress . . .

*Shot 463. Close-up of* EUPHROSYNE. *(Still on page 73)*

EUPHROSYNE : Swear allegiance to Vladimir.

*Shot 464. Close-up of* KURBSKY, *who gives a faint and disdainful smile.*

*Shot 465. Resume on* EUPHROSYNE.

EUPHROSYNE : Money doesn't buy men like you.

*Shot 466. Close-up of* KURBSKY *as she continues off. He raises his eyes reflectively. (Still on page 73)*

EUPHROSYNE *off* : They have to be offered a kingdom.

*Shot 467. Resume on* EUPHROSYNE *in close-up.*

EUPHROSYNE : With Vladimir on the throne it is you who will act
as regent . . .

*Shot 468. Medium close-up of* VLADIMIR *by himself.*

EUPHROSYNE *off* : He is worse than a child. VLADIMIR *catches a
fly in flight and imprisons it in his hand, which he raises to his ear.
He listens and smiles.* EUPHROSYNE *continues off* : He is moronic.

*Shot 469. Close-up of* KURBSKY *from below, looking upwards.*

EUPHROSYNE *off* : You will be absolute master!

*Shot 470. Medium close-up of* KURBSKY *in the same pose.*
EUPHROSYNE'S *head comes into shot on the right. She brings it
close to* KURBSKY *and hisses insidiously in his ear.*

EUPHROSYNE : Swear allegiance to Vladimir.

*The bell tolls again. The noise of a door opening makes them
turn sharply.*

*Shot 471. Medium close-up of* MALYUTA *appearing under the
archway where we saw him previously and gazing before him.
The bell tolls.*

*Shot 472. Close-up of* MALYUTA *raising one of his eyelids with
a finger as he looks ahead.*

*Shot 473. Extreme close-up of* MALYUTA'S *face as he scrutinises*
KURBSKY *and* EUPHROSYNE. *(Still on page 74)*

*Shot 474. Resume on them in medium close-up.* KURBSKY
*retreats behind* EUPHROSYNE *and clasps her hand, which she*

---

Tsar); of his second marriage with Maria Cherbasky there was Vassily,
who lived two months; of his eighth marriage with Maria Nagoy, Dimitri,
born October 19th, 1583, assassinated in May 1591 and canonised in 1606.

*has placed on his shoulder. They exchange glances. Bells.*
*Shot 475. Long shot of the corridor: we see the* BASMANOVS *on the left.* FYODOR *is bending over his father with his hands on his shoulders.* MALYUTA *comes forward in the centre of the shot and makes a quiet announcement.*

MALYUTA : The Tsar is calling. *He bows very low and leaves.\**

*Shot 476. Medium close-up of the baby* DIMITRI *sleeping in his cradle in the royal apartments. Music: ' Ivan petitions the Boyars ', which continues throughout the scene.*

*Shot 477. Medium shot of* ANASTASIA *kneeling beside* IVAN's *motionless body. She touches his hand but he makes no response.*

*Shot 478. Medium long shot of* ANASTASIA *kneeling beside* IVAN's *bed. We see the cradle on the left. She looks off left, then rises slowly to her feet.*

*Shot 479. Long shot of the bedroom, with* ANASTASIA *standing by the bed in the background. Two carpets run diagonally across the stone-flagged floor to the centre of the shot.* EUPHROSYNE *appears in the foreground, back to camera, and advances into the room followed by* VLADIMIR *and some* BOYARS. *They halt and bow.*

*Shot 480. Medium shot of* ANASTASIA *and* EUPHROSYNE, *bowing to each other. We see* IVAN *lying on his bed behind them.* ANASTASIA, *startled by* EUPHROSYNE's *gaze, puts a hand towards* IVAN. *The two women stand eyeing each other for a moment. Then* IVAN *speaks and they both turn towards him.*

IVAN : The end is near . . .

*Shot 481. Close-up of* IVAN's *head resting on the pillows, his eyes closed; he has difficulty in speaking.*

IVAN *continuing*: I bid the world farewell. *His unsteady gaze examines each of the faces about him.* Swear allegiance to my legitimate heir . . . *He opens his eyes wide* . . . Dimitri.

*Shot 482. Medium shot of* VLADIMIR *turning, terrified, to his mother as she pushes him forward.*

*Shot 483. Resume on close-up of* IVAN. *He turns his head and stares at* VLADIMIR.

---

\* End of the sixth reel.

*Shot 484. Close-up of* VLADIMIR. *He looks from* IVAN *to his mother and back again.* EUPHROSYNE'S *hand comes into shot on the right as she lays it on* VLADIMIR'S *shoulder. The music swells.*

*Shot 485. Medium shot, slightly from below, of* VLADIMIR *and* EUPHROSYNE.

*Shot 486. Medium shot of* IVAN, *with* ANASTASIA *partly visible beside him in the foreground.*

IVAN *raising himself painfully*: Swear loyalty to my son . . .
*He raises an arm and falls down on the side of the bed as* ANASTASIA *tries to support him.*

*Shot 487. Close-up of* DIMITRI *sleeping in his cradle. Music.*

*Shot 488. Resume on medium shot of* IVAN *supported by* ANASTASIA. EUPHROSYNE *and* VLADIMIR *pass slowly across in front of camera. Only the backs of their cloaks are visible.* IVAN *and* ANASTASIA *follow them with their eyes.*

*Shot 489. Close-up of the couple.* IVAN, *after gazing for a while at* EUPHROSYNE *and* VLADIMIR, *turns to the right to contemplate the other side of his bed. (Still on page 75)*

*Shot 490. Close-up of the lugubrious gaze of the* BOYAR KOLYCHEV THE UNCONQUERABLE. *Music.*

*Shot 491. Close-up of his son, glancing out of the corner of his eye.*

*Shot 492. Close-up of* KOLYCHEV THE WISE, *scowling.*

*Shot 493. Resume on* IVAN, *still supported by* ANASTASIA, *as he angrily sits up again.*

IVAN *hoarsely*: Swear allegiance to my son! . . . *He sinks back into* ANASTASIA'S *arms.*

*Shot 494. Medium close-up of* IVAN *from below, supported by* ANASTASIA. *As he speaks he starts forward, staring up.*

IVAN *continuing*: Only an undivided, legitimate throne will save Moscow from her enemies and internecine conflict . . .

*Shot 495. Medium close-up of* IVAN *as, staggering with weakness, he succeeds in getting up, his arms outstretched.* ANASTASIA *continues to support him.*

IVAN: . . . without which the Tartars will again violate our frontiers . . .

*Shot 496. Long shot of the room as* IVAN *staggers forward, putting a hand to his brow. The* BOYARS *stand, stolidly in-*

*different, on either side while* ANASTASIA *remains by the cradle in the background. The music swells.*

IVAN : . . . the Poles and Livonians encroach. *He comes forward into medium close-up and looks up into the faces of the* BOYARS. *He raises his hands beseechingly* . . . I don't entreat you for me or my son . . .

Shot 497. *Close-up of* IVAN, *falling to his knees.*

IVAN *continuing* : . . . but for the unity of the Motherland! *He raises a hand and falls down out of shot.*

Shot 498. *Link on the motion. Medium close-up from above as he falls to the ground.*

Shot 499. *Medium shot of the cradle.* ANASTASIA *rushes into frame and places herself protectively in front of it.*

Shot 500. *Close-up of* ANASTASIA *standing anxiously in front of the cradle.*

Shot 501. *Long shot of the room with* IVAN *on the floor in the centre of shot, the three* KOLYCHEVS *standing motionless behind him. Camera tracks out as* IVAN *raises himself and crawls forward to address* IVAN PALITSKY *in the foreground. He stretches out his hand as he speaks.*

IVAN *feebly* : Palitsky! . . . *The* BOYAR *turns away.* Ivan! . . .

Shot 502. *Medium close-up, slightly from above, of* IVAN *kneeling amidst the* BOYARS' *cloaks, his arms outstretched towards* PALITSKY. *He turns towards another* BOYAR.

Shot 503. *Close-up of* IVAN, *clasping the* BOYAR *by the shoulders. (Still on page 75)*

IVAN *beseeching* : Ah! . . . Turuntay-Pronsky! . . .

TURUNTAY-PRONSKY *gazes down at him and looks away uncomfortably.* IVAN *turns and gazes up at another* BOYAR *towards the left. Then he moves out of frame.*

Shot 504. *Link on the motion as* IVAN's *face comes into frame in close-up, gazing up at the* BOYARS.

IVAN : Kolychev the Wise! . . . Daniel Bogdany . . .

Shot 505. *Close-up of* KOLYCHEV *turning away.*

IVAN : You — give an example . . .

Shot 506. *Resume on medium close-up of* IVAN *as he sinks back, looking desperately up. Leaning backwards at the feet of the* BOYARS, *he raises his head.*

*Shot 507. Close-up of* IVAN, *raising his head to look at* KOLYCHEV THE UNCONQUERABLE, *directly above him.*

IVAN *murmuring*: Kolychev the Unconquerable, why don't you speak?

*Shot 508. Low angle close-up of the latter. He gazes down at* IVAN, *then turns away.*

IVAN *continues off*: Kurletov! . . .

*Shot 509. Medium close-up of the* BOYARS, FUNIKOV *and* PALITSKY, *facing camera. In the background* IVAN, *kneeling, stretches out to* FUNIKOV.

IVAN *with a tormented cry*: Funikov!

FUNIKOV *comes round in front of* PALITSKY, *turns and looks sideways down at* IVAN. PALITSKY *turns away. The music swells.*

*Shot 510. Medium shot of* IVAN *lying on the floor beside his bed. He looks from side to side, then draws himself up.*

*Shot 511. Medium close-up of* IVAN, *leaning backwards against the side of his bed.*

IVAN *hoarsely*: You will all be cursed forever. *He tries to rise to regain his bed.*

*Shot 512. Close-up of* IVAN. *He rises to his feet.*

IVAN: Traitors to the Russian Earth.

*Shot 513. Medium shot as he stretches to his full height and shouts.*

IVAN: All of you will be cursed . . .

*Shot 514. Medium close-up of* IVAN. *He makes a slashing movement with his arm, and thunders out.*

IVAN: . . . cursed for all eternity! *He stops, his head thrown back.*

*Shot 515. Medium shot: his strength deserts him, he collapses on his bed.*

*Shot 516. Medium close-up from above of* IVAN, *motionless, lying on his back.*

*Shot 517. Medium shot of* IVAN's *legs hanging over the edge of the bed.* ANASTASIA *hurries into frame from the left and kneels down, gazing anxiously up at* IVAN. *She takes his foot in her hands.*

*Shot 518. Medium close-up of* ANASTASIA *as she carefully*

*raises* IVAN'S *leg onto the bed, and bends forward to look at him.*

*Shot 519. Close-up of* IVAN'S *head, eyes closed, motionless.*

*Shot 520. Close-up of* VLADIMIR *staring down at* IVAN. *He looks uneasily towards the left.*

*Shot 521. Medium close-up of* DIMITRI *sleeping in his cradle.*

*Shot 522. Medium long shot of the cradle.* EUPHROSYNE *comes into frame from the left, one arm raised. Music.*

*Shot 523. Resume on* ANASTASIA *at* IVAN'S *feet. She turns and dashes forward.*

*Shot 524. Medium shot as she pushes* EUPHROSYNE *away from the cradle and bends over the child.*

*Shot 525. Medium close-up as* ANASTASIA *snatches the child from the cradle and turns to face* EUPHROSYNE. *The latter rears threateningly over her and* ANASTASIA, *terrified, rushes off hugging little* DIMITRI *to her breast.*

ANASTASIA *off* : Only Dimitri . . .

*Shot 526. Close-up from above of* IVAN, *lying motionless.*

ANASTASIA *off* : . . . his son . . . can save Russia.

*Shot 527. Medium close-up of* ANASTASIA *in a corner of the room, still clutching* DIMITRI. *She looks round at the assembled* BOYARS.

ANASTASIA : Once you have rejected undivided authority, no matter how strong, courageous, intelligent you may be . . .

*The baby starts to cry.*

*Shot 528. A closer shot of* ANASTASIA, *still clutching* DIMITRI, *who cries as she continues vehemently.*

ANASTASIA : . . . your government will be directionless. Your feuds and hatreds will deliver you up to the foreigner. *She waves an arm in emphasis, then hugs* DIMITRI *to her bosom.*

EUPHROSYNE *off* : The boyars will never submit . . .

*Shot 529. Medium close-up of her in front of the* BOYARS. *She speaks vehemently, her eyes blazing.*

EUPHROSYNE : . . . to the offspring . . . *She points in* IVAN'S *direction.*

*Shot 530. Close-up of* IVAN'S *profile as he lies back on his bed.*

EUPHROSYNE *off* : . . . of the Prince of Moscow !

*Loud music.*

KOLYCHEV THE WISE *off*: Power . . .

    *Shot 531. Medium close-up of him and* VLADIMIR. VLADIMIR
    *looks up at* KOLYCHEV *as he speaks.*

KOLYCHEV: . . . must pass to a Tsar . . .

    *Shot 532. Close-up of* KOLYCHEV THE WISE *as he thunders
    louder and louder.*

KOLYCHEV: . . . who will share it with the boyars . . .

    *Shot 533. Close-up of* VLADIMIR. *He looks round with an
    expression of combined stupidity and haughtiness.*

KOLYCHEV THE WISE *continues off*: . . . and who will serve not
some unknown Russian State but . . .

    *Shot 534. New shot of the two.* VLADIMIR *nods stupidly at*
    KOLYCHEV'S *words.*

KOLYCHEV: . . . the noble boyars.

    EUPHROSYNE *rushes up behind* VLADIMIR *and pushes* KOLY-
    CHEV *aside. As she speaks she stretches out a hand, then lays it
    on* VLADIMIR'S *breast.*

EUPHROSYNE *shouting*: Swear allegiance to the Tsar Vladimir!
    *A bell tolls.*

    *Shot 535. Medium shot of* KURBSKY *entering by the low door
    of the bedroom.**

    *Shot 536. Medium shot of* ANASTASIA *standing by* IVAN'S
    bed,* KURBSKY *at her side. The same music as before starts
    again.* ANASTASIA *starts towards* KURBSKY *then draws aside as
    he goes up to the bed and leans over* IVAN.

    *Shot 537. Close-up of* IVAN, *lying back, motionless, on the bed.*
    KURBSKY'S *face comes into shot from the left. He leans over*
    IVAN *and looks down into his eyes.*

    *Shot 538. Extreme close-up of their two faces.* KURBSKY
    *glances up sideways at the* BOYARS.

    *Shot 539. Resume on close-up (as shot 537). Looking down at*
    IVAN *again,* KURBSKY *draws slowly back and leaves the frame.*

    *Shot 540. Close-up of* ANASTASIA, *three-quarters facing
    camera, and* KURBSKY, *in back view. He turns away from the
    bed and looks up at* ANASTASIA, *then looks away again as she
    raises her head and closes her eyes. Music.*

    *Shot 541. Low angle close-up of* ANASTASIA. *She opens her*

---

\* End of the seventh reel.

*eyes and tears run down her cheeks.*

*Shot 542. Medium close-up of the motionless* IVAN, *from above.*

*Shot 543. Close-up of* KURBSKY *and* ANASTASIA *in profile. She looks imploringly down into his eyes.*

*Shot 544. Medium close-up of the couple in profile.* EUPHRO-SYNE'S *head comes into shot on the left; she looks suspiciously down at* KURBSKY. *The couple raise their eyes to look at* EUPHROSYNE, KURBSKY *turning his head. The music continues loudly.* KURBSKY *lowers his gaze, then looks sideways up at* ANASTASIA *as she and* EUPHROSYNE *eye each other warily across the top of his head.*

*Shot 545. Long shot of the three of them. The two women draw away from* KURBSKY, *who is between them with his head bowed.* VLADIMIR *comes into shot on the left and his mother takes him by the arm and leads him off towards the right.* KOLYCHEV THE WISE *follows on the left.*

*Shot 546. Slightly high angle long shot of* VLADIMIR, *supported by his mother, and* KOLYCHEV THE WISE, *coming towards camera. They pass through the ranks of the* BOYARS, *who stand aside and bow respectfully.*

VOICES *off*: Long live the Tsar of the boyars!

*The* BOYARS *bow the three of them out as they leave the shot in the foreground on the left. In the background we see* KURBSKY *and* ANASTASIA *by* IVAN'S *bed. The* BOYARS *turn to face them.*

*Shot 547. Medium shot of the two of them by the bed. They look at the* BOYARS, *then at each other.* KURBSKY *rises and comes forward into medium close-up.*

*Shot 548. Resume on long shot of the room.* KURBSKY *pauses, then strides forward between the* BOYARS, *who follow him out of the room.*

*Shot 549. Medium close-up of little* DIMITRI *in his cradle. Music.*

*Shot 550. Long shot of* KURBSKY *entering the chapel and coming to a halt before a large image of the Saviour on the wall. The* BOYARS *come in after him and file towards camera.*

*Shot 551. A closer shot of the same scene. The* BOYARS *file past the camera in medium close-up, leaving* KURBSKY *alone in the background, looking up at the image of the Saviour. Music.*

*Shot 552. Medium close-up of* KURBSKY.

KURBSKY : Which road shall I travel? The one . . .

*Shot 553. Close-up of him in profile before the image of the Saviour, looking upwards.*

KURBSKY : . . . which leads to the throne, or the one which leads to marriage? Who should I choose? Anastasia? . . . *He turns towards camera and looks down* . . . Euphrosyne?

*Shot 554. Music. New medium shot of the chapel.* ANASTASIA *comes in, pauses and goes out of frame to the right.*

*Shot 555. Medium shot of* KURBSKY. ANASTASIA *hurries in from the left.* KURBSKY *rushes up behind her and seizes her by the arm. She spins round and he thrusts his face towards her in medium close-up.*

KURBSKY : Anastasia, if you will be mine, I will protect you from the boyars . . .

*Shot 556. A closer shot of the two of them.*

KURBSKY : If you will be mine I will raise you to the throne . . .

ANASTASIA *puts up a hand as if to stop him speaking.*

*Shot 557. Close-up of him, carried away by his enthusiasm.*

KURBSKY : If you will be mine, we will rule Russia together!

*Shot 558. Resume on the two of them in medium close-up.* ANASTASIA *thrusts* KURBSKY *aside in horror and goes off to to the left.*

*Shot 559. Medium shot of* ANASTASIA *hurrying towards the door of the chapel.* KURBSKY *rushes after her and grabs her by the arm, going down on one knee.*

KURBSKY : Without you my life has no meaning . . . *He gets up, grabbing her by the shoulders.* Nor death, either . . .

ANASTASIA *tries to escape back into the chapel; he holds onto her.*

*Shot 560. Medium close-up of the two of them.* ANASTASIA *cowers away from* KURBSKY *as he leans over her.*

KURBSKY : With you, the throne . . . or the scaffold . . . it's all the same!

*Shot 561. Close-up of the huge eye of Christ on the wall.*

KURBSKY *continues off* : My Tsarina of Moscow!

*Shot 562. Medium close-up of them both in front of the icon of Christ,* KURBSKY *in profile,* ANASTASIA *looking up at him.*

ANASTASIA : Prince, one does not bury a man before he is dead.

KURBSKY, *dismayed by* ANASTASIA'S *tone of voice, shrinks back. The music comes to an end.*

*Shot 563. Link on the motion. Medium shot as* KURBSKY *draws away from* ANASTASIA *in front of the image of Christ. He looks wildly from side to side.*

KURBSKY *stupefied* : You mean Ivan isn't dead?

ANASTASIA *leaves frame on the left.*

*Shot 564. Medium long shot of the passage leading out of the chapel.* ANASTASIA *comes into frame from the right and pauses in medium shot, turning back to* KURBSKY.

ANASTASIA : God will be your judge! *She hurries out.*

KURBSKY *follows her for a moment, then stops.*

*Shot 565. Medium long shot of* ANASTASIA *going through the low door of* IVAN'S *bedroom.*

*Shot 566. Medium close-up of* KURBSKY *in the passage leading from the chapel. He recoils in horror as he speaks.*

KURBSKY *in a whisper* : Ivan is not dead!

*Shot 567. Medium shot of* KURBSKY *coming back into the chapel, towards camera. He stops in medium close-up; his eyes widen thoughtfully.*

*Shot 568. Close-up of the huge eye of Christ on the wall. A bell tolls, off.*

KURBSKY *off* : If Ivan is not dead . . .

*Shot 569. Resume on medium close-up of him, looking agonised, the huge eye of the icon on the wall behind him. (Still on page 76)*

KURBSKY : . . . Kurbsky can no longer live. *He turns to look at the icon.*

*Shot 570. Long shot of the chapel, slightly from above.* KURBSKY *hurries towards camera, leaving the chapel in the opposite direction to that taken by* ANASTASIA.

*Shot 571. Long shot of the* BOYARS *and* PRIESTS *assembled in a room in* IVAN'S *apartment. A lectern with candles placed on it stands in the foreground, while on the left we see* PIMEN, VLADIMIR *and* EUPHROSYNE. *The* BOYARS *draw aside as* KURBSKY *hurries into the room at the back. He pauses in front of* EUPHROSYNE, *then comes up to the lectern, opens* a case containing a crucifix and lays his hand on it. *The* BOYARS *turn to watch him from behind.*

KURBSKY: In the name of the Father, the Son and the Holy Ghost . . .

*Shot 572. Medium shot of* PIMEN, EUPHROSYNE *and* VLADIMIR *watching him intently.*

KURBSKY *continues off:* . . . I swear by the Holy Writ to serve faithfully . . .

*Shot 573. Close-up of* KURBSKY. *He looks to the right then off to the left, in the direction of* VLADIMIR.

KURBSKY: . . . the heir to the throne, the legitimate Tsar of Moscow . . .

*Shot 574. Close-up of* VLADIMIR, *looking pleased and expectant.*

*Shot 575. Resume on* KURBSKY *in close-up. He turns to face camera again.*

KURBSKY: . . . Dimitri Ivanovich!

*Shot 576. Close-up of* PIMEN, *starting forward in amazement.*

*Shot 577. Medium close-up of* EUPHROSYNE. *She steps back in dismay.*

*Shot 578. Close-up of* VLADIMIR, *overcome. He looks round with his mouth open. (Still on page 76)*

*Shot 579. Resume on* KURBSKY *in close-up.*

KURBSKY: In evidence of which, I kiss the cross.

*He raises the crucifix to his mouth and kisses it. It covers half his face, leaving one eye staring grotesquely sideways. (Still on page 76)*

*Shot 580. Medium close-up:* EUPHROSYNE *rushes forward and tears the cross away from* KURBSKY. *They glare at each other. They hear a noise and quickly turn round.*

*Shot 581. Medium shot from the same angle as everyone turns with them.*

*Shot 582. Medium shot of the doorway. Two* BOYARS *standing on the left retreat out of frame as* IVAN *comes slowly into the room, supported by* MALYUTA *and* ANASTASIA. *He halts in medium close-up and draws himself up. (Still on page 76)*

*Shot 583. Close-up of* IVAN'S *face from below. He looks suspiciously round at the* BOYARS. *(Still on page 76)*

IVAN: The Holy Sacrament has cured me!

*Shot 584. Medium shot of the* BOYARS *bowing and crossing themselves.* IVAN *passes amongst them.*

*Shot 585. Medium shot of* EUPHROSYNE *and* KURBSKY *by the lectern, looking round at* IVAN. EUPHROSYNE *moves out of frame to the left as* IVAN *comes up to* PIMEN *in the background and bows low before him.*

*Shot 586. Link on the motion.* IVAN *bows before* PIMEN. *The latter watches him warily, then blesses him, while* VLADIMIR *watches, mystified, in the background.*

*Shot 587. Resume on medium shot of* KURBSKY *standing by the lectern. On the left* IVAN *looks up sideways at him as he straightens up in front of* PIMEN, *then comes across to him.* KURBSKY *looks warily up at* IVAN *as the latter addresses him.*

IVAN *hesitating slightly*: You . . . have always been close to the Tsar. *He claps a hand on* KURBSKY'S *shoulder.* I shall raise you higher still . . .

*Shot 588. Medium close-up of the two men.* KURBSKY *sinks to his knees and* IVAN *leans towards him.*

IVAN : . . . for at the hour of the supreme test . . . KURBSKY *closes his eyes.*

*Shot 589. Close-up of the two men,* IVAN *in profile, leaning over* KURBSKY, *who opens his eyes again and looks up at the Tsar.*

IVAN *continuing*: . . . you alone remained faithful. I shall invest you with a sacred mission. *They both rise.*

*Shot 590. Link on the motion. They rise in medium close-up and* IVAN *comes round to the right. The two men are seen in profile looking towards the left.*

IVAN : We have consolidated the East . . . KURBSKY *turns to face* IVAN, *who continues* . . . you will lead the Russian forces to the West . . . *They both look upwards towards the left, their eyes alight* . . . to the Baltic !

KURBSKY *turns his back to camera, facing* IVAN. *The music 'The High Seas' begins, as* IVAN *embraces* KURBSKY.

*Shot 591. Reverse shot of the two men, embracing in close-up. They place their cheeks together, first on one side then on the other. As they do so,* KURBSKY *looks over* IVAN'S *shoulder towards* ANASTASIA, *off-screen to the right.*

*Shot 592. Close-up of* ANASTASIA; *she watches them, then*

*looks away.*

*Shot 593. Resume on close-up of* KURBSKY *watching* ANA-
STASIA *over* IVAN'S *shoulder. He frowns slightly.* IVAN *embraces him on the other cheek and his gaze settles on someone else. His eyes widen.*

*Shot 594. Close-up of* MALYUTA'S *rugged face as he watches
suspiciously. (Still on page 76)*

MALYUTA *sarcastically* : Flying like an arrow? . . .

*Shot 595. Resume on* KURBSKY *looking over* IVAN'S *shoulder.*

MALYUTA *continues off* : . . . Well, fly !

KURBSKY *ducks behind* IVAN'S *shoulder.*

*Shot 596. Close-up from above, as he sinks down past* IVAN'S
*body to kneel at his feet.*

IVAN *off* : And to defend . . .

KURBSKY *looks up at* IVAN *standing behind him. The music
ends.*

*Shot 597. Medium close-up of* IVAN. *The* BOYARS *move
forward expectantly behind him.*

IVAN *continuing* : . . . our southern borders against the Crimean
Khan . . .

*Shot 598. Close-up of* IVAN.

IVAN *emphatically* : . . . I appoint Alexey Basmanov.

*Shot 599. Medium close-up of the* BOYARS *looking at each
other in amazement.*

A BOYAR : Who? . . . Who is he? . . .

*Shot 600. Resume on* IVAN *in medium shot;* VLADIMIR,
EUPHROSYNE *and* KURBSKY *behind him on the left. They
turn as* ALEXEY BASMANOV *enters and comes forward to kneel
at the feet of the* TSAR. IVAN *lays a hand on his shoulder.
(Still on page 76)*

*Shot 601. Medium close-up of* FYODOR BASMANOV *in the
doorway, looking on, enraptured.*

*Shot 602. Close-up of* ALEXEY BASMANOV, IVAN'S *hand on
his shoulder. He raises his head to look at the* TSAR.

*Shot 603. Close-up of* IVAN *looking down at* BASMANOV. *Then
he raises his head and stares across the room.*

*Shot 604. Close-up of* KURBSKY *looking on with a vicious
expression. Fade out.*

*Shot 605. Fade in on close-up of* EUPHROSYNE, *a sour expression on her face.**

VOICE OF A BOYAR *off* : The Tsar trusts no one . . . he sends away the boyars who are closest to him.

*Shot 606. Long shot of* EUPHROSYNE'S *room in the* STARITSKY *apartments.* EUPHROSYNE *is seated on a chair on a dais surrounded by the* BOYARS. *We see* KOLYCHEV THE WISE *on the right.*†

KOLYCHEV THE WISE : He surrounds himself with nobodies . . .

ANOTHER BOYAR : . . . Like these low-born Basmanovs . . .

*Shot 607. Medium close-up of* EUPHROSYNE, *the* BOYARS *behind her on the right.*

ANOTHER BOYAR : . . . and takes them into his confidence.

EUPHROSYNE : I know.

KOLYCHEV THE WISE *coming forward* : He strips us . . .

*Shot 608. Medium shot of the same scene.* KOLYCHEV THE WISE *gesticulates emphatically as he continues. We see* KOLYCHEV THE UNCONQUERABLE *below and behind him to the right.*

KOLYCHEV THE WISE *continuing* : . . . of our hereditary possessions and distributes them to absolutely anyone.

KOLYCHEV THE UNCONQUERABLE : He persecutes the boyars.

ANOTHER BOYAR : Shchenyatov has been arrested!

*Shot 609. Medium close-up of* EUPHROSYNE, KOLYCHEV THE WISE *in soft focus behind her.*

BOYAR *continuing off* : Kurletov has been arrested!

EUPHROSYNE : I know.

KOLYCHEV THE WISE *steps forward in the background.*

A VOICE : I'm going to escape.

ANOTHER VOICE : I daren't . . .

*Shot 610. Medium close-up of a white-bearded* BOYAR. *He looks anxiously from side to side as he speaks.*

BOYAR : I'm frightened . . . I shall flee . . .

---

\* End of the eighth reel.

† Historically speaking, the following scene took place several months later. From the moment he was better, Ivan returned to his hectic round of work and debauchery, giving the impression he had forgotten the betrayal. The truth, probably, was that he was planning the most considerable revenge possible without harming his programme for the absolute unification of Russia.

*Shot 611. Resume on* EUPHROSYNE *in medium close-up. Behind her,* KOLYCHEV THE WISE *watches the* BOYAR *as he continues off.*

BOYAR *off* : . . . to Livonia.

KOLYCHEV THE WISE *turns back to* EUPHROSYNE.

EUPHROSYNE *severely, turning towards the* BOYAR, *off-screen* : Ivan Ivanovich, aren't you ashamed? *She gets up.*

*Shot 612. Medium shot of the same scene. Link on the motion as* EUPHROSYNE *rises from her chair.*

EUPHROSYNE : The Archbishop has gone to see the Tsar . . . He'll get us pardoned . . .

*Shot 613. Noise of a door opening and the sound of footsteps. Long shot of* PIMEN, *followed by his acolyte,* PETER VOLY- NETS, *hurrying into the room. He throws himself down on a bench. The* BOYARS *gather round.*

*Shot 614. Medium shot of* PIMEN *sprawled across the bench,* PETER VOLYNETS *beside him.*

PIMEN : The Tsar pardons no one.

*Shot 615. Medium close-up of* PIMEN *and* PETER VOLYNETS.

PIMEN *gesticulating* : He has stripped me, his confessor . . . *He shakes his head in despair.*

*Shot 616.* EUPHROSYNE *appears under the arch of the inner chamber and comes into close-up.*

PIMEN *continues off* : . . . of everything.

*Shot 617. Resume on close-up of him. (Still on page 76)*

PIMEN : He's sending me from Moscow to Novgorod.

*Shot 618. Medium long shot of* EUPHROSYNE *going forward and falling to her knees before* PIMEN. *The white-bearded* BOYAR, *who is standing in the background on the left, raises his arms and shakes his fists in despair.*

BOYAR *running to the door* : I'm going to get away!

*Shot 619. Medium shot of the doorway. The* BOYAR *rushes into frame from the left, halts and comes back towards camera.*

BOYAR : For God's sake fly.

*Shot 620. Resume on* EUPHROSYNE *in medium close-up, getting up in fury.*

EUPHROSYNE : Let cowards run away!

*Shot 621. A closer shot of her. She raises her head.*

EUPHROSYNE : Those who stay . . .

    *Shot 622. Medium shot of* VLADIMIR *from above, sitting under an arch; he looks up anxiously as his mother continues off.*

EUPHROSYNE *off* : . . . will fight !

    *Shot 623. Close-up of* VLADIMIR, *listening in alarm.*

PIMEN *off* : Whilst the Tsar's best friend . . .

    *Shot 624. Medium close-up of* PIMEN; EUPHROSYNE *and the assembled* BOYARS *behind him.*

PIMEN *continuing* : . . . Kurbsky is away . . . *The* BOYARS *crowd forward to listen,* KOLYCHEV THE WISE *in the middle* . . . we must take him firmly in hand. *He wags a finger, then stretches out his hand in an imperious gesture.* To start with we must curb Ivan's power.

    *Shot 625. Close-up of* PETER VOLYNETS. *His face comes into shot from the right as he leans forward in order to hear better.*

PIMEN *continues off* : We must oppose his military campaigns . . .

    *Shot 626. Close-up of* PIMEN, *one finger raised.*

PIMEN : . . . refuse the money for the war in the Baltic provinces. *He lowers his hand.*

EUPHROSYNE *off* : But above all else . . .

    *Shot 627. Medium close-up of her in profile.*

EUPHROSYNE : . . . we must separate Anastasia . . . *She raises her head with a sinister expression* . . . from Ivan.

    *Beginning of the music ' The Poisoning '.*

    *Shot 628. Close-up of* EUPHROSYNE. *She looks darkly round at the* BOYARS.

EUPHROSYNE : It is I who will take charge of that.

    *Loud music. She puts her hand up in front of her face then turns away from camera. Fade out.*

    *Shot 629. Fade in on a close-up of the cockerel emblem of Ivan the Third in* IVAN'S *stateroom.\* It is the same hall in which the wedding feast took place earlier.*

IVAN *off* : I need the maritime towns, the Baltic towns . . .

    *Shot 630. Medium close-up, slightly low angle, of the emblem of Riga: an armed figure carrying a model of a building in*

---

\* Ivan the Third, known as Ivan the Great (1462-1505), did not know his grandson Ivan the Fourth, known as Ivan the Terrible.

*its hand, a name-plate in front of it.*

IVAN *off*: Riga . . .

*Shot 631. Close-up of a similar emblem bearing the name of Reval.*

IVAN *off*: Reval . . .

*Shot 632. Close-up of the emblem of Narva.*

IVAN *off*: I need Narva . . .

*Shot 633. Medium shot of* IVAN *surrounded by his models.*

IVAN: Once again the Rigans and the Hanseatics have intercepted the English ships . . . *He seizes a candlestick and hurls it to the ground, with a crash* . . . Once again . . . *He kicks another candlestick.*

*Shot 634. Medium close-up of* IVAN, *the cockerel emblem behind him.*

IVAN: . . . they deprive me of lead, of sulphur . . . and my artillery of trained gunners!

*Shot 635. Close-up of the emblem of Riga (as shot 630).*

*Shot 636. The emblem of Reval (as shot 631).*

IVAN *continues off*: I shall . . .

*Shot 637. The emblem of Narva (as shot 632).*

IVAN *off*: . . . use force . . .

*Shot 638. Low angle medium close-up of* IVAN, *looking down to the right.*

IVAN: . . . to stop these treacherous neighbours . . . *He raises his eyes* . . . from throttling our commerce . . . *He twists a string of beads angrily in his hands* . . . Not only . . .

*Shot 639. Close-up of* IVAN *in profile.*

IVAN: . . . the Germans are stumbling-blocks to our ambitions, but also you boyars! In opposing my campaigns . . .

*Shot 640. Medium close-up of the* BOYARS *standing at the end of the stateroom.*

IVAN *continuing off*: . . . in the Baltic you are worse than the Germans and the Livonians . . .

*Shot 641. Medium shot of the* BOYARS *seen under an archway.*

IVAN *off*: . . . you are Russia's worst enemies.*

---

* This war against the Baltic Provinces was very important for Ivan. Karl Marx has noted in his writings: 'Ivan IV persevered in his intensive efforts against the Baltic States. His aim was clear: by access to the Baltic he wished to provide Russia with a way of communication with Europe. This

*Shot 642. High angle long shot of the great room:* IVAN *leaves his throne at the far end and strides towards the* BOYARS, *who stand paralysed. His shadow looms on the wall above them.* IVAN *stops suddenly and stamps with fury. The* BOYARS *turn and flee. Sound of their hasty footsteps.* IVAN *comes towards camera and stands in front of a desk, bearing maps and a metal globe, on a dais in the foreground. The music 'The Tents of Ivan' begins. He sits down and we see the gigantic shadow of his head and pointed beard projected on the far wall.*

*Shot 643. Medium long shot of* NEPEYA, *who has been standing on some steps to the right of the desk throughout the preceding shot.* IVAN'S *shadow looms on the wall behind him.*

*Shot 644. Resume on long shot of the room (as shot 642).* NEPEYA *comes across to the desk and bows.*

IVAN : You see, Nepeya, just why I have to bring about this alliance.

*He gives a sign. A* SERVANT *comes slowly down some steps on the right bearing a superb chess-set.*

*Shot 645. Medium shot of the desk,* IVAN *seated,* NEPEYA *standing in the background. Link on the motion as the* SERVANT *lays the chess-set down on the table, then retires. The music stops. (Still on page 109)*

IVAN *pointing to the chess-set* : Take this present to the gracious Queen Elizabeth of England . . .

*Shot 646. Medium close-up of* IVAN, *slightly high angle, the chess-set in front of him.*

IVAN : You will demonstrate to her with these pieces . . . *He picks up the queen and, as he continues to speak, moves it across the board to illustrate his words. He bangs it down again on the left* . . . just how the English boats can cross the Baltic . . . *He moves the board away and points at a map on the desk* . . . to reach us by the White Sea . . .

*Shot 647. Close-up of* IVAN.

IVAN : . . . in the teeth of the Germans and Livonians. *He looks up at* NEPEYA.

*Shot 648. Resume on medium close-up of* IVAN *at the desk,*

is why Peter I, known as Peter the Great, so admired him.' (Marx and Engels Archives)

*his finger on the map.*

Ivan : And remind her that Tsar Ivan in Moscow . . . *He gets up and his head goes out of frame at the top* . . . is solely in charge of negotiations . . .

*Shot 649. Medium shot of* Nepeya. *The shadows of* Ivan *and the metal globe loom above him on the wall.*

Ivan *off*: That he orders and controls all commerce. He accords privileges to whosoever pleases him . . .

*Shot 650. Shot of shadows on the wall.* Ivan's *huge shadow on the left, the globe in the middle,* Nepeya's *tiny shadow at the bottom on the right. (Still on page 109)*

Ivan *off*: . . . and whosoever does not please him will never enter Moscow . . . *The shadow of* Ivan's *hand moves across the top of the frame* . . . On the other hand, his friends will have the route to the West completely open.

*Shot 651. Medium shot of* Ivan *holding out a parchment.**

*Shot 652. Long shot of the room, slight high angle,* Ivan *at his desk in the foreground.* Nepeya *takes the parchment and goes off, followed by the* Servant, *who has picked up the chessboard.*

*Shot 653. Medium long shot of the two men going off down the room. Their tiny shadows pass under the vast shadow of* Ivan's *head on the wall behind them. The music ' Anastasia's Illness' begins.*

*Shot 654. Medium shot of* Ivan, *seated at the desk. He wraps his cloak around him and leans back, looking thoughtful.†*

*Shot 655. Medium close-up of an embroidered picture of the*

---

* End of the ninth reel.

† There is no dissolve to separate this sequence and the next, which, historically, are situated at a great distance from each other in time. In fact Anastasia fell ill during a great pilgrimage undertaken by the Tsar for political ends, which had a great success throughout Russia. This ' propaganda tour' was, however, very tiring and it resulted in the death of the young Tsarevich, Dimitri (aged eight months). When, shortly afterwards, the Tsarina fell ill, Ivan ordered the return to Moscow. The illness lasted a long time and during it Anastasia gave birth to Fyodor. She succumbed to it on August 7th, 1560. This is the day on which the scene starts. It should be noted, moreover, that the poisoning theory is much disputed by the historians, the majority of whom dismiss it. Eisenstein, in order to develop his argument against the boyars, relies solely, historically speaking, on Ivan's letters written to Kurbsky a few years later. (*The Great Soviet Encyclopedia*)

*Virgin hanging on the wall in* ANASTASIA'S *room.*

*Shot 656. Medium shot of the same, lamps burning in front of it. The music continues.*

*Shot 657. Medium close-up of* ANASTASIA *lying ill in bed.*

*Shot 658. Close-up of* EUPHROSYNE *in profile, shrouded in black, seated beside the bed, looking down at* ANASTASIA.

*Shot 659. Medium shot of the two women. Lighted lamps hang above the bed.* ANASTASIA *stirs in her sleep.*

*Shot 660. Close-up of* ANASTASIA'S *head on the pillow. She stirs slightly. The music grows louder.*

*Shot 661. Medium shot of the room,* EUPHROSYNE *sitting by the bed.*

*Shot 662. Medium shot of* IVAN *walking across his stateroom, having got up from his armchair. The shadow of the globe looms on the wall in the background.* IVAN'S *shadow follows him across from right to left.*

*Shot 663. Resume on medium shot of* EUPHROSYNE *by* ANASTASIA'S *bed. She turns abruptly and looks off to the right.*

*Shot 664. Medium long shot of a small door at the top of the steps leading out of the stateroom. Preceded by his shadow,* IVAN *comes into shot from the left and goes up the steps and out of the door.*

*Shot 665. Long shot of* ANASTASIA'S *room, a flight of steps leading from the corridor in the foreground,* EUPHROSYNE *by the bed in the background.* EUPHROSYNE *gets up and comes towards camera and down the steps. A door opens off-screen, casting a shaft of light across the steps.* IVAN *enters from the right and* EUPHROSYNE *bows as he comes towards her.*

*Shot 666. Medium shot of the two of them as* IVAN *passes* EUPHROSYNE *and goes up the steps. He suddenly pauses and turns, and puts an arm round* EUPHROSYNE, *gazing at her intently. The music continues. Then he turns again and goes on into the room, dropping his cloak on the stone balustrade beside the steps.* EUPHROSYNE *backs away down the steps to the right.*

*Shot 667. Medium shot of* EUPHROSYNE *as she backs down the steps and hides in a corner at the bottom, just under the stone balustrade. She peeps over the top of it.*

*Shot 668. Medium long shot of* ANASTASIA *lying in bed.* IVAN

*comes into frame from the right, back to camera, and goes up
to the bed. He sinks to his knees beside it, then after a pause
lowers his head onto* ANASTASIA's *breast.*

*Shot 669. Close-up of* IVAN *lowering his head onto* ANA-
STASIA's *breast and closing his eyes. She strokes his head.
(Still on page 110)*

ANASTASIA *with difficulty*: Are you troubled, Tsar Ivan?

IVAN: I am alone. *Raising his head.* There is no one I can trust.
Kurbsky is far away . . . ANASTASIA *opens her eyes wide at the
mention of his name* . . . fighting in the Baltic States. Fyodor
Kolychev is even further away: he is praying in the Solovyets
monastery . . . I only have you. *He lays his head on her breast
again. She kisses him gently.*

*Shot 670. Close-up of* EUPHROSYNE, *watching with a sinister
expression.*

*Shot 671. Long shot from above of* IVAN *cradled in* ANA-
STASIA's *arms.*

*Shot 672. Medium close-up of the same scene. They look up
as they hear the sound of footsteps.*

*Shot 673. Medium shot of* EUPHROSYNE, *hiding by the door,
as a* COURIER *runs in and up the steps.*

*Shot 674. Long shot of the room. The* COURIER *pauses half-
way up the steps and holds out a parchment.* IVAN *hurries
forward from beside the bed and bends over the balustrade
to take it.*

COURIER: It's from Ryazan!

IVAN *unrolls the scroll.*

IVAN *to* ANASTASIA: It's from Basmanov! *The music ends. He
gets up.*

*Shot 675. Medium shot of* IVAN *going over to a candle in a
corner to see the parchment more clearly.*

IVAN *looking up from the letter*: Again the boyars! They have
disobeyed my orders again! *He turns angrily and goes towards the
bed in the background.*

*Shot 676. He sits down on the bed in medium close-up and
continues to read the parchment.* ANASTASIA *looks anxiously
up at him. (Still on page 110)*

IVAN: They betray Russia. They are preventing Basmanov and
the people from defending Ryazan. They are ready to surrender

the city . . .

> *Shot 677. Close-up of the two of them.* IVAN *clenches his fist and presses it to his forehead.*

IVAN : . . . to the Emperor of the Crimea.

ANASTASIA *looking up at him* : Be firm !

> *Shot 678. Resume on medium close-up of the two of them.* IVAN *looks angrily round as he speaks.*

IVAN : I will be. So much the worse for the boyars ! . . . *He gets up.*

> *Shot 679. Shot of the arched ceiling of the bedroom from below.* IVAN *comes forward into medium close-up and glares down at the* MESSENGER, *off-screen. (Still on page 110)*

IVAN : I shall confiscate all their estates. *He throws down the parchment furiously, then leans forward on the balustrade* . . . The only concessions I will make . . .

> *Shot 680. Medium close-up of* EUPHROSYNE, *listening in her hiding-place.*

IVAN *continues off* : . . . will be for services to the State.

> *Shot 681. Long shot of the room.* ANASTASIA *lies on the bed in the background. In the foreground,* IVAN *moves further along the balustrade to the right and leans forward again.*

IVAN : But those who dishonour themselves on the battlefield . . .

> *Shot 682. Medium shot of* EUPHROSYNE *in her hiding-place by the door.*

IVAN *continues off* : . . . will lose everything !

> *The* COURIER *hurtles past* EUPHROSYNE *down the steps and out of the door. She moves forward into the doorway.*
>
> *Shot 683. Close-up of* EUPHROSYNE. *She gazes up towards* IVAN *in a cold rage.*

EUPHROSYNE *muttering to herself* : You go too far, Tsar Ivan !

> *She turns away. Loud sinister music: 'The Poisoning'.*
>
> *Shot 684. Medium close-up of* EUPHROSYNE *in the doorway. She produces a silver goblet and empties a phial of poison into it, then conceals it under her sleeve. She glances sinisterly up the steps. We hear the voice of* MALYUTA, *off.*

MALYUTA *off* : Bad news . . .

> *Shot 685. Resume on* IVAN *in medium shot at the top of the steps with* MALYUTA *beside him, holding out a parchment.*

MALYUTA *continuing* : The Russian troops at Revel have been beaten. *In the background* ANASTASIA *tries to raise herself.* Kurbsky is beaten.

IVAN *in astonishment* : Kurbsky?

*In the background,* ANASTASIA *falls back on the pillow with a cry. She tries to raise herself again but falls half out of the bed. The two men look round and* IVAN *runs to her. Music.*

*Shot 686. Medium shot of* ANASTASIA. IVAN *rushes into frame from the right and, kneeling down beside the bed, lifts her gently back onto the pillow.*

*Shot 687. Close-up of* EUPHROSYNE *holding up the goblet*

*with the sleeve of her cloak draped over it.*

*Shot 688. Medium close-up of* IVAN, *looking anxiously down at* ANASTASIA, *who is breathing heavily. He looks round, wide-eyed, and reaches out an arm.*

*Shot 689. Link on the motion as* IVAN'S *hand appears in close-up and tips up a goblet by the bed. It is empty.*

*Shot 690. Resume on medium close-up of* IVAN *and* ANASTASIA. *Link on the motion as he withdraws his hand and looks wildly round, then goes off to the right.*

*Shot 691. Long shot of the room. In the foreground* MALYUTA, *in medium close-up, gazes grimly in front of him. Behind him,* IVAN *comes forward from the bed and casts around frantically, looking for some water. He goes off to the right.*

*Shot 692. Close-up from above of* ANASTASIA *in bed, her*

101

*breast heaving. She opens her eyes.*

ANASTASIA *murmuring weakly*: Could he have betrayed us? *She closes her eyes again.*

*Shot 693. Close-up of* EUPHROSYNE'S *hand uncovering the goblet she is holding. She moves it out of frame.*

*Shot 694. Medium close-up of the balustrade by the door.* EUPHROSYNE'S *hand appears, holding the goblet. She sets it down on the top of the balustrade and pushes it forward. The music gets louder. (Still on page 110)*

*Shot 695. Close-up of* IVAN'S *face from below as he searches frantically round for some water. Suddenly he catches sight of the goblet and moves out of frame to the right.*

*Shot 696. Medium shot of the balustrade from the steps below, the goblet standing on top of it,* EUPHROSYNE'S *face in medium close-up at bottom of frame.* IVAN *appears behind the balustrade, picks up the goblet, looks into it (Still on page 110), then goes off, cradling it in his hands. Camera holds on* EUPHROSYNE, *hiding beneath the balustrade. She turns and looks upwards. Sinister music.*

*Shot 697. Long shot of the room with* MALYUTA *staring ahead in the foreground as* IVAN *hurries past with the goblet.*

*Shot 698. Medium shot of the bed.* IVAN *comes in from the right and kneels down beside* ANASTASIA, *holding out the goblet. She sits up and takes it with both hands, looking towards camera.*

*Shot 699. Close-up of* IVAN, *in profile, looking up at his wife.*

*Shot 700. Close-up of* ANASTASIA, *slowly raising the goblet to her lips, staring ahead. She pauses, then lowers the goblet again.*

*Shot 701. Close-up of the top of the balustrade.* EUPHROSYNE'S *head appears, shrouded in black. She turns and looks across towards* ANASTASIA.

*Shot 702. Close-up of* ANASTASIA, *the goblet raised. She seems to have noticed* EUPHROSYNE *and her eyes are wide with alarm. (Still on page 111) Slowly she raises the goblet in front of her face and drinks. We hear a short, sinister phrase on the violin. Fade out.*\*

---

\* End of the tenth reel.

*Shot 703. Fade in on a high shot of* ANASTASIA'S *body, lying in a coffin in the cathedral of Moscow, surrounded by candles. (Still on page 111) The camera cranes slowly down to show* IVAN, *prostrate with grief, on the floor beside the coffin. Hymns are being sung off.* PIMEN'S *voice is heard off, reading.*

PIMEN *off*: God be my salvation . . .

*Shot 704. Close-up of* ANASTASIA *from above, elaborately dressed.*

PIMEN *continuing off*: . . . for the waters are come in unto my soul. I sink . . .

*Shot 705. Medium close-up of* IVAN *at the foot of the coffin. (Production still on page 112)*

PIMEN *off*: . . . beneath the deep waters where nothing can save me.

*Shot 706. Medium close-up of* PIMEN, *who is standing reading at a lectern. The coffin is in the background.*

PIMEN *continuing*: I am in the depths of the flood and its current . . .

*Shot 707. Medium shot of* IVAN *by the coffin. He is leaning forward, staring at the ground.*

PIMEN *off*: . . . bears me away . . .

*Shot 708. Close-up of* IVAN.

PIMEN *off*: . . . I no longer have the strength to groan . . .

*Shot 709. Resume on medium close-up of* PIMEN.

PIMEN: My tongue is dry, my eyes no longer see . . . *A bell tolls.*

*Shot 710. Medium shot of* MALYUTA *as he comes slowly forward beneath the tall candles surrounding the coffin. He is holding out a sheet of parchment.*

MALYUTA: Prince . . .

*Shot 711. Close-up of* IVAN *by the coffin, staring downwards.*

MALYUTA *continuing off*: . . . Ivan Mikhailovich Shuisky has fled . . .

*Shot 712. Resume on* MALYUTA.

MALYUTA: . . . to Livonia. *He glances down at* IVAN, *off-screen* . . . Prince Ivan Vassilievich Sheremetyev . . .

*Shot 713. Medium close-up of* MALYUTA *from below. He looks down at* IVAN *again as he speaks.*

MALYUTA: . . . was captured in flight. Boyar Tugoy Luk-Suzdalsky has fled . . .

*Shot 714. Medium shot of the scene,* PIMEN *in the foreground* on the left, MALYUTA *and the coffin in the background. The hymn singing continues off.*

MALYUTA : . . . to Livonia.

PIMEN : Those who hate me without cause . . .

*Shot 715. Medium close-up of* PIMEN; *in the background* IVAN *and* MALYUTA.

PIMEN *continuing* : . . . are more numerous than the hairs on my head.

MALYUTA : Prince Mikail Vorotynsky . . .

*Shot 716. Close-up of* MALYUTA.

MALYUTA *continuing* : . . . has fled. Prince Ivan Ivanovich Turuntay-Pronsky has been recaptured, arrested and brought to Moscow. *He lowers the parchment and turns away.*

*Shot 717. Medium long shot of* IVAN *beside the coffin. He gets up slowly. The hymns continue.*

IVAN : Have I done wrong? . . . *He stretches up an arm and leans against the side of the coffin* . . . Is it God's punishment? . . . *He collapses on the steps of the catafalque. Sound of the fall* . . . Ah! . . .

*Shot 718. Medium close-up of* PIMEN *at the lectern.*

PIMEN : I have become a stranger unto my brethren and without significance to the sons . . .

*Shot 719. Medium close-up of* MALYUTA.

PIMEN *continues off* : . . . of my own mother.

    *Hymns. The two* BASMANOVS *come up behind* MALYUTA. ALEXEY BASMANOV *whispers urgently in his ear.* MALYUTA *claps his hand over* BASMANOV'S *mouth and looks anxiously off to the right.*

    *Shot 720.* IVAN *rises slowly into view from bottom of frame, in medium close-up, as he struggles to his knees beside the coffin. He looks beseechingly upwards.*

IVAN : Am I right in my heavy struggle? *His head drops forward.*

    *Shot 721. Close-up from above of* ANASTASIA *in the coffin.*

    *Shot 722. Close-up of* EUPHROSYNE, *looking on warily.*

    *Shot 723. Medium close-up of her, leaning on her staff, watching* IVAN, *off-screen.*

    *Shot 724. Medium long shot of her, standing in a corner of the cathedral. Hymns.*

    *Shot 725. Low angle medium long shot of* IVAN, *standing by the coffin. He runs a hand along the side of it, looking upwards, then drops his hand and bows his head.* MALYUTA *and the* BASMANOVS *stand in the background.* MALYUTA *comes forward on the left and sinks down on the steps of the catafalque.*

    *Shot 726. Medium close-up of* IVAN *from below, leaning against the coffin. He turns abruptly as* MALYUTA *addresses him.*

MALYUTA *off* : Great Sovereign, Kurbsky has fled to King Sigismund.

    IVAN *looks round, wide-eyed, and falls wearily against the side of the coffin.*

IVAN *painfully* : What? . . . My friend Kurbsky! . . . What have I done to him? *He looks up towards* ANASTASIA.

    *Shot 727. Close-up from above of* ANASTASIA *in the coffin.*

IVAN *off* : What more could he have wanted? . . . Or could it be . . .

    *Shot 728. Resume on low angle medium close-up of* IVAN *against the coffin.*

IVAN : . . . that he coveted my crown? *He falls against the coffin again.*

    MALYUTA *rises into shot on the left and whispers urgently to him.*

MALYUTA *in a hoarse whisper* : Taking advantage of the defeat in the Baltic States, the boyars are rousing the people against you.

IVAN *turns, masking* MALYUTA *as the latter sinks down again out of shot.*

PIMEN *off* : Shame . . .

*Shot 729. Close-up of* IVAN, *leaning his head back against the side of the coffin.*

PIMEN *continuing off* : . . . has eaten into my heart and I am full of weariness. I have looked for mercy . . . IVAN'S *head drops forward* . . . but it has not been granted me . . . IVAN *turns and leans his forehead against the side of the coffin.* I have sought . . .

*Shot 730. Medium close-up of* IVAN, *seen between two candles. He turns slowly as* PIMEN *continues off, then suddenly bounds forward.*

PIMEN *continuing off* : . . . consolation but without finding it.

*Shot 731. Link on the motion: close-up of* IVAN *thrusting his face forward.*

IVAN *shouting* : You lie !

*Shot 732. Medium close-up of* PIMEN *recoiling, terrified, and snatching up his book.*

*Shot 733. High-angle medium close-up of* EUPHROSYNE, *who reacts similarly.*

*Shot 734. High angle long shot of* IVAN *standing by the coffin. He hurls aside two of the great candlesticks, which crash to the ground one after the other.*

IVAN : The Tsar of Moscow has not yet been brought to heel !

*In the foreground on the left,* PIMEN *hurls aside the lectern and bible and strides off to the right.*

*Shot 735. Medium shot of* EUPHROSYNE. *She ducks down and disappears through a small doorway.*

*Shot 736. The hymns get louder. Long shot of* PIMEN *striding angrily out of the cathedral.*

*Shot 737. Medium close-up of* IVAN *beside the coffin, with* MALYUTA *in the background on the left.* IVAN *gazes suspiciously round, then turns and leans forward, his hands grasping the top of the coffin behind him.*

*Shot 738. Medium long shot of the* BASMANOVS. *They come forward.*

*Shot 739. Resume on* IVAN *in medium close-up.*

IVAN : You are few ! . . . *He comes down a step* . . . Send for my last and only remaining faithful friend, Fyodor Kolychev . . . *He looks upwards* . . . He is praying for us in the far-off Solovyets monastery.

*Malyuta comes up behind Ivan on the left and addresses him.*

Malyuta : Tsar, do not trust Boyar Kolychev.

*He leaves again and his place is taken by Alexey Basmanov.*

Basmanov : Surround yourself with new men . . .

*Shot 740. Close-up of* Basmanov, *looking up at* Ivan, *his son* Fyodor *beside him.*

Basmanov *continuing* : . . . who have sprung from the people and who owe you everything. With them, forge about you an iron ring, a circle of spears pointing towards the enemy.

*Shot 741. Close-up of* Basmanov's *face, raised towards* Ivan.

Basmanov : Choose men who will renounce everything, who will deny father and mother to serve only the Tsar and the dictates of his will. *He turns towards* Fyodor, *off-screen.*

*Shot 742. Close-up of the two* Basmanovs. *Link on the motion as the father turns towards his son and puts an arm round his shoulder. Then he turns and looks up at* Ivan *again.*

Basmanov : The first link of the iron ring will be my son. *He caresses* Fyodor's *head.* To these noble ends I donate my only son ! *He hurls* Fyodor *forward.*

*Shot 743. Medium shot of the three men as* Fyodor *falls at* Ivan's *feet.*

Basmanov : With these men alone you will be able to retain power, break the boyars . . . Ivan *lays a hand on* Fyodor's *head.* Basmanov *continues* . . . overthrow treachery and achieve great ends.

Ivan *looks down at* Fyodor, *then back at* Basmanov, *and puts an arm round the latter's shoulder.*

Ivan : You are right, Alyoshka ! I shall bind myself about with iron. We will form a brotherhood of iron. Outside the brotherhood we will trust no one. *He leans back against the coffin* . . . I shall be an iron leader . . . *He turns away from them* . . . I shall leave Moscow . . .

*Shot 744. Medium close-up of* Ivan *gazing fiercely downwards.*

Ivan : . . . and withdraw to the hamlet of Alexandrov !

Malyuta *coming into frame on the right* : You will take Moscow by assault !

BASMANOV *coming into frame from the left*: You will return to Moscow as a conqueror.

IVAN *raises his head slowly.*

*Shot 745. Close-up of* IVAN *raising his head.*

IVAN: No, it is not as a soldier I will return . . . *He leans forward again. . . .* not as a soldier . . .

*Shot 746. Resume on medium close-up of the three of them.*

IVAN: . . . but summoned by the entire populace.

BASMANOV: Don't rely on the people.

MALYUTA: Don't listen to beggars . . . don't trust vagabonds.

IVAN *angrily*: You are getting above yourself, cur! You presume to instruct the Tsar! BASMANOV *and* MALYUTA *go out of frame.* By the people's summons . . .

*Shot 747. Close-up of* IVAN.

IVAN: . . . I shall gain limitless power. It will be like a new coronation, enabling me relentlessly to consummate my great task!

*The 'Poisoning' theme music starts very loudly.* IVAN *looks off at* MALYUTA.

*Shot 748. Medium close-up of* MALYUTA, *turning away.*

*Shot 749. Resume on* IVAN. *He looks round at* BASMANOV.

*Shot 750. Close-up of* BASMANOV, *turning away.*

*Shot 751. Medium close-up of* IVAN. *The music swells. His confidence seems to waver; then he turns and looks up into the coffin.*

*Shot 752. Rapid close-up of* ANASTASIA *in the coffin, seen from above.*

*Shot 753. Resume on* IVAN. *He turns from the coffin. We hear the same violin phrase which accompanied* ANASTASIA'S *poisoning as his eyes light upon* FYODOR, *off-screen.*

*Shot 754. Close-up of* FYODOR, *watching him in admiration.*

*Shot 755. Close-up of* FYODOR *in profile.* IVAN'S *face comes into shot on the right, also in profile.*

IVAN: What do you say?

FYODOR: You are right!

*Shot 756. Medium shot of the two men.* IVAN *turns and strides up to the coffin. The 'Poisoning' theme music continues loudly.*

*Shot 757. Medium shot of three of the candles round the coffin.* IVAN *leans backwards against the top of the coffin and*

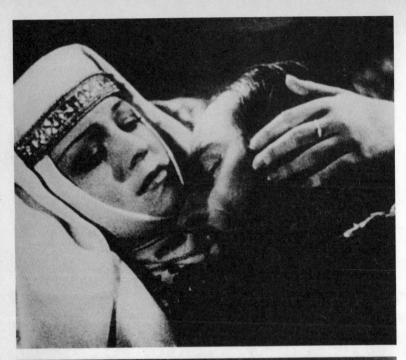

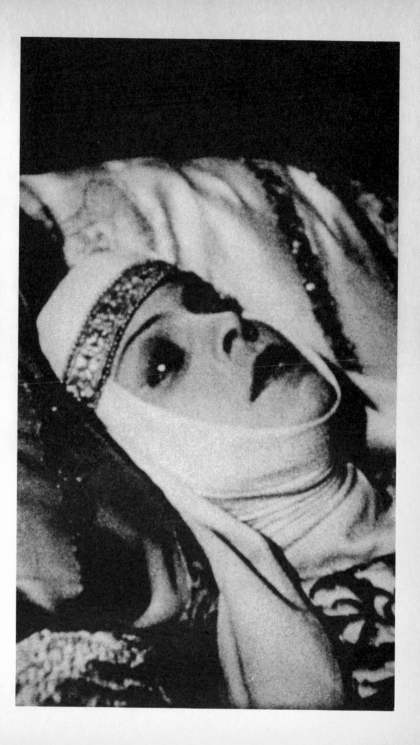

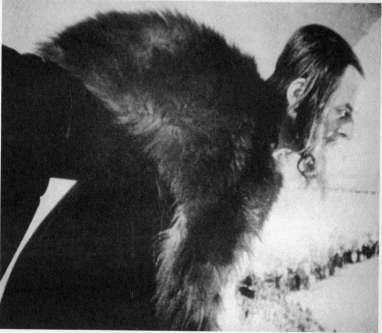

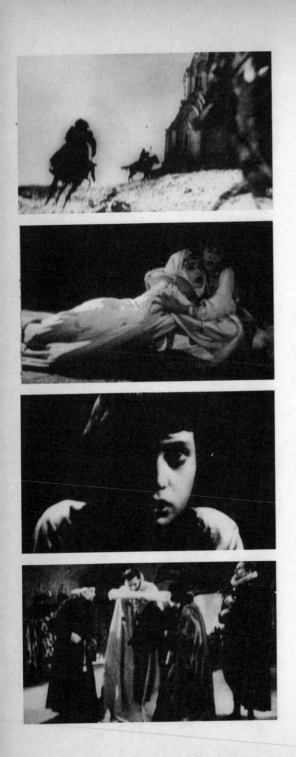

*raises an arm.*

IVAN : The call of the people will express God's will. I shall accept the sword of vengeance from God's hand. *He gazes down at the three men, off-screen.*

*Shot 758. Close-up of* IVAN. *He brings his arm down and stretches out his hand.*

IVAN : I shall accomplish great things.

*Shot 759. Medium close-up of* IVAN *in front of the candles. He throws both arms in the air and thunders at the top of his voice.*

IVAN : Two Romes have fallen. Moscow is the third. She will stand firm, for there will never be a fourth !

*Shot 760. The 'Poisoning' theme ends, and is replaced by the even more violent theme of 'Ivan the Terrible'. Very high angle long shot of the cathedral. In the centre* IVAN *stands over the coffin, and* ANASTASIA'S *white robes gleam in the dim light. From the far end of the cathedral a crowd streams in, bearing torches.*

*Shot 761. High angle medium shot of* IVAN, *standing over* ANASTASIA. *The crowd surge round him.*

*Shot 762. Close-up of* FYODOR, *slightly low angle. He gazes up at* IVAN, *lost in admiration, his head framed by flaming torches.*

*Shot 763. Similar close-up of* ALEXEY BASMANOV.

*Shot 764. Close-up of* MALYUTA. *In contrast to the others he looks unimpressed.*

*Shot 765. Close-up of* IVAN, *the torches behind him. He turns sideways and bends down towards* ANASTASIA.

*Shot 766. Close-up of* ANASTASIA *from above.* IVAN'S *head comes into frame. He kisses her on the forehead, then lays his head on hers. Loud music and fade out.\**

*Shot 767. Fade in on a low angle medium shot of a* HERALD *in the middle of the Kremlin Square. It is day. The* HERALD *is reading a proclamation by the* TSAR *from a parchment. We hear the noise of the crowd.*

HERALD : ' These princes and boyars have amassed great wealth,

---

\* End of the eleventh reel.

but not a thought do they spare for the Tsar . . .'

*Shot 768. Medium shot of the* HERALD *reading to the people.*

HERALD *continuing* : '. . . or the State, and they are even indifferent to religion . . .'

*Shot 769. Long shot of the* HERALD, *and the people and the* BOYARS *gathered in the square. Murmuring of the crowd.*

HERALD : '. . . since they refuse to defend themselves against our enemies, the Tartars, the Livonians, the Germans . . .'

*Shot 770. Resume on medium shot of the* HERALD *and the people.*

HERALD : '. . . and oppress the people This is why the Tsar, Sovereign and Grand Duke . . .'

*Shot 771. Long shot (as shot 769).*

HERALD : '. . . is abandoning the State and Moscow, the capital.'
*Movements and murmurs of reaction in the crowd.*

*Shot 772. Low angle medium close-up of the* HERALD. *He turns from side to side. (Still on page 113)*

HERALD : ' But the Tsar bears no malice against the citizens, shop-keepers and orthodox Christians of Moscow . . .'

*Shot 773. Medium long shot of the* HERALD, *the* BOYARS *and the people in the square.*

HERALD : '. . . and in no way holds them responsible.'
*The* HERALD *starts to roll up the parchment. An* OPRICHNIK *comes round from behind him.*

OPRICHNIK : As for those good Christians . . .

*Shot 774. Low angle medium close-up of the* OPRICHNIK. *He gesticulates enthusiastically as he speaks.*

OPRICHNIK : . . . who don't side with the boyar princes . . . *He points to them, behind him.* . . . or the well-known families, and are of humble origin and ready to serve the Tsar faithfully . . .

*Shot 775. Medium close-up of two* YOUTHS, *listening intently. Murmurs of the crowd.*

OPRICHNIK *continuing off* : . . . the Tsar summons them to join his bodyguard . . . *The two* YOUTHS *exchange enthusiastic glances.* . . . and to swear allegiance to him . . .

*Shot 776. Long shot of the crowd whilst the* OPRICHNIK *continues off.*

OPRICHNIK *off* : . . . at the hamlet of Alexandrov.*

*The musical theme 'The Oath of the Oprichniks' comes in loudly. Fade out.*

*Shot 777. On the final words of the* OPRICHNIK, *fade in on a medium close-up of* IVAN, *sitting despondently in a chair in the Alexandrov Palace. He is bent over, leaning his head on his fists on the arm of the chair. A* CHOIR *sings gently off. The camera tracks towards him. He straightens up and holds his fists to his brow, then shakes his head desperately. He is wrinkled and sombre. The thirty-five year old* TSAR *looks like a man of fifty.*

MALYUTA *off* : Are you waiting for a message from MOSCOW?
IVAN *turns towards him.*
*Shot 778. Close-up of* MALYUTA, *wearing the long black robe of the* OPRICHNIKS. *He listens attentively, turning his head as the* CHOIR *sings louder, off.*

CHOIR : ' Have pity O Lord . . .'
*Shot 779. Medium close-up of* MALYUTA. IVAN *comes into shot behind him and puts his hands on his shoulders, looking at him with an expression of suppressed excitement. The singing continues.* MALYUTA *turns towards* IVAN *and the two men smile at each other briefly, then look off to the left.*
*Shot 780. High angle long shot of a procession advancing like a long serpent across a snow-covered plain. The* CHOIR *sings.*
*Shot 781. A closer shot of the procession, carrying banners. The singing gets louder.*
*Shot 782. Medium long shot of the procession, slowly advancing and singing as it goes.*
*Shot 783. Close-up of* IVAN *listening.*
*Shot 784. Medium shot of* IVAN *standing by his chair, his head raised, listening. He turns as* NEPEYA *suddenly runs in from*

---

* In historical fact. Ivan left Moscow by sledge without explanation on December 3rd, 1594 accompanied by Maria, his second wife, his two sons by Anastasia (Ivan and Fyodor) and a large number of attendants. He took with him in a hundred carriages the treasury funds, icons, crosses, gold and silver plate, in a word all the portable fortune of the imperial family . . . and only reached the Alexandrov Palace, north of Vladimir, on Christmas Eve.

the left and falls to his knees in front of the chair. IVAN *bends towards him across the chair.*

NEPEYA : The first . . .

*Shot 785. Medium close-up of the two men.*

NEPEYA : . . . English boats laden with consignments of arms and munitions have just entered the White Sea.

*Shot 786. A closer shot of the two of them.*

IVAN *looking up* : We have outwitted you, Germans and Livonians ! *He moves out of frame to the right.*

*Shot 787. Link on the motion as* IVAN's *head comes up into shot in medium close-up.*

IVAN : The day is coming when you will drop to your knees before the authority of Moscow.

*Shot 788. Reverse angle medium shot of* IVAN, *seen from the back: in front of him are the* OPRICHNIKS. *A curtain is drawn aside behind* IVAN *off-screen and a ray of light casts the shadow of a lattice-work on the opposite wall. The* CHOIR *bursts in.*

CHOIR : ' Have mercy, O Lord ! '

IVAN *turns towards camera, drawing himself up.* MALYUTA *and* FYODOR *come up behind him and throw a cloak over his shoulders.* MALYUTA *hands him a staff. He takes it and raises his head in an imperious gesture.*

*Shot 789. Link on the motion. Close-up of* IVAN *raising his head. He moves forward.*

*Shot 790. Link on the motion again. Medium close-up of* IVAN *as he goes off to the left, followed by* MALYUTA *and* FYODOR. *The* OPRICHNIKS *follow behind with lighted candles.*

*Shot 791. Long shot of the procession winding its way across the snow, seen from above through an archway in the palace.* IVAN *comes into shot from the right and bends forward to look out through the archway.*

*Shot 792. Medium close-up of* IVAN *in profile, bending forward and looking down at the procession, which can be seen in the background. (Still on page 113) He turns to the left.*

*Shot 793. Medium shot of* IVAN *by the archway, turning and looking off to the left. The singing continues.* IVAN *turns right round and goes off down some steps to the left.*

*Shot 794. Medium long shot of a flight of steps leading down from the palace. We see the procession winding its way across the plain in the background.* IVAN *appears from under the archway and pauses.*

*Shot 795. A slightly closer shot of* IVAN, *standing on the steps. He bows low before the procession, off-screen. Loud music; the theme is 'O Return'.*

*Shot 796. Close-up of* IVAN *in profile; in the background the people.* IVAN *raises his head.*

CHOIR : ' O return ! O return ! '

*Shot 797. High angle long shot of the crowd falling to its knees. (Still on page 114)*

*Shot 798. Medium shot of the people falling to their knees beside an icon of the Blessed Virgin.*

CHOIR : ' O return ! '

*Shot 799. Long shot of another part of the procession, falling to its knees.*

*Shot 800. Close-up of* IVAN. *His long pointed beard comes down across the frame as he lowers his head. (Still on page 114) A pause.*

CHOIR : ' The father of us all ! '

*Music of the finale.*

*Shot 801. Medium shot of* IVAN *on the steps. He straightens up, leaning on his staff.*

*Shot 802. Medium close-up of* IVAN *in profile. The music swells.* IVAN *puts on his fur-trimmed hat, pauses, turns towards camera, pauses again and with an imperious sweep of his staff goes off to the right.*

*Shot 803. Low angle medium shot of* IVAN *climbing the steps into the palace under the archway. Halfway up he pauses and turns back. The music continues.*

*Shot 804. Long shot of the crowd getting to its feet.*

*Shot 805. Similar long shot of the crowd.*

*Shot 806. Resume on* IVAN *in medium shot on the staircase. He turns and goes on up.*

*Shot 807. Medium shot as* IVAN *arrives at the top of the staircase. The procession can be seen through the archway on the plain below.* FYODOR *appears from behind* IVAN, *who stops and puts a hand on his shoulder.*

121

Ivan: Get the horses saddled, we are going back to Moscow . . .*

    Fyodor *turns and hurries off down the stairs.* Ivan *puts a hand to his breast.*

    *Shot 808. Close-up of* Ivan.

Ivan: . . . to work for the future of the Great Russian State.

    *His image fades out as the following words cross the screen:*

*END OF PART ONE.*

---

* It was in fact on February 2nd, 1565, that Ivan left the Palace of Alexandrov to return to Moscow.

# IVAN THE TERRIBLE

## PART II

### THE BOYARS' PLOT

*Shot 1. Music. Very brief credits come up over a shot of swirling clouds. Then a voice recapitulates the principal scenes from Part I, at the same time giving the names of the actors.*

*Shot 2. High angle close-up of the Monomakh crown. The music continues as the voice of the* SPEAKER *begins off.*

SPEAKER *off*: This story about Ivan the Terrible . . .

*Shot 3. High angle shot of the crown, the orb and the sceptre on an embroidered cushion. The music fades gradually.*

SPEAKER *off*: . . . the founder of . . .

*Shot 4. High angle long shot of the cathedral at the Coronation.* PIMEN *advances at the head of the procession.*

SPEAKER *off*: . . . the Tsardom of Muscovy . . . PIMEN *mounts the dais* . . . tells of his struggle against the foes of Russian unity. *The* CHOIR *begins to sing ' The Black Cloud'.*

*Shot 5. Low angle medium close-up of* PIMEN *blessing* IVAN.

*Shot 6. Medium close-up of* IVAN, *back to camera, putting on his crown.*

*Shot 7. Close-up of* IVAN *looking about him.*

*Shot 8. Low angle medium shot of* IVAN *standing;* PIMEN *on the dais, behind him, surrounded by* PRIESTS.

*Shot 9. Longer shot of the same scene.*

*Shot 10. Rapid close-up of* EUPHROSYNE *watching sourly, with* VLADIMIR *looking over her shoulder.*

*Shot 11. Quick close-up of* VLADIMIR *who gazes stupidly about him.*

*Shot 12. Close-up of the* VISIONARY *whom we saw at the end of the banquet scene.*

*Shot 13. Close-up of* KOLYCHEV THE UNCONQUERABLE *looking sideways.*

*Shot 14. Close-up of his son.*

*Shot 15. Close-up of* Kolychev the Wise.

*Shot 16. Low angle medium shot of the cannons ranged on the hill opposite Kazan, gunners standing at the ready, a pile of cannonballs in the foreground. The* Choir *continues to sing off.*

*Shot 17. Low angle medium shot of* Ivan *coming to the threshold of his tent and gazing across to Kazan.*

Speaker *off* : In the role of Ivan the Terrible . . .

*Shot 18. Medium close-up of* Ivan *at the door of his tent.*

*Shot 19. Close-up of* Ivan *gazing across to Kazan.*

Speaker *off* : . . . Nikolai Cherkasov.

*Shot 20. Long shot of the walls of Kazan, lined with Tartar soldiers.*

Speaker *off* : The Oprichniks . . .

*Shot 21. Another long shot of the walls of Kazan, low angle. An explosion sends a column of earth into the air.*

*Shot 22. Close-up of another explosion.*

Speaker *off* : Malyuta . . .

*Shot 23. Medium shot of a third explosion.*

Speaker *off* : . . . Skuratov . . .

*Shot 24. Close-up of* Malyuta *as we saw him at the end of the banquet scene, throwing his arm in the air and shouting.*

Speaker *off* : . . . Mikhail Zharov.

*Shot 25. Medium shot of the cavalry galloping across the screen in the assault on Kazan, an assault tower on the left.*

Speaker *off* : Alexey Basmanov . . .

*Shot 26. Close-up of* Alexey Basmanov *in armour.*

Speaker *off* : . . . Amvrosy Buchma.

*Shot 27. Low angle long shot of the walls and gateway of Kazan; black spirals of smoke coil upwards.*

Speaker *off* : His son, Fyodor Basmanov . . .

*Shot 28. Close-up of the young* Fyodor, *as we saw him in the assault on Kazan, gazing across at* Ivan *in admiration.*

Speaker *off* : . . . Mikhail Kuznetsov.

*Shot 29. Medium shot of black-robed* Priests *grouped in* Ivan's *apartments at the time of his illness,* Pimen *in white in the background.*

Speaker *off* : Philip, the Archbishop of Moscow . . .

*Shot 30. A closer shot of the same scene.*

SPEAKER *off* : . . . and of all the Russias . . .

*Shot 31. Close-up of* PHILIP, *the former* BOYAR, FYODOR KOLYCHEV.

SPEAKER *off* : . . . Andrei Abrikosov . . .

*Shot 32. Close-up of the Bible open across the face of the reclining* IVAN.

SPEAKER *off* : Pimen, the Bishop of Novgorod . . .

*Shot 33. Medium close-up of* PIMEN *turning his head, one arm raised.*

SPEAKER *off* : . . . Alexander Mgebrov.

*Shot 34. Close-up of* PETER VOLYNETS.

SPEAKER *off* : Peter Volynets : Vladimir Balashov.

*Shot 35. Medium close-up of* EUPHROSYNE'S *hand pushing the poisoned goblet across the top of the balustrade in* ANASTASIA'S *bedroom.*

SPEAKER *off* : Euphrosyne Staritsky . . .

*Shot 36. Close-up of* ANASTASIA *raising the poisoned goblet.*

SPEAKER *off* : . . . the Tsar's aunt . . .

*Shot 37. Close-up of* EUPHROSYNE, *shrouded in black, looking sideways from her hiding place at the bottom of the stairs which lead from* ANASTASIA'S *bedroom.*

SPEAKER *off* : . . . Seraphima Birman.

*Shot 38. Medium close-up of* VLADIMIR *catching a fly.*

SPEAKER *off* : Her son, Vladimir Staritsky : Pavel Kadochnikov.

*Shot 39. Close-up of* KURBSKY.

SPEAKER *off* : Prince Andrew Mikhailovich Kurbsky : Mikhail Nazvanov.

*Shot 40. Medium close-up of* KING SIGISMUND *seated on his throne.*

SPEAKER *off* : Sigismund, King of Poland : Pavel Massalsky.

*Shot 41. Very high angle long shot of* IVAN *standing beside* ANASTASIA'S *coffin on the catafalque in the cathedral. The crowd, bearing torches, streams in from the background.*

*Shot 42. High angle medium shot of the same scene.* IVAN, *standing over* ANASTASIA, *puts one hand to his breast while the crowd gather round with their torches.*

SPEAKER *off* : It is the year fifteen hundred . . .

*Shot 43. Close-up of* IVAN, *the torches behind him.*

SPEAKER *off* : . . . and sixty-four . . .

*Shot 44. Close-up of* FYODOR BASMANOV, *against a background of flaming torches, looking up at* IVAN.

SPEAKER *off* : . . . the year in which . . .

*Shot 45. Similar close-up of* ALEXEY BASMANOV.

SPEAKER *off* : . . . the Tsar formed his special bodyguard . . .

*Shot 46. Similar close-up of* MALYUTA *looking straight ahead.*

SPEAKER *off* : . . . the Oprichniks.

*Shot 47. Low angle medium shot of the* HERALD, *reading from his parchment, in the Kremlin Square, the people gathered around him.*

SPEAKER *off* : The year in which . . .

*Shot 48. A longer shot of the same scene: the crowd listen in the foreground as the* HERALD *finishes reading from the parchment and the* OPRICHNIK *comes forward to address them, waving his hat.*

SPEAKER *off* : . . . Tsar Ivan withdrew to Alexandrov.

*Shot 49. High angle long shot of the procession to Alexandrov, winding like a long dark ribbon across the snow-covered plain, carrying banners and icons.*

SPEAKER *off* : The year in which the people . . .

*Shot 50. Another similar shot of the procession.*

SPEAKER *off* : . . . organised a procession . . .

*Shot 51. Close-up of* IVAN *in profile, the advancing procession in the background.*

SPEAKER *off* : . . . to beg the Tsar to return.

*Shot 52. Medium shot of* IVAN *at the top of the stairs at Alexandrov, giving the order to* FYODOR *to saddle the horses for the return to Moscow. In the background the procession is seen through the archway on the plain below.*

SPEAKER *off* : . . . the year in which Prince Kurbsky . . .

*Shot 53. Medium close-up of* IVAN, *leaning on his staff, his left hand on his heart. The music, which has continued in the background throughout the sequence, comes to an end.*

SPEAKER *off* : . . . committed the base treachery of surrendering the Russian armies to the Poles and . . . *Fade out.*

*Shot 54.*

SPEAKER *off* : . . . transferred his allegiance to King Sigismund.

*With these last words fade in to a high angle long shot of the great throne room of* SIGISMUND'S *palace. The floor is tiled* like a chessboard, and an immense tapestry of mounted knights at a tournament is visible on the far wall. In the background, in the centre, KING SIGISMUND lounges on his throne. The richly-ornamented chamber also contains a group of magnificently attired COURT LADIES on the right; and on the left three MONKS, two in white, one in black. Two KNIGHTS in armour stand beside an imposing statue in the foreground on the left. A fanfare of trumpets greets KURBSKY as he appears in back view in the foreground, clad in a white cloak, and goes down the hall towards KING SIGISMUND. Half-way down the hall, KURBSKY drops to one knee, just level with the group of COURT LADIES. The fanfare continues.

Shot 55. *Medium shot of the three* MONKS *standing by an elaborate candelabra, watching him.*

Shot 56. *Medium shot of the* COURT LADIES *looking on.*

Shot 57. *Medium shot of* KURBSKY, *still in back view, as he rises to his feet, then walks forward and kneels at the foot of* SIGISMUND'S *throne. (Production still on page 115) He is seen in profile as he looks up at the* KING, *then bows his head in submission. The fanfare ends.*

Shot 58. *Medium shot of* SIGISMUND, *lounging affectedly on his throne, which is elaborately carved with three crenellated turrets. Insipid court music begins to play as* KURBSKY *draws his sword slowly out from its scabbard and holds it out to the* KING, *who puts out a hand to receive it.*

Shot 59. *Medium close-up of* SIGISMUND *on his throne, wearing an enormous white ruff. He receives the sword, runs his hand along the blade, looks at it, then hands it back to* KURBSKY, *all with a supremely affected and pompous expression. (Production still on page 115)*

Shot 60. *Medium close-up of* KURBSKY, *his helmet in his hand. With equally affected gestures, he takes back the sword, kisses it, then gazes up at* SIGISMUND *and starts to put the sword back in its scabbard.*

Shot 61. *Medium shot of* SIGISMUND, *seated on his throne on right of frame. Two* COURTIERS, *with enormous puffed sleeves making them look like butterflies, come from the left and present a cushion bearing a white sash, from the end of which hangs a cross.* SIGISMUND *takes it and turns towards* KURBSKY.

*Shot 62. Medium close-up of* SIGISMUND *with link on the motion as he takes the cross and holds it out to* KURBSKY, *off-screen.*

*Shot 63. Close-up of* KURBSKY, *gazing upwards at the cross, as it comes dangling into view, followed by* SIGISMUND'S *hands as the latter lays the sash around* KURBSKY'S *neck.*

*Shot 64. Close-up of a* COURT LADY *watching coyly and raising her head.*

*Shot 65. Medium close-up of* KURBSKY, *with* SIGISMUND *partly visible on the left holding out his elaborately gloved hand.* KURBSKY *kisses the hand with an affected gesture and* SIGISMUND *sits down again on his throne, his head coming into shot. The* LIVONIAN AMBASSADOR *appears between them from behind and addresses* KURBSKY.

LIVONIAN AMBASSADOR : There are certain defeats that are more resounding . . . than victories. *He draws back.*

KURBSKY *rising to his feet and speaking in strong, ringing tones*: The defeat of my Russian army near Revel . . .*

*Shot 66. Medium close-up of the two* MONKS *in white, who listen with lugubrious faces.*

KURBSKY *continues, off*: . . . will spark off the revolt. *The two* MONKS *exchange glances. (Still on page 115)* Tsar Ivan has fled the wrath of the boyars and taken refuge . . .

*Shot 67. Medium close-up of two* KNIGHTS *in black armour with white ruffs, watching with cruel faces. (Still on page 115)*

KURBSKY *off*: . . . in Alexandrov.

*Shot 68. Medium close-up of a* KNIGHT *in armour, lance in hand, almost drowned by his luxuriant plumes. (Still on page 115)*

*Shot 69. Medium close-up of* SIGISMUND *lounging back on his throne.* KURBSKY *leans towards him from the right.*

KURBSKY : The Moscow boyars, the Kolychevs, have managed to get some messages through . . .

*Shot 70. Close-up of one of the* MONKS, *clad in white, bald as an egg, his mouth permanently drooping.*

KURBSKY *off* : The Tsar is assailed on every side . . .

*Shot 71. Close-up of the other* MONK *in a starched white cap.*

---

* Capital of the Baltic State of Estonia, also spelt Reval. It is now called Tallinn.

*His long face creases in a half-smile.*

KURBSKY *off* : . . . like a baited bear.

*Shot 72. Resume on medium close-up of* SIGISMUND *and* KURBSKY.

KURBSKY : The boyars are seething with revolt; the Tsar will fall . . .

*Shot 73. Close-up of a* COURT LADY *listening with a smile.*

KURBSKY *continues, off* : . . . without a blow being struck . . .

*Shot 74. Close-up of a* SECOND COURT LADY *listening with a haughty expression.*

*Shot 75. Medium close-up of* KURBSKY, *slightly low angle, the* LIVONIAN AMBASSADOR *lurking in the background.*

KURBSKY : . . . and the throne of Moscow . . . *He leans forward and places a hand to his breast, looking up at* SIGISMUND, *off-screen to the left.* . . . will be free for a new Tsar well-disposed towards Poland.

*Shot 76. Close-up of a* THIRD COURT LADY, *the* SECOND *slightly behind her. They are both looking admiringly across at* KURBSKY. *The* THIRD COURT LADY *hides her face coyly in her fan, then turns and exchanges a meaningful glance with her companion.*

*Shot 77. Low angle medium shot of* SIGISMUND *getting to his feet.*

SIGISMUND : God in his wisdom decreed that Lithuania, Poland and the Baltic States should serve . . . *He raises an elegant hand, holding his brocaded glove.* . . . as the outposts of Europe . . .

*Shot 78. The music ends. Low angle medium close-up of* SIGISMUND.

SIGISMUND : . . . in order that the civilised nations of the West might be protected . . . *He wags a delicate finger* . . . from the Muscovite barbarians. *He tilts his head back affectedly.*

THIRD COURT LADY *off* : They say . . .

*Shot 79. Medium close-up of the* FIRST *and* THIRD COURT LADIES, *another behind them.*

THIRD COURT LADY : . . . the Muscovites eat children alive. *Her two companions raise their eyes to heaven and gasp in horror.*

*Shot 80. Low angle close-up of* SIGISMUND. *His small, effeminate face, with pointed beard and moustache, is almost lost in his vast white ruff. His hat is set at a jaunty angle.*

SIGISMUND : Russian soil is fertile. The herds are well-fed.

*Shot 81. Close-up of the* THIRD COURT LADY, *listening. She sighs admiringly and her well-endowed bosom heaves under her low-cut dress.*

SIGISMUND : The sub-soil conceals inexhaustible riches.

*Shot 82. Resume on close-up of him.*

SIGISMUND : Of course, the Russians have to be kept down. *He looks stern.* But a strong man on the throne of Moscow would shatter the most cherished dreams of all the European sovereigns.

*Shot 83. Medium close-up of the* LIVONIAN AMBASSADOR. *He leans forwards and speaks in* KURBSKY'S *ear.*

AMBASSADOR : We need the dim-witted Vladimir Staritsky . . .

*Music. He looks off left at* SIGISMUND . . . on the throne of Moscow.

*Shot 84. Resume on close-up of* SIGISMUND. *He leans forward to address* KURBSKY *and the* LIVONIAN AMBASSADOR, *off-screen to the right.*

SIGISMUND : We must support the rebel boyars. The solitary reins . . .

*Shot 85. Close-up of the two* KNIGHTS *in armour.*

SIGISMUND *continues, off :* . . . of absolute power must be wrenched from the Tsar and . . .

*Shot 86. Low angle medium close-up of the two* MONKS.

SIGISMUND *off :* . . . returned to the feudal princes.

*Shot 87. Medium shot of* SIGISMUND, *seated on his throne. He raises his voice, and his finger.*

SIGISMUND : We must destroy the unity of Ivan's Russia . . . *He throws up his hand again in an affected gesture.* Once that has been done . . .

*Shot 88. Low angle medium shot of* SIGISMUND *standing in front of his throne, the* LIVONIAN AMBASSADOR *on the right, the* MONKS *on the left. As he speaks,* SIGISMUND *gesticulates in a grotesque and unintended parody of* IVAN.

SIGISMUND : . . . the Christian kings will embark on a new crusade. We will force the Muscovite to serve the West.

*Shot 89. A longer shot of the same scene, taking in* KURBSKY *in the foreground on the right.*

SIGISMUND : We will drive the Russians out of Europe and force them back to their Asian steppes. *He throws up his arms.*

*Shot 90. Medium close-up of the two* KNIGHTS *in armour. Like iron robots, they raise their fists twice in a gesture of approval. A fanfare rings out.*

130

*Shot 91. Medium shot of the* COURT LADIES. *They fling their hands daintily in the air as they cry out.*

LADIES : Hurrah! Hurrah! Hurrah!

*Shot 92. Resume on long shot of the throne room. A* MESSENGER *in a cloak runs in from left foreground and hurries down the room towards* KURBSKY.

*Shot 93. Link on the motion. Medium shot of* KURBSKY *as the messenger falls to his knees in front of him, back to camera, and holds out a message.* KURBSKY *grabs the message and the* MESSENGER *turns to face camera and shouts.*

MESSENGER *shouting* : Tsar Ivan is on his way back to Moscow!

*Shot 94. The music 'Ivan the Terrible' comes in. Medium shot of* SIGISMUND *as he hurries down from his throne, the three* MONKS *behind him on the left. He stands for a moment, looking furious, his hand on his sword, then turns and with an angry wave of his hand goes out of frame to the left. The* MONKS *begin to follow him.*

*Shot 95. Resume on long shot of the hall. The court hurries out to the left leaving* KURBSKY *alone with the* MESSENGER; *a solitary* KNIGHT *in armour stands in the foreground on the left.*

*Shot 96. Medium shot of* KURBSKY, *slightly low angle, standing reading the message. The* MESSENGER *is crouched in front of him, back to camera.* KURBSKY *thrusts away the message and looks round furiously, then as the* MESSENGER *starts towards him, puts out a foot to kick him.*

*Shot 97. Resume on high angle long shot of the throne room. Link on the motion as* KURBSKY *kicks the* MESSENGER *onto the floor. While the latter remains sprawled across the tiles,* KURBSKY *throws the message down and stands gazing bitterly off in the direction taken by* SIGISMUND *and his court. Fade out.*

*Shot 98. There is a crash of drums and a new theme strikes up loudly. Long shot of snow-covered countryside outside Moscow, a church tower in the background. Black-clad* OPRICHNIKS *ride across at full gallop, moving right to left away from camera, and circle round past the church tower in the background.*

*Shot 99. A closer shot of the same scene. (Still on page 116)*

131

IVAN's *coach races by, drawn by six horses and mounted on a sledge.*

*Shot 100. The music continues. Reverse angle long shot of the church, the countryside stretching away behind it.* OPRICHNIKS *gallop across from left to right at the bottom of frame.*

*Shot 101. A slightly longer shot of the same scene as* IVAN's *coach races past.*

*Shot 102. Medium close-up of a low doorway opening into the throne room of the Kremlin. One of the double doors opens and* IVAN *appears, clad in his fur-trimmed cape and hat, his staff in his hand. He bends down and peers through the doorway, with a sly, fox-like expression.*

IVAN: So I've caught you! *He starts to open the other door.*

*Shot 103. Medium shot of the doorway. Link on the motion as* IVAN *opens the second door and comes through, bending low. The camera tracks out in front of him as he advances into the room, revealing* MALYUTA *and* FYODOR *standing on either side of the doorway.* IVAN *stops, leaning on his staff and gazes down at the* BOYARS, *off-screen.*

IVAN: You didn't expect me back, eh? MALYUTA *and* FYODOR *come forward to stand on either side of him.* You were delighted . . .

*Shot 104. Medium close-up of the three of them gazing suspiciously down at the* BOYARS, MALYUTA *to the left of* IVAN, FYODOR *on the right.*

IVAN: . . . by the Tsar's departure! *He strikes the ground with his staff.* You've shown yourselves for what you are . . .

*Shot 105. Medium shot of the* BOYARS *lining the wall and the stone staircase. They stand looking sheepish in their fur capes and heavily embroidered robes.*

IVAN *off*: . . . Traitors!

*Shot 106. Close-up of* IVAN *gazing down at the* BOYARS.

*Shot 107. Close-up of* FYODOR *doing likewise. The fur of* IVAN's *cape can be seen in left foreground.*

*Shot 108. Medium close-up of* IVAN *and* MALYUTA.

IVAN: The rogues . . . *He glances meaningfully at* MALYUTA *and continues sarcastically* . . . They wanted to govern the land themselves! . . . MALYUTA *bursts out laughing.*

*Shot 109. Medium close-up of a group of aged* BOYARS

*watching apprehensively, leaning on their staffs.*
*Shot 110. High angle long shot of the room, the* BOYARS *in the background.* IVAN *steps forward in profile, just in front of camera.*

IVAN: All right. *He turns and walks down towards the* BOYARS, *away from camera. He stands facing them while* MALYUTA *appears in right foreground, back to camera . . .* If that's what you want! From now on I'll give you land to govern!

*Shot 111. Medium shot of a group of* BOYARS. IVAN *comes into frame from the left and goes up to one of them, who is particularly aged and bent. He takes him by the chin, raising his head, and thrusts his face at him.*

IVAN *between his teeth*: I'll give you land. *He forces the* BOYAR *to his knees.*

*Shot 112. Reverse angle shot of black-clad* OPRICHNIKS *lined up on the opposite side of the room,* FYODOR *in front of them on the left.* IVAN, *who is partly visible in back view on the left of frame, turns to face* FYODOR *and places his hand on his shoulder. (Still on page 116) As he speaks* IVAN *comes slowly towards camera, one hand on* FYODOR'S *shoulder, the other holding his staff.*

IVAN: But as the widower, I shall keep the widower's portion . . .
*Shot 113. Medium close-up of the two.*

133

IVAN: . . . the towns along our borders.* From there . . .

*Shot 114. Medium shot of* IVAN *coming up some steps towards camera, accompanied by* FYODOR. *We see the* BOYARS *ranged against the wall in the background.*

IVAN: . . . I will watch over the security . . .

*Shot 115. Reverse angle medium shot of* IVAN *mounting the steps away from camera, leaning on his staff.*

FYODOR *and* MALYUTA *follow slightly behind him.*

IVAN: . . . of the State . . . MALYUTA *stops and turns to look back, then* FYODOR *and finally* IVAN, *who shouts at the* BOYARS . . . and guard the integrity of Russian frontiers. *He turns and moves on up the steps.*

*Shot 116. A closer shot of* IVAN *at the top of the steps, more* BOYARS *lining the wall behind him. Link on the motion as he turns under an archway and looks back again.*

IVAN: And I shall stamp out treason!

*Shot 117. Reverse angle long shot of* IVAN *at the top of the steps, seen in three-quarter back view under the arch,* FYODOR *and* MALYUTA *on either side of him, backs to camera. In the background on the left, the* BOYARS *retreat through several archways while the* OPRICHNIKS *come forward from the right and gather round* IVAN. *The* TSAR *turns and comes forward again under the arch as he speaks.*

IVAN: I have no confidence in you boyars . . . *He stops and turns again.*

*Shot 118. Medium shot of more* BOYARS, *ranged against the wall. They sink to their knees as* IVAN *continues off.*

IVAN *off*: Therefore as God created man in his own image . . .

*Shot 119. Long shot of the room, slightly high angle.* IVAN'S *throne stands on a dais, in the foreground.* EUPHROSYNE *is seen on the left of frame. As he continues to speak,* IVAN *advances towards camera from the archway and the kneeling* OPRICHNIKS *rise to their feet on the right.*

---

* The Oprichniks, as has been shown, were created much earlier by Ivan. He is merely ratifying their creation to the boyars. The reference to 'widower' relates to an untranslatable pun; Oprichnik is derived from the words 'except, separated'; whilst the Oprichina designates both the dowry accorded to the widows of great princes and the militia created and directed by Ivan, i.e. that which is outside the general organisation.

IVAN: ... so I have created men in mine. They will carry out my orders ...

*Shot 120. Reverse angle medium shot of* IVAN *as he mounts the dais and stands facing his audience. Black-robed* PRIESTS *stand in the background, on the right.*

IVAN: ... and only they will enjoy my confidence. *With a sweep of his staff he turns towards the* OPRICHNIKS, *off-screen to the left.*

*Shot 121. Reverse angle medium shot of the* OPRICHNIKS *ranged against the wall. They rise to their feet as* IVAN *continues off.*

IVAN *off*: That is why I have christened them Oprichniks.*

*Shot 122. High angle long shot of the other end of the room, the* BOYARS *lining the wall on the left.* PHILIP *enters through an archway in the background and comes towards camera, followed by a* NOVICE. *He mounts the steps under the arch and halts, banging his crozier on the ground.*

PHILIP *shouting*: These plans come not from God ... *He comes forward under the arch, the camera tracking out in front of him, then halts, banging his crozier on the ground again and waving it in the air as he shouts* ... but from the devil ... *(Still on page 116) He moves forward again.*

*Shot 123. Medium shot of* IVAN. *He sits down on his throne and leans forward as* PHILIP *continues to shout, off.*

PHILIP *off*: He who defies ancestral traditions ...

*Shot 124. Medium shot:* PHILIP *stands in the foreground, facing camera, with* EUPHROSYNE *slightly behind him to the right.* PIMEN *stands in the background, robed in white, with four black-robed priests behind him. On the left,* IVAN *sits leaning forward on his throne.*

PHILIP *continuing loudly, pointing his crozier at* IVAN: ... shall not remain sovereign for long.

IVAN: Fyodor Kolychev! ... *As he speaks,* IVAN *throws his arms in the air and comes down from the dais towards* PHILIP, *who raises his crozier.*

*Shot 125. Medium close-up of* PHILIP, *his crozier raised,* PIMEN *and* EUPHROSYNE *behind him. Link on the motion as* IVAN *comes up to him and takes him by the wrist, addressing*

---

* End of the first reel (300 metres).

*him in an undertone.* MALYUTA *comes into frame on the right.*

IVAN *quietly*: Say no more.

*Shot 126. High angle medium long shot from beside* IVAN'S *throne.* IVAN *leads* PHILIP *off to the right, glancing back at the assembled company as he goes.*

IVAN *almost whispering*: Say no more.

MALYUTA *mounts the dais and leans on the arm of the throne, watching them go suspiciously.* EUPHROSYNE *moves forward behind him.*

*Shot 127. Medium close-up of* MALYUTA. EUPHROSYNE *hurries out behind him, followed by* PIMEN *and his priests.*

*Shot 128. Medium shot of* PHILIP *and* IVAN *in front of the throne.* PHILIP *takes a step to the left, clutching his crozier, as* IVAN *comes round behind him towards the right, and looks him up and down.* PHILIP *glances at him, then looks away again.* IVAN *mounts the dais to sit on his throne in the background.*

*Shot 129. Medium close-up of* IVAN *as he sinks back on his throne and looks across at* PHILIP, *off-screen to the left.*

IVAN *quietly*: Why are you so severe with me, Fyodor Kolychev? Why, my good friend, are you so cruel?

*Shot 130. Medium shot of the two of them,* PHILIP *in the foreground on the left.*

IVAN: You should really pity me! . . .

PHILIP *replies without looking at him*: I am not Kolychev, I am Philip the monk. I carry out the will of God . . . *He turns slightly, raising his voice* . . . not the designs of the Tsar.

IVAN *raising a pacifying hand*: Listen . . .

*Shot 131. Close-up of* PHILIP. IVAN *continues off.*

IVAN *off*: Ever since I was a child . . .

*Shot 132. Shot of swirling clouds. Music.*

IVAN *off*: The boyars showed their hatred . . .

*Shot 133. Flashback of* IVAN'S *youth. Close-up of* IVAN *as an eight-year-old boy, in his night-shirt. He looks terrified.**

IVAN *off*: . . . of the Grand Duke of Moscow.

*The* YOUNG IVAN *glances from side to side in alarm, his face*

---

* The occasion is the death of his mother, the regent, on April 3rd, 1538.

*lit by flickering lights. (Still on page 116)*

*Shot 134. Long shot of a darkened room in the royal apart-ments. The* YOUNG IVAN *is crouched on the floor in a pool of light. As* IVAN *continues off, the camera tracks out, revealing a doorway on the left.*

IVAN *off* : After my father's death . . . *The door opens, casting a shaft of light into the room.* My mother . . .

*Shot 135. Medium close-up of the* YOUNG IVAN *cowering on the floor.*

IVAN *continuing, off* : . . . was killed.

*Shot 136. On the sound of a dreadful female shriek the camera cuts to a medium close-up of the door, through which* PRINCESS GLINSKAYA *appears, screaming.*

GLINSKAYA *screaming* : They have poisoned me! *She clutches at her throat.* Ah! . . . I am dying! *She falls.*

*Shot 137. High angle medium close-up. Link on the motion as the* PRINCESS *measures her length on the stone floor in the shaft of light coming from the doorway.*

*Shot 138. Medium close-up of the* YOUNG IVAN. *He crawls forward on his knees. The music gets louder.*

*Shot 139. Resume on high angle medium close-up of the* PRINCESS. *The* YOUNG IVAN *crawls towards her and touches her. She raises her head and hugs him to her bosom. (Still on page 116)*

GLINSKAYA : My son!

*Shot 140. Close-up of them both.*

GLINSKAYA *continuing* : They have killed me! . . . Watch out for poison! . . . Beware of the boyars!

*A shadow falls across them from the doorway. The* PRINCESS *turns.*

*Shot 141. Medium close-up of three* WOMEN, *shrouded in black, advancing in the doorway.*

*Shot 142. Resume on the* YOUNG IVAN, *crouched over his mother on the floor. The three* WOMEN *come into shot from the left and raise the* PRINCESS *up, thrusting the boy aside. Suspended in the three* WOMEN'S *arms, the* PRINCESS *stretches out to her son on the floor.*

*Shot 143. Close-up of the* YOUNG IVAN *gazing up at his mother, his arms round her neck. She is dragged off, out of frame to the left.*

*Shot 144. Close-up, slightly high angle, of the* PRINCESS'S *hands sliding along the ground.*

*Shot 145. Medium shot, with link on the motion as the* PRINCESS *is carried off to the left, leaving the* YOUNG IVAN *crouched on the floor. The door closes, shutting off the shaft of light.*

VOICE *off*: Helena Glinskaya . . .

*Shot 146. Close-up of the* YOUNG IVAN, *his eyes wide with terror.*

VOICE *off*: . . . is dead! *The music fades.*

*Shot 147. Close-up of* TSAR IVAN *recalling his memories, his eyes dim. (Still on page 116)*

IVAN *slowly*: That's how I came to be an orphan, alone and abandoned . . . *He turns to look up at* PHILIP, *off-screen to the left. The music 'The Tents of Ivan' begins quietly . . .* whilst the boyars governed in my name and handed over Russian territory . . .

*Fade out.*

*Shot 148. Another flashback: medium shot of the doorway into the throne room. One of the doors opens to reveal the* YOUNG IVAN *wearing an enormous crown.*

IVAN *off*: . . . to foreign enslavement.

*Shot 149. Medium close-up of the* YOUNG IVAN *cautiously looking round the half-open door.*

*Shot 150. Resume on medium shot of the doorway. The other door opens and the* YOUNG IVAN *advances into the reception room as* TSAR IVAN *did previously. He is wearing full ceremonial robes and carries a staff. He halts in medium close-up and looks off to the right. (Still on page 116)*

*Shot 151. Reverse angle medium shot of the* BOYARS *ranged along the wall. They bow deeply, looking towards him. The music swells.*

*Shot 152. Medium long shot, looking towards the end of the throne room. The diminutive figure of the* YOUNG IVAN *walks along the carpeted floor, away from camera, and up to the throne on the dais at the end. On either side of him,* FOREIGN AMBASSADORS *bow deeply, backs to camera, and most deeply of all, the two Boyars* SHUISKY *and* BYELSKY *who are facing camera on either side of the throne. Having reached the throne, the* YOUNG IVAN *turns to face camera also.*

*Shot 153. Medium shot of the* YOUNG IVAN *standing in front of his throne.* SHUISKY *and* BYELSKY, *slightly behind him, straighten up with exaggerated gestures. The former, on the right, is vastly corpulent with a flowing white beard. The latter, on the left, is thin and goat-like, with a long pointed nose.* BYELSKY *raises his hand and a* SCRIBE *comes in behind them from the left, carrying a book.*

*Shot 154. Medium close-up of* BYELSKY. *He speaks solemnly, his nose in the air, waving his staff from side to side. A second* SCRIBE *stands behind him, holding a scroll.*

BYELSKY : Ivan Vassilievich, Grand Duke of Moscow . . .

*Shot 155. Reverse angle long shot of the room, slightly from above, the* YOUNG IVAN *in back view in the foreground. His head seems weighed down by the large crown, his slender neck emerges from a heavy gold collar. He looks from side to side as* BYELSKY *continues off.*

BYELSKY *off* : . . . has graciously ratified a commercial treaty . . .

*Shot 156. Resume on medium close-up of* BYELSKY.

BYELSKY : . . . and agrees to pay duties for the transit of goods via the Baltic to . . .

*Shot 157. Rapid close-up of a vast, bearded Hanseatic*

MERCHANT.

BYELSKY *off* : . . . the great . . .

> *Shot 158. Medium close-up of the* MERCHANT'S *fat hand as he fingers his purse.*

BYELSKY *off* : . . . Hanseatic league . . .

> *Shot 159. Resume on medium close-up of* BYELSKY.

BYELSKY : . . . of the German merchant towns.

> *He smiles ingratiatingly across at the Hanseatic representatives, then turns to the* SCRIBE *behind him.*
>
> *Shot 160. Medium shot of the end of the room with the* YOUNG IVAN *on his throne on the left,* SHUISKY *in the centre, the first* SCRIBE *just behind him and the* HANSEATIC AMBASSADOR, *thin, scrawny-necked and dressed in black, in the foreground on the right.* BYELSKY'S SCRIBE *comes into frame from the left, carrying his scroll. The* HANSEATIC AMBASSADOR *stretches out claw-like hands to receive it. As he is about to do so,* SHUISKY *strikes the ground with his staff. The* SCRIBE *whips round with the scroll, leaving the* HANSEATIC AMBASSADOR *clawing at the air.*

SHUISKY *leaning forward on his staff* : The Grand Duke of Moscow . . .

> *Shot 161. Reverse angle medium shot of the Livonian representatives: the* LIVONIAN AMBASSADOR *in the centre, a* KNIGHT *on either side of him.*

SHUISKY *off* : . . . has reconsidered his decision.

> *As* SHUISKY *speaks, the other* SCRIBE *comes into frame from the left, bearing another scroll which he hands to the* LIVONIAN AMBASSADOR, KASPAR VON OLDENBOCK, *looking younger but no less sly. As* SHUISKY *continues, the* AMBASSADOR *holds it up to one of the* KNIGHTS *wearing a white cloak, on the left, who kisses the scroll. (Still on page 116)*

SHUISKY *off* : He has concluded the treaty with . . .

> *Shot 162. Medium close-up of the* LIVONIAN AMBASSADOR *and the* KNIGHT *kissing the parchment.*

SHUISKY *off* : . . . the Order of Livonian Knights.

> *The* LIVONIAN AMBASSADOR *puts the scroll under his cloak, peering slyly out over the top of his square-rimmed spectacles.*
>
> *Shot 163. Medium close-up of the Hanseatic group muttering and looking hostilely across at the Livonians.*

VOICE *off* : Someone . . .

> *Shot 164. Close-up of the* LIVONIAN AMBASSADOR. *He grins slyly across at the Hanseatic representatives, then turns and looks straight at camera.*

VOICE *off* : . . . has certainly been lining Shuisky's pockets.

BYELSKY *off* : The Hansa.

> *Shot 165. Medium close-up of the* YOUNG IVAN *on his throne,* SHUISKY *behind him to the right.*

BYELSKY *off* : The Hansa . . . *He comes into frame from the left and points an accusing finger at* SHUISKY . . . It was the Boyar Council's decision . . .

> *Shot 166. Medium shot of* SHUISKY *and* BYELSKY. *The* YOUNG IVAN, *seated in front of them, looks doubtfully from side to side as they continue their argument with ponderous gestures. (Still on page 149)*

SHUISKY : The Grand Duke is free to annul the council's decisions.

BYELSKY *pointing at the* YOUNG IVAN : But he has pledged his word.

SHUISKY *doing likewise* : The Grand Duke is the sole arbiter of his word . . .

> *Shot 167. A slightly longer shot of the same scene. As they continue their argument,* SHUISKY *and* BYELSKY *turn to face the assembled company.*

SHUISKY : He gives it or rescinds it as he pleases. It is the Grand Duke's will which constitutes the law.

BYELSKY *raising his fist* : But the will . . .

> *Shot 168. Medium close-up of* BYELSKY, *staff in hand, growing progressively angrier. One of the* SCRIBES *stands behind him.*

BYELSKY : . . . of the Grand Duke is to conclude a treaty with the Hansa.

> *Shot 169. Resume on medium shot of the two* BOYARS, *arguing angrily on either side of the* YOUNG IVAN. *Slouched on his throne, the latter is eyeing them with increasing suspicion.*

SHUISKY : The Grand Duke's will is to concede the privileges to the Livonian Order.

> *Shot 170. Medium shot of the* BOYARS *ranged along the wall. They sink to their knees.*

VOICE *off* : The Grand Duke's will is law !

141

*Shot 171. Medium close-up of the* BOYARS *baring their heads. Music.*

*Shot 172. Resume on medium shot of the throne.* SHUISKY *and* BYELSKY *prostrate themselves at the* YOUNG IVAN'S *feet; the* SCRIBES *bow on either side.*

*Shot 173. Close-up of the* YOUNG IVAN *looking down at the two* BOYARS *off-screen at his feet. His eyes flick uncomfortably from side to side and he heaves a sigh. The music continues. Behind him, two enormous eyes gaze down from a fresco on the wall.*

*Shot 174. Close-up of his feet swinging backwards and forwards in a vain attempt to reach the ground.*

*Shot 175. Another close-up of the* YOUNG IVAN, *back in the royal apartments. He gazes thoughtfully off to the left.*

*Shot 176. Medium shot of the door into the royal apartments, two* BOYARS *prostrated on either side.* SHUISKY *staggers through mopping himself with a large handkerchief, followed by* BYELSKY, *who waves a finger at him angrily as they continue their argument, coming towards camera.**

---

* The following scene has no date, historically speaking. Eisenstein uses it to represent the undying hatred which existed between the Shuisky and Byelsky families and to sum up the position of the young Ivan in the face of personal interests which were not his own.

BYELSKY: We must pay the Hansa!

SHUISKY: No, we'll pay the Livonians!

> *Shot 177. Medium close-up of the* YOUNG IVAN. *Two black-robed* WOMEN *divest him of his ceremonial robes, leaving him in his shirt. He gazes solemnly in front of him as the argument continues off.*

BYELSKY: The Hansa will be more profitable to the State!

SHUISKY: You mean more profitable to yourself!

BYELSKY: And you have been bribed by the Livonians! The money must go . . .

> *Shot 178. Medium close-up of* BYELSKY, *in profile, and* SHUISKY, *three-quarters back to camera, arguing.*

BYELSKY: . . . to the Hansa!

SHUISKY: We'll pay the Livonians.

YOUNG IVAN *off*: We will pay no-one!

> SHUISKY *and* BYELSKY *turn, stupefied.*
>
> *Shot 179. Medium close-up of the* YOUNG IVAN *sitting in his shirt, the crown in front of him;* SHUISKY *is partly visible in soft focus in the background.*

YOUNG IVAN *with sudden decisiveness*: We're not obliged to pay. The coastal towns were built by our ancestors . . .

> *Shot 180. Close-up of him.*

YOUNG IVAN: Those lands are our inheritance; they must be returned to Moscow. *He turns to look at the two* BOYARS.

SHUISKY *off*: Who would be fool enough . . .

> *Shot 181. Medium close-up of* SHUISKY *and* BYELSKY. *The latter laughs patronisingly at the* YOUNG IVAN *and lays a hand on* SHUISKY'S *shoulder.*

SHUISKY: . . . to give them back?

BYELSKY: Anything that falls off the back of a wagon is lost.

> *Shot 182. Close-up of the* YOUNG IVAN *rising to his feet and speaking with fierce determination.*

YOUNG IVAN: If they won't return them voluntarily, we shall take them back by force.

> *Shot 183. Close-up of* SHUISKY.

SHUISKY: By force? *He bursts out laughing.*

> *Shot 184. Close-up of* BYELSKY *leaning forward on his staff and grinning patronisingly at the* YOUNG IVAN.

BYELSKY: And where will we find this force?

*Shot 185. Medium close-up of* BYELSKY *as the* YOUNG IVAN *comes in from the right and moves in front of him to the left of frame.* BYELSKY *listens with a mocking expression as the* YOUNG IVAN *continues.*

YOUNG IVAN : You have wasted Russia's strength . . . *He turns to face* BYELSKY . . . it has been frittered away by the boyars!

*BYELSKY, laughing helplessly, moves away from camera. The* YOUNG IVAN *turns to watch him.*

*Shot 186. Medium shot of the* YOUNG IVAN *standing in his shirt, back to camera. The mocking laughter of* SHUISKY *and* BYELSKY *continues off. Two more* BOYARS, *standing in back view in the foreground, burst out laughing also. The* YOUNG IVAN *whips round angrily. (Still on page 149)*

*Shot 187. Medium shot of a bed as* SHUISKY *comes in from the left and collapses onto it, laughing helplessly.*

SHUISKY : O Lord! I'll die laughing.

*Shot 188. Close-up of* SHUISKY'S *boot on the bed. The* YOUNG IVAN *comes into frame from the right and gazes indignantly at the boot, then up at* SHUISKY'S *face which is off-screen to the left. (Still on page 149)*

YOUNG IVAN *furiously* : Take it off.

*Shot 189. Close-up of* SHUISKY. *He stops laughing abruptly and raises his head from the bed.*

*Shot 190. Medium close-up of the* YOUNG IVAN, SHUISKY'S *boot in the foreground. He looks down at the boot, then back at* SHUISKY, *off-screen.*

YOUNG IVAN : Off, I say.

*Shot 191. Another close-up of* SHUISKY. *He raises his head and glares off at the* YOUNG IVAN.

*Shot 192. Low angle close-up of the* YOUNG IVAN *glaring down at* SHUISKY, *off-screen.*

YOUNG IVAN : Get off my mother's bed! *He looks towards the other* BOYARS. My mother, who was murdered by you, you dogs!

SHUISKY *off* : A dog, am I?

*Shot 193. Close-up of him getting up and glaring at the* YOUNG IVAN.

SHUISKY : Well your mother was a bitch.

*Shot 194. Close-up of the* YOUNG IVAN *as* SHUISKY *grabs him by the front of his shirt and towers over him like an angry bear.*

144

(Still on page 149)

SHUISKY : She used to sleep with that dog Telepnev. *He pushes him violently off to the right.*

*Shot 195. Link on the motion. Close-up of the* YOUNG IVAN *as he backs into a doorway, looking off left towards* SHUISKY.

*Shot 196. A closer shot of the* YOUNG IVAN; *his eyes narrow harshly as* SHUISKY *continues off.*

SHUISKY : No one even knows who your father was! . . .

*The* YOUNG IVAN *starts forward.*

*Shot 197. Close-up of* SHUISKY. *He starts back and lunges with his staff.*

SHUISKY : Race of dogs!

*Shot 198. Medium close-up of the* YOUNG IVAN *as he backs into the doorway. He flings his arms up to protect himself and cries out.*

YOUNG IVAN : Seize him!

*Loud music.*

*Shot 199. Close-up of* SHUISKY. *He starts back in alarm.*

*Shot 200. Close-up of the* YOUNG IVAN *in the doorway, the shirt torn from his bare shoulder. He gazes off at* SHUISKY *with eyes narrowed, and raps out a command.*

YOUNG IVAN *shouting* : Seize him.

*Shot 201. Close-up of* SHUISKY, *wide-eyed with terror.* (Still on page 149)

*Shot 202. High angle medium shot of the doorway, which is now open, the* YOUNG IVAN *standing beside it,* SHUISKY *in the foreground on the left. The music continues loudly. Two* KENNELMEN *rush in with whips, pause in front of* IVAN, *then seize hold of* SHUISKY, *followed by a third.*

*Shot 203. Medium close-up of* BYELSKY *in front of the opposite door, looking on with mingled fear and amazement.*

BYELSKY : The leading boyar handed over to the kennelmen!

*Shot 204. A slightly longer shot of the same scene. As* BYELSKY *continues to stare in alarm, the other* BOYARS *back hurriedly out through the door, jostling him as they go.* BYELSKY *also backs towards the door, pauses to look anxiously off in the direction of the* YOUNG IVAN, *then turns and hurries out.*

*Shot 205. Medium close-up of the* YOUNG IVAN *rising to his feet by the bed. He seems momentarily bewildered by the*

145

*sudden turn of events and one of the* KENNELMEN *crouches behind him, watching him anxiously. The music continues. As he rises to his feet, the camera tilts up, cutting out the* KENNELMAN. *Then the 'royal look' returns to his eyes; he jerks the shirt back onto his shoulder with an imperious gesture and takes hold of the cross hanging round his neck.*

YOUNG IVAN : I shall reign alone ! Without the boyars ! *The camera tracks in to a close-up of his face as he gazes steadily in front of him.* I will be Tsar !

*Fade out.**

*Shot 206. Shot of swirling clouds. We hear the voice of* TSAR IVAN, *off.*

IVAN *off* : Now . . .

*Shot 207. Close-up of* PHILIP, *who stands listening to* IVAN, *in the throne room.*

IVAN *off* : . . . I hold great power.

*Shot 208. Close-up of* IVAN, *seated.*

IVAN : The people support me. My personal guard form an iron ring about me . . . My enemies are kept at bay. *Music;* IVAN *stares into space for a moment and drops his voice as he continues.* But I have no close friends.

*Shot 209. Close-up of* PHILIP *who listens, crozier in hand.*

IVAN : God refuses me the sweet consolations of friendship . . . On whose shoulders . . .

*Shot 210. Resume on close-up of* IVAN, *slightly low angle.*

IVAN : . . . can I rest my head? With whom can I share my joys and sorrows? I am alone, abandoned . . . *He closes his eyes for a moment.* I had a single close friend—Anastasia . . . She has left me. I had a friend, Kurbsky . . . *He shakes his head, raising his voice.* He has betrayed me. *Raising his head.* No, not just myself . . .

*Shot 211. High angle medium shot of* IVAN, PHILIP *standing in the foreground. The* TSAR *gets up brusquely, raising his hand.*

IVAN : . . . but our great cause . . . *He sits down on the steps in front of the throne . . .* I don't fear the trouble-makers.

*Shot 212. Close-up of* IVAN *sitting with his back against the*

---

* The close of this scene is a very free version of what actually took place during a banquet after the Christmas festivities of 1543. The thirteen-year-old Tsar, smarting with humiliation, ordered the arrest of Andrew Shuisky, the head of the Duma, and had him thrown to his hunting dogs.

*throne. He speaks earnestly, reflectively.*

IVAN: I don't fear the sword, poison or betrayal. *He looks up at* PHILIP, *off-screen to the left.* I fear nothing for myself. *He stretches out his hand towards* PHILIP. But I tremble for our great cause.

*Shot 213. Medium shot: the* TSAR *sits on the steps by the throne, his arm outstretched towards* PHILIP, *who stands with his back to him in the foreground.*

IVAN *in a tired voice*: A new cause, on which one had hardly embarked . . .

PHILIP *turns abruptly and goes back towards* IVAN. *He leans over the seated figure of the* TSAR, *banging his crozier on the ground.*

PHILIP: There is no higher destiny than to reign according to ancient traditions . . .

*Shot 214. Close-up of* PHILIP *leaning towards* IVAN.

PHILIP: . . . as our ancestors did. Pay heed to the boyars.

*Shot 215. Medium close-up of* IVAN, *huddled at the foot of his throne.*

PHILIP *off*: Share your authority with them.

IVAN *suddenly springs to life and leans back, glaring up at* PHILIP, *off-screen.*

IVAN *savagely*: You lie, monk!

*Shot 216. A reverse angle long shot of the throne room from above,* IVAN *by his throne, glaring up at* PHILIP *in the foreground. (Still on page 150)*

IVAN: These are old wives tales!

PHILIP *shouting angrily*: You reject the counsel of your spiritual guide? Very well! PHILIP *leans towards* IVAN *and spits out his words.* Remain alone! *With an angry sweep of his cloak,* PHILIP *turns to leave, while* IVAN *sits on his throne again.* PHILIP *strides off down the hall, then pauses and turns back to shout at* IVAN. Reviled! *As he speaks,* IVAN *gets up and goes across to the right, stumbling anxiously down from the top of the dais.* PHILIP *takes a few more steps, then turns again.* Condemned, accursed . . . and alone!

IVAN *comes down from the dais and hurries after him as he strides off down the room.**

---

* End of the second reel (300 metres).

147

*Shot 217. Reverse angle long shot of the throne room from under the archway in the middle.* PHILIP *strides in from the right, followed by* IVAN *who catches the end of his flying cloak, holding him back.*

*Shot 218. Medium close-up of* IVAN *tugging at* PHILIP'S *cloak. As he speaks he leans wearily back against a stone parapet at the side of the room.*

IVAN : It is no longer the Tsar who pleads with you, but a friend crushed by the burden of authority.

*PHILIP moves out of frame to the left, tugging forward the* TSAR, *who is still holding onto the end of his cloak.*

*Shot 219. Medium shot of* PHILIP *as he hurries forward under the archway, tugging* IVAN *after him. As he moves out of frame to the left,* IVAN *falls to his knees, bringing him to a halt.*

IVAN *pleading* : Don't leave me . . .

*Shot 220. Medium close-up of* IVAN *hanging on to the cloak, looking imploringly up at* PHILIP.

IVAN : . . . in my isolation. Stay with me . . . *He stretches out an*

*arm and raises his voice* . . . help me to re-establish Russian power, and for this . . . *He puts his hand to his breast* . . . accept the office . . .

*Shot 221. Close-up of* PHILIP.

IVAN : . . . of Metropolitan Bishop of Moscow.

Philip *reflects and looks round.*

Philip : Will you allow me the right to plead ...

*Shot 222. Medium shot of the two of them in front of the arch,* Philip *standing, crozier in hand, the* Tsar *on his knees, hanging on to his cloak.*

Philip *continuing* : ... in favour of those you accuse?

*In a sudden burst of anger,* Ivan *flings aside the cloak.*

Ivan *shouting* : I never accuse the innocent.

Philip *moves angrily off to the right, his cloak flying.* Ivan *rises and stamps on the end of it, bringing* Philip *to an abrupt halt.*

Ivan *shouting* : Wait!

*A* Novice *appears in the background under the archway. Suppressing his anger,* Ivan *sinks to his knees on the end of* Philip's *cloak, his head bowed.*

*Shot 223. Medium shot of the same scene,* Ivan *and* Philip *in the foreground, the* Novice *behind them.*

Ivan : Very well. It shall be as you say.*

Philip *helps* Ivan *to his feet and embraces him.*

*Shot 224. Link on the motion. Close-up of* Philip *embracing* Ivan, *first on one cheek, then on the other,* Ivan *with his back to camera.*

*Shot 225. Reverse angle medium shot from above as* Philip *and* Ivan *go down the steps at the end of the throne room, accompanied by the* Novice, *and out through an archway on the left. Fade out.*

*Shot 226. Medium shot of* Ivan *standing in front of a carved chair in another chamber in the Kremlin, three-quarters facing camera. He turns as* Malyuta *speaks, off.*

Malyuta *off* : Why give the bishop ...

*Shot 227. Close-up of* Ivan, *listening to* Malyuta.

---

* Philip Kolychev, the son of a boyar, member of an ancient and noble family, cup-bearer to Ivan IV, entered a monastery at his own request (see the scene at the beginning of the first part of the film). He was recalled by Ivan in 1566, but he did not return very hopefully. He imposed as a condition the suppression of the Oprichina which, under Ivan's orders, was engaging in a reign of terror. Ivan agreed, but did not keep his word. Philip was installed on July 25th, 1566, but three years later was condemned to penal servitude for life, then strangled. After the Tsar's death, the deposed Archbishop was canonised in 1652.

MALYUTA *off* : . . . such power over you? IVAN *turns to the right.* Why let yourself be humiliated by an ignorant priest?

IVAN *brutally* : None of your business, dog! *He turns back again.*

MALYUTA *off* : I know . . .

> *Shot 228. High angle medium shot of* MALYUTA, *dressed in the black of the* OPRICHNIKS, *coming forward under an archway.*

MALYUTA *off* : I am a dog . . . But a faithful dog.

> *Shot 229. Close-up of* MALYUTA.

MALYUTA *gruffly* : You are wrong, Tsar, to prefer a priest to a dog. *He goes off to the right.*

> *Shot 230. Medium close-up of* IVAN, *slightly low angle, as* MALYUTA *comes up behind him on the right.*

MALYUTA : I know, you want friendship . . . You languish without friendship . . . For friendship you are ready to bow at his feet. *He bends down and kisses the hem of the* TSAR's *robe. Camera tilts down with him. As he continues he holds up the robe, then tosses it angrily away.* Do you not see that Philip has only one idea : to conceal your enemies under his own skirts? A friend, eh? . . . *He laughs and gets up again, camera tilting with him.* He's hardly worth more than Kurbsky! . . .

> IVAN *throws his head back desperately and presses his fists to his brow.*

IVAN *shouting* : You dare pronounce that name.

MALYUTA *triumphantly* : Ah! . . .

> *Shot 231. Close-up of the two of them,* IVAN *with his head thrown back,* MALYUTA *behind him, speaking in his ear.*

MALYUTA : I know you love Kurbsky! It's not his treachery which wounds you . . . It's the loss of a friend! . . . You don't sleep at night!

> IVAN *starts to turn towards him.*

> *Shot 232. Link on the motion. Medium close-up of the two of them as* IVAN *turns and with a violent push sends* MALYUTA *sprawling back on the floor, under the archway.*

IVAN : Hold your tongue, dog!

MALYUTA *sitting up where he has landed* : You don't show any gratitude or affection . . . IVAN *sits down in his chair and leans over the side towards* MALYUTA . . . to those who are loyal to you . . . MALYUTA *starts forward.*

154

*Shot 233. Close-up of the two of them,* MALYUTA *kneeling by the arm of the chair,* IVAN *with his head bent, listening.*

MALYUTA: . . . who'd give their lives for you . . . MALYUTA *shakes his fist angrily* . . . who carry the weight of your power on their strong shoulders.

IVAN *leans back.*

*Shot 234. Link on the motion. Close-up of* IVAN *leaning back thoughtfully in his chair.*

IVAN: My power is carried by the shoulders of the people. *He leans his head against the back of the chair* . . . and their will is my strength. *He starts forward, looking upwards.* I hear the voice of God through them and I carry out His holy designs. *He looks down at* MALYUTA *off-screen.*

MALYUTA *off*: Tsar, I beg you . . .

*Shot 235. Medium close-up of him, standing, clutching his staff.*

MALYUTA: . . . don't let the priest do as he pleases. Don't trust anyone. *He raises his staff in both hands.* You have power . . .

*Shot 236. Medium close-up of* IVAN, *sunk in his chair. He sits up as* MALYUTA *finishes, off.*

MALYUTA *off*: Use it! MALYUTA'S *head comes into frame on the left as he leans towards the listening* TSAR. I understand. You've given your word to the priest. You've made him promises . . . You can't go back on your word . . . I understand . . . So we must see that the Tsar's word is respected and . . . wipe out the traitors too. *A pause.* IVAN *sinks back in his chair again.* MALYUTA *draws the* TSAR's *fur cape around his neck and strokes it soothingly. (Still on page 151)* It's just going back on your word that worries you, isn't it? There is a way out . . . use a cat's paw . . . No, a red-headed dog — me, Malyuta. IVAN *looks up, hope dawning in his eyes.* I'll take the Tsar's sins on my shoulders. MALYUTA *moves away.*

*Shot 237. Medium close-up of* MALYUTA, *his right hand on his chest,* IVAN *in profile in the foreground.*

MALYUTA: I'll give my soul for the Tsar. I'll go to hell if need be, but I'll keep the Tsar's word.

*He raises his eyes to heaven and crosses himself, then bows his head.* IVAN *puts out a hand and takes him by the chin.*

*Shot 238. Close-up of* MALYUTA. *Link on the motion as* IVAN's *hand lifts him by the chin.*

MALYUTA : What does the hound do when the game tries to go to earth? Flies straight as an arrow to the lair.

*Shot 239. Medium close-up of the two of them, slightly high angle, MALYUTA gazing up at IVAN.*

IVAN *looking up thoughtfully* : He outwits it . . . heads it off . . . outruns it . . . *A pause. He bends close to MALYUTA and whispers.* Outstrip the priest?

MALYUTA *agreeing* : Uh huh !

IVAN : Is that what you're suggesting?

MALYUTA : Uh huh !

IVAN *raising his voice excitedly* : Head him off in such a way that he won't have time to double back?

MALYUTA *triumphantly* : Ah ! . . .

> IVAN *turns towards MALYUTA, away from camera and strokes his head.*

IVAN *mockingly* : You'd give your soul for the Tsar ! . . . *A pause.* Eh, dog? . . . MALYUTA *laughs.* You complain the Tsar doesn't spoil you?

*Shot 240. Close-up of MALYUTA's face. IVAN's hand continues to caress his hair; it raises his forelock. The smile freezes on MALYUTA's face. He stares up at the TSAR. IVAN's other hand comes into shot and takes him by the chin. (Still on page 151)*

*Shot 241. Reverse angle medium close-up of the two of them. IVAN bends forward and kisses MALYUTA firmly on the forehead. (Still on page 151) Then, as MALYUTA bends down to kiss IVAN's hand, he smites him on the back.*

IVAN : Be off with you ! . . . MALYUTA *disappears at bottom of frame. IVAN continues, staring off to the right.* Do what you have to do. By God's will, be judge and executioner . . .

MALYUTA *off* : And to outstrip the priest . . .

*Shot 242. Medium close-up of MALYUTA drawing a parchment from his sleeve and unrolling it. He reads the parchment, pointing at it with his stubby fingers.*

MALYUTA : We'll start on some of his distant relatives, the Koly-chevs . . . We'll tame them . . .

*He cackles with laughter, looking up at IVAN off-screen, but his face freezes as he notices the TSAR's expression. He turns to go.*

*Shot 243. Link on the motion. Medium shot of the two of them as* MALYUTA *creeps away on the left, leaving* IVAN, *who has started forward in his chair, staring upwards.* MALYUTA *turns to look anxiously at the* TSAR, *then goes out through an archway in the background, pausing once again to look anxiously back. Alone,* IVAN *rises slowly to his feet, camera tilting up with him, and claps his right hand to his forehead.*

IVAN : By what right do you set yourself as a judge, Tsar Ivan? *He presses the other hand to his cheek, then raises his right arm in the air.* By what right do you wield the sword of justice?*

*A cry is heard off-screen.* IVAN *turns abruptly, looking off to the right, then bends down, leaning on his chair, camera tilting down with him. Loud music as he turns again and hurries off towards the left, pausing for a moment in the archway, then disappearing.*

*Shot 244. High angle medium shot of the stairs leading up into* ANASTASIA's *bedroom.* IVAN *runs in through the archway at the bottom, pauses to look back, then hurries up the stairs, towards the left.*

*Shot 245. Long shot of the room from the top of the stairs with link on the motion as* IVAN *runs in from the right and throws himself on the bed in the background.* FYODOR BASMANOV *appears after him and pauses at the top of the stairs, three-quarters back to camera.*

*Shot 246. Medium shot, slightly high angle, of* IVAN *lying on the bed, his head buried in the pillow.* FYODOR *appears in back view on the left and moves hesitantly towards the bed.*

*Shot 247. Medium close-up of* IVAN *raising his head from the pillow, under the lamps hanging over the bed. The music stops.*

IVAN : Let me not drink of this cup.

FYODOR *off* : You cannot avoid it . . . IVAN *whips round at the sound of his voice* . . . Even though . . .

---

* Most historians reject the idea that Ivan ever suffered any attacks of conscience with respect to his personal code of justice. On the contrary, it is generally conceded that at this period Ivan was at the height of his persecution mania and that he committed innumerable crimes. It is possible that Ivan the man felt occasional qualms about the way he wielded his ' sword of justice ' . . . they did not, however, hinder him from indulging in even more murders and orgies.

*Shot 248. Close-up of* FYODOR, *lit from below, staring down at* IVAN.

FYODOR : . . . some cups contain poison !

*Shot 249. Resume on close-up of* IVAN. *He turns away and looks off to the left.*

IVAN : The cup? . . .

*Shot 250. Close-up of a goblet, on the table by the bed. It is the one which* IVAN *found empty when he was looking for water for* ANASTASIA, *just before her poisoning.*

*Shot 251. Resume on close-up of* IVAN *as he turns and looks off to the right.*

*Shot 252. Close-up of* EUPHROSYNE's *poisoned goblet, standing on the top of the balustrade by the stairs.*

IVAN *off* : The goblet . . .

*Shot 253. Close-up of* IVAN *turning back again.*

*Shot 254. Close-up of the first goblet on the table.*

*Shot 255. Medium close-up of* IVAN. *He shrinks back in horror and grabs hold of* FYODOR's *sleeve, which is partly visible on the right.*

IVAN : They poisoned her !

*' Poisoning' music.* IVAN *looks up at* FYODOR *and leaps up.*

*Shot 256. Medium close-up of the two of them in profile, with link on the motion as* IVAN *starts up and grabs* FYODOR *by the shoulders, then clasps his head in both hands.*

IVAN : They poisoned my little heifer ! *As he cries out in anguish, he clasps* FYODOR's *head to his breast.*

*Shot 257. Close-up of them both, in profile.\**

FYODOR : Who gave the fatal goblet to the Tsarina?

IVAN *looks at* FYODOR, *then away again, his eyes wide. He sinks slowly downwards.*

*Shot 258. Medium shot with link on the motion as* IVAN *sinks down onto the bed.*

*Shot 259. Close-up of him. He looks up at* FYODOR, *then away, his eyes staring.*

*Shot 260. Close-up of his hands as he runs them slowly across*

---

\* It is interesting to recall that in 1561, during the course of a banquet, Ivan himself stabbed Prince Ovchina-Obolensky who had called Fyodor Basmanov, the Tsar's favourite, a sodomite. Perhaps Eisenstein was hinting at the possibility of ambiguity in this scene.

*the white fur bed cover. The music stops.*

IVAN *off*: She received it from my own hands!

 *Shot 261. Close-up of* IVAN, *prostrate on the bed, staring into space.* FYODOR *comes into frame and bends over him, speaking in his ear. (Still on page 151)*

FYODOR: And who gave it to you?

IVAN *realising*: Euphrosyne! ... *He starts up.*

 *Shot 262. Medium close-up of them both with link on the motion as* IVAN *leaps to his feet, taking* FYODOR *with him.*

IVAN: Euphrosyne? ... *He puts a hand to his head and turns away.* Is it possible? The Tsar's aunt? *He turns back to* FYODOR. My own blood relation? ...

 FYODOR *tries to say something, but the* TSAR *hastily claps his hand over his mouth.*

 *Shot 263. Close-up of the two of them with link on the motion as* IVAN *claps his beringed hand over* FYODOR'S *mouth and glares at him.*

IVAN: Silence! Not a word of your suspicions to anyone ... *He stares off left* ... until I have ferreted out the truth. Come!

 *He hurries off left, followed by* FYODOR.

 *Shot 264. Long shot of the bedroom as* IVAN *dashes towards camera, dragging* FYODOR *with him. Loud music. They pause at the top of the stairs, then turn and go over to a window on the left.*

 *Shot 265. Medium shot of the two of them, bending down and looking out of the window, three-quarters back to camera.*

 *Shot 266. The music continues. Medium shot of black-clad* OPRICHNIKS *dragging struggling* BOYARS *down a staircase into a courtyard in the Kremlin. One of the* BOYARS *is thrown to the ground.*

 *Shot 267. High angle medium shot of the* OPRICHNIKS *pushing or dragging the wildly struggling* BOYARS *down some more stone steps.* *

 *Shot 268. High angle long shot of a snow-covered courtyard outside the Kremlin. The music continues. Three* BOYARS *are dragged in from the left and forced to their knees in the foreground facing camera.* MALYUTA, *wearing a black cloak over*

---

\* End of the third reel (300 metres).

*an embroidered kaftan, stands under an image of Christ on
a wall in the background, watching the scene; two* OPRICHNIKS
*stand behind him.*

*Shot 269. Medium shot of* MALYUTA *and the two* OPRICHNIKS
*by the wall. They walk forward.*

*Shot 270. Low angle medium shot of the scene with two of the*
BOYARS, KOLYCHEV THE WISE *and* KOLYCHEV THE UN-
CONQUERABLE, *in the foreground, facing camera. Flanked by
the two* OPRICHNIKS, MALYUTA *comes up behind them and
unrolls a parchment.*

MALYUTA: In the name of the Father, the Son and the Holy
Ghost . . . *He glances down at the* BOYARS *and begins to read.*

*Shot 271. Close-up of* MALYUTA *in profile, reading.*

MALYUTA: . . . Our Sovereign Ivan Vassilievich, Tsar and Grand
Duke of all the Russias, has pronounced these boyars . . . *He looks
down at them.*

*Shot 272. Close-up of the* BOYAR KOLYCHEV THE WISE, *his
head bowed.*

MALYUTA: . . . of the Kolychev family to be traitors. *He raises his
head.*

*Shot 273. Close-up of the* BOYAR KOLYCHEV THE UNCONQUER-
ABLE *in profile.*

MALYUTA: . . . the aforementioned boyars having been in communication . . .

*Shot 274. High angle close-up of the son of* KOLYCHEV THE
UNCONQUERABLE, *his head bowed.*

MALYUTA: . . . with the king of Poland . . .

*Shot 275. High angle medium shot of the three* KOLYCHEVS
*kneeling on the ground, the two elder* BOYARS *nearest camera,
holding their heads up stiffly, the* YOUNGER KOLYCHEV *overcome, his head buried in his fur cape.*

MALYUTA *continues off*: . . . with a view to what?

*Shot 276. Medium close-up of two* OPRICHNIKS *listening.*

MALYUTA: With the aim of submitting to foreign . . .

*Shot 277. Close-up of one of the* OPRICHNIKS.

MALYUTA: . . . domination.

*Shot 278. Resume on high angle medium shot of the three
kneeling* BOYARS.

MALYUTA: Ivan Vassilievich, Tsar of all the Russias . . .

Shot 279. *Music. Low angle close-up of the two elder* KOLYCHEVS *in profile.*

MALYUTA : . . . has condemned them to be beheaded . . .

Shot 280. *Medium close-up of* MALYUTA, *stern-faced. He rolls up the parchment and hands it to an* OPRICHNIK *behind him on the left.*

MALYUTA : . . . for high treason.

*With a quick movement of his shoulders,* MALYUTA *slips off his cloak, which is caught by an* OPRICHNIK *behind him on the right. Without turning he takes a long curved sword from the* OPRICHNIK *on the left. He runs his hand along the blade. (Still on page 151)*

Shot 281. *Resume on medium close-up of the two elder* KOLYCHEVS; *they turn to face the front again, holding their heads up arrogantly.*

Shot 282. *Close-up of* MALYUTA *as he swings the sword rapidly upwards, then suddenly pauses, the sword above his head. He lowers it slowly, looking down at the* BOYARS.

Shot 283. *Close-up of the neck of* KOLYCHEV THE WISE *in three-quarter back view, his head stiffly raised.*

Shot 284. *Resume on close-up of* MALYUTA. *The music comes to a crescendo. Throwing his shoulders back, he raises his sword and, bending forward, delivers the blow.*

Shot 285. *On the noise of the sword cutting into flesh, cut to medium shot of* IVAN *at the bottom of the staircase leading into the courtyard,* FYODOR *standing just behind him. Camera tracks slowly with him from left to right as he comes down some more steps and across to* MALYUTA, *who is standing nonchalantly with one foot up on a step, waiting for the* TSAR'S *approval.* IVAN *pauses in front of him without looking at him, then advances towards camera, staring at the beheaded* BOYARS, *off-screen to the right. Camera pans slightly to the right as he comes into medium close-up while* FYODOR *goes up to* MALYUTA *in the background.*

Shot 286. *A slightly longer shot of the same scene; in the foreground,* IVAN, *staring off to the right, takes off his hat and bows low before the dead men off-screen. In the background,* FYODOR *and* MALYUTA *lean forward, watching him. The music ends and a church* CHOIR *intones the anthem 'Lament ye not . . .'*

*Shot 287. Close-up of* IVAN *as he straightens up and begins to cross himself. Suddenly he stops and points at the ground, off-screen, a gleam of madness in his eyes.*

IVAN *hoarsely*: Too few! . . .

*Shot 288. High angle medium shot of* BOYARS *kneeling in the cell of the Metropolitan Bishop, their hands outstretched, candles burning in the foreground. The* CHOIR *sings off. (Still on page 152)*

*Shot 289. Medium close-up of* PETER VOLYNETS *staring off to the right, the* BOYARS *and flaming candles behind him.*

*Shot 290. Medium close-up of* PHILIP *between the coffins of the dead* BOYARS, *crozier in hand, staring grimly off to the right. The bare feet of one of the* BOYARS *stick out from a coffin in the foreground.* PIMEN *stands in the background, crozier in hand. (Still on page 152)*

*Shot 291. Low angle medium shot of* PIMEN, *standing motionless, robed in white, a row of burning candles on the right, a skull painted on the ceiling above him.\* (Still on page 152)*

*Shot 292. High angle close-up of* PHILIP *in silent contemplation.*

*Shot 293. Medium close-up of two of the coffins against a background of flaming candles, the naked feet of the dead* BOYARS *sticking out of the end. The* CHOIR *sings loudly, off.*

*Shot 294. Medium shot of* PHILIP *leaning forward over one of the coffins, the others on either side,* PIMEN *in the background. Smoke from the flaming candles drifts across the screen. (Still on page 152)*

*Shot 295. Resume on low angle medium shot of* PIMEN. *He moves slowly forward to the right, past the flaming candles.*

*Shot 296. Resume on medium shot of* PHILIP *amongst the coffins.* PIMEN *moves forward behind him.*

*Shot 297. Medium close-up of the two of them,* PHILIP *in the foreground gazing ahead,* PIMEN *slightly behind, towering over him like an avenging angel. There is a vast wing painted on*

---

\* After Philip's assassination, Ivan rehabilitated Pimen despite past errors and appointed him Archbishop of Moscow. The appointment lasted from 1569 to 1570.

*the ceiling above.*

PIMEN : By God's power invested in you, bring the Tsar to heel. *He stretches out an arm imperiously, then the camera tracks briefly to the left as he comes round behind* PHILIP *and speaks vehemently in his ear.* I charge you to excommunicate him.

PHILIP *stubbornly* : I shall return to my monastery.

*Shot 298. Close-up of* PIMEN, *who comes into view at the bottom of frame as he steps back.*

PIMEN : You daren't. If you don't bring the Tsar to heel . . . *He grips his crozier with both hands, then bends forward and stretches one arm out behind him in a theatrical gesture, raising his eyes to heaven as he continues. . . .* you will answer for it before God! . . . *There is a noise off.*

*Shot 299. Long shot of the room.* EUPHROSYNE *hurries in from the back and comes towards camera, sinking to her knees in close-up and clutching at her head with both hands.*

EUPHROSYNE : Ah! . . . my lord!

*She sinks forward, disappearing at the bottom of frame. Two* BOYARS *hurry towards camera and bend over her in close-up.*

*Shot 300. High angle medium shot of the assembled* BOYARS *rising to their feet.*

*Shot 301. Medium close-up:* PHILIP *sits motionless on the right of frame while on the left the two* BOYARS *help* EUPHROSYNE *up.*

EUPHROSYNE *clutching at her throat* : I ask for justice against the Tsar, and protection . . .

*Shot 302. Close-up of her, slightly low angle, supported by the two* BOYARS.

EUPHROSYNE : I ask that the boyars' cause be defended . . . No, I do not ask, my lord, I demand! *Suddenly she stares off to the right and her jaw drops.*

*Shot 303. High angle medium shot of two of the coffins, the bare feet of the executed* BOYARS *sticking out of the end, candles flaming in the background.*

*Shot 304. Close-up of* EUPHROSYNE *staring down at the coffins,* PIMEN *in the background.*

EUPHROSYNE : That's not all I'm demanding . . . *She turns towards the left and bares her teeth, shaking her fist as she continues grimly.* I demand that the Tsar be humbled. *She gets up.*

*Shot 305. Low angle shot:* PHILIP *in the foreground on the left,* PIMEN *towering over him in the background, on the right.* EUPHROSYNE *rises to her feet between them and looks down at* PHILIP *as she continues grimly.*

EUPHROSYNE : I do not ask . . .

*Shot 306. High angle close-up of* PHILIP, *seated, looking morose.*

EUPHROSYNE, *behind him, shouts* : I demand !

*Shot 307. Low angle close-up of* PIMEN *staring grimly down, the skull on the ceiling behind him.*

*Shot 308. Close-up of* PETER VOLYNETS *gazing up at* PHILIP.

PHILIP *off* : God . . .

*Shot 309. Resume on low angle close-up of him,* EUPHROSYNE *behind.*

PHILIP : . . . be my witness . . . *A pause. It is not for myself . . . He looks to the right . . .* nor for the members of my family who have been executed . . . *He looks up towards camera . . .* that I take up the sword. *He gets up.*

*Shot 310. Similar shot from a slightly higher angle, taking in* PIMEN *in the background. Link on the motion as* PHILIP *rises to his feet in the foreground.*

PHILIP : It is on behalf of the boyars. *He leans forward, his face coming into extreme close-up, staring straight at camera.* Justice must be done against the Tsar. Beneath my priestly robes . . . *He straightens up again and bangs his crozier on the ground . . .* beats the heart of a Kolychev ! And a Kolychev . . . who is a prince of the Church !

*Shot 311. Low angle medium close-up of him,* EUPHROSYNE *and* PIMEN *in the background. A vast fresco of an angel seems to float above them on the ceiling.*

PHILIP : Even the Tsar can do nothing against the Church . . .

*Shot 312. Close-up of* PHILIP. *He looks fiercely from side to side as he speaks.*

PHILIP : Come tomorrow to the cathedral ! I shall humble the Tsar . . . *He bangs his crozier on the ground . . .* I shall crush him with the weight of the Church.

*Shot 313. Close-up of* PETER VOLYNETS. *He kisses* PHILIP's *hand feverishly and gazes upwards.*

*Shot 314. Close-up of the latter, gazing austerely before him.*

*The singing of the* CHOIR *dies away. Fade out.*

*Shot 315. A bell tolls loudly. Long shot of the cathedral interior,* BOYARS *ranged on either side. In the centre, on the dais where* IVAN *delivered his coronation speech long ago, stands a ' Chaldean furnace ' — a platform on stilts surrounded by miniature walls — erected for the ' Fiery Furnace play'.*
*Shot 316. A longer shot of the same scene.* EUPHROSYNE *stands in medium shot on the left, a small child beside her.*

CHOIR *singing loudly* : ' God be praised . . .'
*Shot 317. Medium shot, slightly high angle, of the* STARITSKYS. EUPHROSYNE *stands holding her staff on the right,* VLADIMIR *behind her, the child in the centre.*
*Shot 318. Medium close-up of the child with* EUPHROSYNE *behind him. He turns to the left.*

CHILD : Mother . . . What's the story of the fiery furnace? . . .
EUPHROSYNE *leans forward to explain.*
*Shot 319. Close-up of* EUPHROSYNE. *She puts her hand on the child's shoulder and looks upwards as she speaks.*

EUPHROSYNE : The story tells how a heavenly angel led three youths called Shadrach, Meshach and Abednego . . .
*Shot 320. Low-angle medium close-up of the ' furnace', candles burning in front of it.*

EUPHROSYNE *continues, off* : . . . out of the fiery furnace of Babylon . . .
*Shot 321. Close-up of* EUPHROSYNE.

EUPHROSYNE : . . . into which the ferocious heathen Tsar, Nebuchadnezzar, had thrown them.
*Shot 322. Close-up of* VLADIMIR, *who has grown a scanty beard, standing beside an old Staritsky* BOYAR—PENINSKY.

PENINSKY : Now, there are no such angels.
*Shot 323. High angle medium shot of the* CHILD. *Two* BOYARS *bend down and lift him into the air. (Still on page 152)*
*Shot 324. Medium shot with link on the motion as the two* BOYARS *hoist the* CHILD *onto their shoulders. The rest of the congregation bow low behind them.*
*Shot 325. Long shot of the congregation bowing in another part of the cathedral. The* CHOIR *continues to sing, off.*

*Shot 326. Medium long shot of the 'furnace'. The* CHOIR *stops singing and the bell starts to toll as two 'CHALDEANS' with painted faces and pointed caps lead three* YOUTHS *in from the left with exaggerated clown-like gestures. The* YOUTHS *are wearing white cassocks and artificial haloes bound to their heads, and are tied together by a long sash, the* CHALDEANS *holding each end. The* CHALDEANS *leap in the air and land with a crash of cymbals. At the same time the bells stop tolling and the* YOUTHS *begin to sing in chorus. (Still on page 152)*

*Shot 327. Medium close-up of the three* YOUTHS *starting to sing, the* CHALDEANS *behind them.*

YOUTHS *singing*: ' Innocent, we were flung into the burning, fiery furnace . . .'

*Shot 328. Close-up of them.*

YOUTHS : '. . . lit by the Chaldeans . . .'

*Shot 329. Medium shot of the three* YOUTHS *in front of the furnace. The two* CHALDEANS *leap forward with a crash and, walking comically with bent legs, lead the* YOUTHS *round behind the furnace.*

YOUTHS *singing*: '. . . for having disobeyed the heathen Tsar . . .'

*Shot 330. Medium close-up of the* BOYARS *bowing.*

*Shot 331. A close-up of the furnace. One of the* CHALDEANS *comes in from the left and leans against the side of it.*

CHALDEAN : Chaldean! Hey! Chaldean!

*The* SECOND CHALDEAN *comes in from the right and leans against the other side of the furnace.*

SECOND CHALDEAN : What is it?

*Shot 332. Close-up of the two* CHALDEANS *as they come together in front of the furnace. As they speak, they twist their mouths grotesquely, the effect exaggerated by their painted faces. (Still on page 152)*

FIRST CHALDEAN : Is this the Tsar's work?

SECOND CHALDEAN : The Tsar's!

*Shot 333. Close-up of the* FIRST CHALDEAN.

FIRST CHALDEAN : They disobeyed the Tsar?

*Shot 334. Close-up of a young woman laughing.\**

---

\* This shot was used in the coronation scene in Part I.

Second Chaldean *off* : They disobeyed !

>*Shot 335. Close-up of another young woman looking on.\**

First Chaldean *off* : So, we . . .

>*Shot 336. Medium close-up of the* Child *poised on the shoulders of the* Boyars; *he laughs as the* Chaldean *continues.*

First Chaldean *continuing, off* : . . . are going to hurl them . . .

>*Shot 337. Medium close-up of the two* Chaldeans *in front of the furnace. They throw up their arms.*

First Chaldean : . . . into the burning, fiery furnace !

>*Shot 338. Medium shot of the same scene. Link on the motion as the two* Chaldeans *throw their arms in the air; then they come down from the dais and turn somersaults in front of it, accompanied by the crash of cymbals. At the same time, the back of the furnace opens and the* Youths *climb into it, singing.*

Youths : ' We are given into . . .'

>*The* Chaldeans *turn and go towards the furnace.*

>*Shot 339. Long shot of the same scene. Link on the motion as the* Youths *come forward and stand in the centre of the furnace while the* Chaldeans *crawl underneath it to light the fire. The crowd starts forward on either side to watch.*

Youths : '. . . the hands of lawless princes . . .'

>*Shot 340. Close-up of the* Youths' *hands as they light tapers from the candles in front of the furnace, continuing to sing.*

Youths *singing in unison* : '. . . wretched apostates . . . into the hands . . .'

>*Shot 341. Medium close-up of the* Chaldeans *stoking the fire with comic gestures.*

>*Shot 342. Medium shot, showing the* Young Men *standing singing above them. The* Chaldeans *continue to stoke the fire.*

Youths : '. . . of an unjust Tsar . . .'

>*Shot 343. Medium shot of the* Youths *singing on top of the furnace. The* Chaldeans *rise up with torches in their hands.*

Youths : '. . . who is the wickedest in the world . . .'

>*Shot 344. Long shot of the* Youths, *seen over the heads of the congregation. As they continue to sing, the* Tsar's *great laugh*

---

\* See footnote to Shot 334.

*echoes through the cathedral, off.*

*Shot 345. High angle medium shot of an archway at the bottom of some steps.* IVAN *comes through, clad in a black cassock and cowl, accompanied by* MALYUTA *and several other* OPRICHNIKS *similarly dressed. They have just recounted to him an incident concerning* EUPHROSYNE.

IVAN: With her staff . . . MALYUTA *turns away sulkily.* Ha! ha! ha! . . . the old lady . . . Ha! ha! Hands off the Tsar's aunt! She's Tsarina in her own house! Ha! ha! ha! *He mounts the stairway.* So she . . .

*Shot 346. Close-up of* IVAN *laughing, leaning towards* MALYUTA, *who looks down morosely.*

IVAN: . . . slapped your faces, you and your henchmen! *He takes* MALYUTA *by the chin as he continues to laugh, but* MALYUTA *looks away angrily.* Ha! ha! ha! I recognise the family spirit right enough! IVAN *gives* MALYUTA *a push with his staff.*

*Shot 347. Close-up of* MALYUTA *pushing the staff aside, still sulking.*

ALEXEY BASMANOV *off*: Perhaps this is the right moment . . .

*Shot 348. Medium close-up of* IVAN *leaning towards* BASMANOV. FYODOR *is behind him on the left.*

BASMANOV *continuing*: . . . to polish off the Staritskys with one blow. *He makes a clawing motion with his hand.*

IVAN *straightens up angrily while* FYODOR *comes forward and tugs at his cowl from behind, speaking in his ear.*

FYODOR: They've opposed the Tsar's will!

IVAN *turning angrily towards* BASMANOV: It is not for you, Alexey, to tell the Tsar what he should do. *Turning to* FYODOR. Not for you, Fyodor, to raise your hand against the Tsar's family. *He moves forward.*

*Shot 349. High angle medium shot from the top of the stairs.* IVAN *comes up another step, then pauses,* FYODOR *on the left.*

IVAN: No harm shall come to Euphrosyne . . .

BASMANOV *moves forward from behind* IVAN *and stands beside* FYODOR.

*Shot 350. Medium close-up of* IVAN, *slightly low angle, the two* BASMANOVS *behind him on the left.*

IVAN: . . . so long as she calls herself the Tsar's aunt . . . *He drops his voice* . . . so long as she does not take it into her head to become the mother of a Tsar . . . a Tsar who submits to the boyars. *He glances angrily down at the* BASMANOVS. As for you, Basmanovs . . .

*Shot 351. Close-up of* BASMANOV *and* FYODOR *contemplating the* TSAR *sulkily as he continues off.*

IVAN *off* : . . . learn to keep your place !

*Shot 352. Medium close-up of the archway at the top of the stairs;* IVAN *comes in from the right, bending under the arch.* FYODOR *follows him and comes under the arch on the left.*

FYODOR : And the poisoned goblet . . . have you forgotten that?

IVAN *claps his hand over* FYODOR'S *mouth and looks back. Then he comes round to the left of* FYODOR, *still keeping his hand over his mouth.*

*Shot 353. Link on the motion. Close-up of the two of them as* IVAN *comes round to the left of* FYODOR, *his hand over his mouth.*

IVAN *very quietly* : Be quiet . . . Be quiet, Fyodor. Don't mention that grave charge ! *He looks off left.* God grant it was not she who was guilty ! . . . *He goes off left.**

*Shot 354. High angle long shot of the interior of the cathedral. The* BOYARS *turn and draw back in confusion. Music.*

*Shot 355. Medium long shot of black-cowled* OPRICHNIKS *hurrying forward from right to left under the vaulted entrance to the cathedral.*

*Shot 356. Another high angle long shot of the interior of the cathedral.* IVAN *strides in from the right between the ranks of* BOYARS *and advances down the aisle, followed by the* OPRICH-NIKS.

*Shot 357. New long shot as* PHILIP *emerges from the Sanctuary at the other end of the cathedral, followed by a* DEACON *and assistants. The latter take one look at the* OPRICHNIKS *and flee back into the sanctuary.* PHILIP *strides purposely forward, going out of frame to the right.*

*Shot 358. Very high angle long shot of the central nave, the Chaldean furnace at the far end. As* PHILIP *comes forward from behind it,* IVAN *appears in right foreground and the two men stride forward simultaneously to meet in the centre of the*

---

* End of the fourth reel (300 metres).

*nave, where* PHILIP *mounts a small dais. The music comes to a climax as the* OPRICHNIKS *follow* IVAN *in and form a semicircle round him. The music ends.*

*Shot 359. Low angle medium close-up of the three* YOUTHS *standing on the furnace, holding their candles. They exchange questioning glances then face forwards, and, taking a deep breath, start to sing.*

YOUTHS : ' Why, shameless Chaldeans . . .'

*Shot 360. Medium close-up of* IVAN *in profile, his face hidden by his black cowl.* PHILIP *stands, dominating him, in the background on the right. As the* YOUTHS *continue to sing,* IVAN *turns slowly towards the left and holds out his staff.*

YOUTHS *continuing off* : '. . . do you serve a lawless Tsar?'

*Shot 361. Close-up of* FYODOR. *Link on the motion as* IVAN'S *hand comes in from the right and gives him the staff.* FYODOR *stands holding it, looking sideways at the* TSAR.

YOUTHS *off* : ' Why, bewitched Chaldeans . . .'

*Shot 362. Close-up of* EUPHROSYNE *and* VLADIMIR *looking on.*

YOUTHS *continuing off* : '. . . do you serve . . .'

*Shot 363. Resume on a low angle close-up of* IVAN *walking off to the left, listening,* PHILIP *behind him on the right. He turns away from camera, to face* PHILIP.

YOUTHS *off* : '. . . a devilish, blaspheming and despotic Tsar?'

*Shot 364. Medium close-up of* PHILIP, *standing, crozier in hand, gazing stonily ahead.* IVAN *comes in from the left, in profile, and bows before him, stretching out a hand to receive his benediction. (Still on page 152)*

*Shot 365. Close-up of* IVAN *in profile, head bowed, hand held out. He looks out from under his cowl.*

YOUTHS *off* : ' Why do you torment us with fire?'

*Shot 366. Low angle close-up of* PHILIP, *staring off to the right, ignoring the* TSAR.

YOUTHS *continuing, off* : ' Why do you burn us?'

*Shot 367. Resume on close-up of* IVAN *in profile. He raises his head to look at* PHILIP, *withdraws his hand, reflects for a moment, then offers it again, bowing his head.*

YOUTHS *off* : ' And now, bear witness to a miracle.'

*Shot 368. Resume on low angle close-up of* PHILIP. *He looks away.*

Youths *off*: 'The terrestrial lord will be humbled by the Lord of Hosts.'

Fyodor *off*: The Tsar . . .

> *Shot 369. Low angle close-up of* Fyodor, *standing just beside* Philip, *looking up at him.*

Fyodor: . . . of all the Russias begs your blessing. *He bows his head.*

Youths *off*: We languish, O Lord . . .

> *Shot 370. Medium close-up of* Fyodor *looking up at* Philip. *He turns away haughtily.*

Philip *loudly*: I do not recognise the Tsar in these borrowed garments!*

> *Shot 371. Close-up of his face, slightly low angle.*

Philip *continuing*: I do not recognise the orthodox Tsar in his pagan actions!

> *Shot 372. Low angle medium close-up of* Ivan, *looking up at* Philip, *his arms crossed on his chest, the three* Youths *in the background.*

Ivan: In what way, monk, do my actions . . .

> *Shot 373. Low angle medium close-up of* Philip.

Ivan *continuing off*: . . . concern you?

> Philip *turns and thrusts his face forward, coming into close-up.*

Philip *shouting*: Your actions are those of a bloodthirsty beast!

> *Shot 374. Close-up of* Ivan *in profile, also starting forward.*

Ivan *shouting*: Silence, Philip. If you question my sovereignty . . .

> *Shot 375. Low angle medium close-up of* Ivan *and* Philip *glaring at each other.*

Ivan *continuing*: . . . you will incur my anger!

> Ivan *and* Philip *move off on opposite sides of the frame. Camera tracks forward to a low angle medium shot of the three* Youths, *standing on the furnace, as they start to sing again.*

Youths: 'Now bear witness to a miracle . . .'

---

* Historically speaking the Tsar, after his retreat at Alexandrov, had transformed his palace into a monastery, though the resemblance was purely nominal, for the most monstrous orgies took place daily. His idea had been to create a religious order comprising three hundred of his most savage Oprichniks as monks, and himself as abbot. This explains his cassock and cowl of rough black serge in this scene.

*Shot 376. Low angle close-up of two of the* YOUTHS : *the one on the right stops singing, the other continues, then stops also, staring down at the confrontation, off-screen.*

YOUTHS : ' The terrestrial lord will be humbled . . .'

*Shot 377. Low angle close-up of the third* YOUTH *who sings alone.*

YOUTH : '. . . by the Lord of Hosts . . .' *His voice trails away as he realises that he is the only one singing.*

PHILIP *off* : Ivan, like Nebuchadnezzar . . .

*Shot 378. Close-up of* PIMEN, *leaning forward, listening.*

PHILIP *continuing, off* : . . . you cast . . .

*Shot 379. High angle close-up of* EUPHROSYNE *and* VLADIMIR *listening with satisfaction.*

PHILIP *off* : . . . those who are close to you into the fire.

*Shot 380. Medium close-up of* PHILIP. *He raises his eyes to heaven.*

PHILIP : But the avenging angel will descend from heaven . . . *He raises his crozier* . . . and free them from their prison. *He bangs the crozier on the ground.*

*Shot 381. Medium close-up of* IVAN, *three-quarters back to camera, his face hidden by his black cowl. The* YOUTHS *stand*

*above the flickering flames of the furnace in the background.*
IVAN *flinging his arms in the air and shouting*: Silence . . .
    *Shot 382. Close-up of* FYODOR *starting forward, wide-eyed, the*
    YOUTHS *in the background.*
IVAN *off*: . . . Philip! . . .
    *Shot 383. Resume on low angle medium close-up of* PHILIP.
    *He steps down from the dais, coming into close-up.*
PHILIP: Submit to the authority of the Church, Ivan! . . . Repent!
*He leans forward. Dissolve the Oprichina . . .*
    *Shot 384. Close-up of* IVAN *slowly raising his head, looking*
    *suspiciously sideways at* PHILIP.
PHILIP *continuing*: . . . before it's too late! . . . Ivan . . .
    *Shot 385. Resume on low angle medium close-up of* PHILIP
    *as he steps back onto the dais again, striking the ground angrily*
    *with his crozier. Music.*
PHILIP *shouting*: . . . dissolve the Oprichina . . . before it is . . .
    *Shot 386. Low angle medium close-up of the two of them as*
    IVAN *steps forward on the left and seizes* PHILIP'S *crozier.*
PHILIP: . . . too late!
    IVAN *thrusts his face towards* PHILIP *and the two of them glare*
    *at each other in profile.*
IVAN *shouting*: Silence!
    *Shot 387. Close-up of the two of them glaring at each other.*
    *Music. We hear the piping voice of the* CHILD, *off.*
CHILD *off*: Mother, is that the terrible . . .
    *Shot 388. Resume on medium close-up of* IVAN *and* PHILIP;
    *the latter tears his crozier away from* IVAN'S *grasp as* IVAN
    *whips round at the sound of the* CHILD'S *voice. The two of*
    *them stare off to the left.*
CHILD: . . . and godless Tsar?
    *Shot 389. Medium close-up of the* CHILD *perched on the*
    BOYARS' *shoulders; laughingly he points at* IVAN.
CHILD: Mother, it is the terrible and godless Tsar!
    *Shot 390. Low angle close-up of* VLADIMIR *laughing inanely.*
    *Shot 391. The music gets louder. Close-up of* IVAN *glancing*
    *towards him in fury.*
    *Shot 392. Resume on close-up of* VLADIMIR. *The smile is wiped*
    *from his face as he catches* IVAN'S *eye and he lowers his head.*
    *Shot 393. Close-up of* IVAN *in profile, turning his scrutiny on*

EUPHROSYNE.

*Shot 394. Close-up of* EUPHROSYNE. *She looks away, unable to meet his gaze.*

*Shot 395. Low angle close-up of* FYODOR *staring off, holding* IVAN'S *staff, one of the* YOUTHS *behind him.* IVAN *rushes in from the right and seizes him by the shoulders, staring across at* EUPHROSYNE.

IVAN: It is her, Fyodor! . . . *Shouting in agony.* It is her. *He presses his head against* FYODOR'S *shoulder in an agonised spasm while the* YOUTH *cowers in terror behind them. Then his hand gropes blindly for his staff and he grips the top of it, thrusting* FYODOR *off, to the right, while the* YOUTH *scuttles away to the left.* IVAN *stands, holding his staff, glaring madly across at* EUPHROSYNE. From now on . . . *He thrusts his face forward.* I will be . . .

*Shot 396. Close-up of* EUPHROSYNE, *starting in alarm.*

IVAN *continues, off* : . . . just what you . . .

*Shot 397. Close-up of* VLADIMIR *in profile, petrified, gazing up at* IVAN.

IVAN *continues, off* : . . . say I am!

*Shot 398. Close-up of* IVAN *in his black cowl, his hands resting on the top of his staff, supporting his chin. A sly, fox-like expression comes over his face and his eyes switch to and fro as he utters the following words.*

IVAN: I will be Terrible! . . . *He looks straight towards camera and his eyebrows lift slightly as the music climaxes and dies away. Fade out.*


*Shot 399. Fade in on long shot of the* STARITSKY *apartments. The door opens in the background and* EUPHROSYNE *hurries in, coming straight towards camera until she is in close-up.*

EUPHROSYNE *crying out* : Philip . . .

*Shot 400. Medium shot of the* BOYARS *at table,* EUPHROSYNE *in the background.*

EUPHROSYNE : . . . has been arrested.

*The* BOYARS *rise from the table and hurry back towards* EUPHROSYNE.

*Shot 401. Long shot of* EUPHROSYNE, *the* BOYARS *hurrying towards her, backs to camera in the foreground.*

EUPHROSYNE : He's been forbidden . . .

*Shot 402. High angle medium close-up of* Euphrosyne *surrounded by the* Boyars.

Euphrosyne *continuing*: . . . to go back to the monastery. *She moves forwards.* He'll be given a savage trial. *The* Boyars *draw back behind her.*

*Shot 403. Close-up of* Euphrosyne *falling to her knees.*

Euphrosyne : He will be condemned . . .

*The* Boyars *move away, looking at her, in soft focus in the background.*

A Voice *off*: In the old days . . .

*Shot 404. Close-up of the old* Boyar, Peninsky, *leaning forwards.*

Peninsky : . . . they would have handed Philip over to us for trial. We'd never have let him . . .

*Shot 405. High angle medium shot of* Euphrosyne *seated on some steps, the* Boyars *in the background.*

Peninsky : . . . be humiliated.

Euphrosyne : It's no good living in the past. *She leans forward.* We must . . .

*Shot 406. Close-up of* Vladimir, *standing by an archway. He starts back and looks from side to side, anxiously following the conversation.*

Euphrosyne *off*: . . . find a solution.

Peninsky *off*: There is no solution . . .

*Shot 407. High angle close-up of* Euphrosyne.

Euphrosyne : There is a solution. Just one . . .

*Shot 408. Medium close-up of an icon on the wall.*

Euphrosyne *continues, off*: The last . . .

*Shot 409. Extreme close-up of her.*

Euphrosyne : Kill the Tsar. *She turns suddenly.*

*Shot 410. Reverse angle medium close-up, with link on the motion as she turns round.*

Euphrosyne : Either kill the Tsar . . . *She gets up.*

*Shot 411. Medium close-up of* Peter Volynets *seated on a stone bench, leaning forward, looking from side to side.*

Euphrosyne : . . . or lay our own heads on the block.

*Shot 412. High angle medium close-up of* Vladimir, *cowering beside a chair, a candelabra in front of him on the left.*

Vladimir *terrified*: But who will do it? *He turns as* Pimen *speaks.*

175

PIMEN *off* : Only the pure in heart . . .

    *Shot 413. High angle close-up of him, also seated on the stone bench,* PETER VOLYNETS *behind him in the background.*

PIMEN : . . . would be worthy of carrying out so elevated a mission !

    *He turns towards the left.*

    *Shot 414. Medium close-up of* VLADIMIR *watching anxiously from behind the candelabra.* PETER VOLYNETS *rises into view in close-up, looking off towards* PIMEN.

PIMEN *off* : Peter Volynets.

    *Shot 415. Close-up of* PIMEN, *three-quarters facing camera,* EUPHROSYNE *in soft focus behind him.*

PIMEN : I consecrate this mission to you . . .

    *While* EUPHROSYNE *moves forward and goes out of frame to the left,* PIMEN *turns and looks away from camera, his hand on* PETER VOLYNETS' *shoulder.*

    *Shot 416. Close-up of* VLADIMIR *peering in terror from behind the candles.*

PIMEN *off* : Come, my brothers . . .

    *Shot 417. Long shot of the room, the table in the foreground. In the background,* PETER VOLYNETS *kneels in front of* PIMEN, *who extends his hands to bless him.*

PIMEN : . . . embrace for the last time . . . EUPHROSYNE *approaches the table from the right and picks up a long, pointed knife, looking sinisterly off towards the right* . . . God's servant Peter, who lately dwelt among us. EUPHROSYNE *turns and walks back towards* PIMEN *and* PETER VOLYNETS.

    *Shot 418. Low angle medium close-up of* PIMEN *blessing* PETER. *There is a fanatical gleam in his eye. (Production still on page 185)*

PIMEN : He has vowed himself to the grave, he will repose beneath a cold slab . . .

    *Shot 419. Close-up of* PETER *gazing upwards,* PIMEN's *hands extended in blessing over his head.*

PIMEN : He is entering into the shades.

    *Shot 420. Close-up of* EUPHROSYNE *glancing towards the left, slowly holding out her knife.*

PIMEN : He bids farewell . . .

    *Shot 421. Medium close-up of* PETER, *his head raised. Link on the motion as* EUPHROSYNE's *hand comes slowly in from the right, holding out the knife.*

PIMEN : . . . to friends and relations.

PETER *slowly takes the knife with both hands, still gazing upwards.*

*Shot 422. Rapid low angle close-up of* PIMEN *making the sign of the cross.*

PIMEN : He will lie . . .

*Shot 423. High angle medium shot of the icon on the wall, burning lamps in front of it.* PETER *advances towards it from the right on his knees.*

PIMEN *off* : . . . with the dead. PETER *bows low before the icon.* PIMEN *comes into frame from the right and advances towards camera, coming down a step so that he is in close-up, masking* PETER. *He continues viciously.* He confiscated Church property . . .

*Shot 424. Low angle medium shot of* PIMEN, EUPHROSYNE *behind him on the right.*

PIMEN : . . . We will exterminate the beast ! *He turns towards her.*

*Shot 425. Close-up of* PIMEN *with* EUPHROSYNE *speaking over his shoulder on the left.*

Euphrosyne : We must save Philip, because he has incurred Ivan's wrath for our sake.

Pimen : That will depend on Philip's judges. *He turns and goes out of frame to the right.* Euphrosyne *turns after him.*

Euphrosyne : Who will preside at the tribunal?

*Shot 426. Medium shot:* Pimen *crosses frame from left to right, followed by* Euphrosyne.

Euphrosyne : To whom must we send . . .

*Shot 427. Medium close-up of* Pimen *walking away from camera.*

Euphrosyne *off* : . . . our gold, plate and furs?

Pimen *stopping and turning back* : It is I who will preside at the tribunal.

*Shot 428. Close-up of* Euphrosyne.

Euphrosyne : That means he's saved!

*Shot 429. High angle medium close-up of* Pimen*: he points a bony finger.*

Pimen : That means he's lost!

*Shot 430. High angle close-up of him. He leans forward slightly.*

Pimen : Philip is more useful to our cause as a martyr.

*Shot 431. High angle medium close-up of* Pimen *facing* Euphrosyne, *who stands three-quarters back to camera in the foreground. As he speaks, he comes forward into close-up while she retreats out of frame to the left.* Pimen *looks grotesque: the lighting accentuates his toad-like mouth and wrinkled, warty nose.*

Pimen : A corpse, a martyr, a saint is much more valuable to our struggle. *He makes the sign of the Cross.*

*Shot 432. Close-up of* Euphrosyne, *who draws back in alarm.*

Pimen *off* : A dead man . . . A saint . . .

*Shot 433. Low angle medium shot of* Pimen, *turned towards* Euphrosyne, *off-screen,* Peter *standing in profile just behind him.*

Pimen : . . . is invincible, even for the Tsar! *He raises a finger then turns and goes slowly towards the door in the background, his hand on* Peter's *shoulder.*

*Shot 434. Close-up of* Euphrosyne *staring after* Pimen. *As she speaks she removes her black shawl, revealing a white wimple like* PIMEN'S *cowl underneath.*

EUPHROSYNE *to herself*: His cowl is white but his soul is black.
*She backs towards an archway.*\*

*Shot 435. Medium shot of* EUPHROSYNE, *slightly high angle,
as* VLADIMIR *hurries towards her and into her arms. She
hugs him tight.*

*Shot 436. Medium shot of the two of them,* VLADIMIR *looking
up at his mother, his head on her breast.*

VLADIMIR *pathetically*: Why are you always trying to make a
leader of me, mother?

EUPHROSYNE *stares down at* VLADIMIR. *He backs away.*

*Shot 437. Link on the motion. High angle close-up of*
VLADIMIR *as he backs away and looks up at his mother.*

VLADIMIR: Why do you want to sacrifice me?

EUPHROSYNE *hurries into frame from the right and passes in
front of him so that she is on the left, in close-up, hugging
him to her bosom.*

*Shot 438. Close-up of* VLADIMIR *pressed against his mother's
breast; he looks up at her as she gently strokes his hair. Music.*

*Shot 439. Medium close-up of the two of them.* EUPHROSYNE
*looks towards camera and pushes* VLADIMIR *slightly away from
her.*

*Shot 440. Medium shot of the two of them. We see the icon on
the wall in the background.* VLADIMIR *settles his head comfortably on* EUPHROSYNE'S *knee. She draws her cloak gently over
him and begins to sing. Their richly embroidered robes gleam
in the lamplight. (Still on page 186)*

*Shot 441. Medium close-up of the two of them. As she sings,*
EUPHROSYNE *strokes* VLADIMIR'S *head. He looks upwards for
a while then closes his eyes.*

EUPHROSYNE *singing*:  'A black beaver was bathing
In the river.
In the frozen Moskova River.'

*Shot 442. Close-up of the two of them,* VLADIMIR *with his eyes
closed.* EUPHROSYNE *gazes off to the right.*

EUPHROSYNE *continuing*: 'He didn't wash himself cleaner
He only got blacker . . .'

---

\* End of the fifth reel (300 metres).

*Shot 443. Close-up of* VLADIMIR. *He opens his eyes and listens,*
*(Still on page 186) then slowly closes them again.*

EUPHROSYNE *off* :     'Ah! . . . Ah! Ah! Ah! Ah!
        Having taken his bath, the beaver . . .'

*Shot 444. Close-up of* EUPHROSYNE.

EUPHROSYNE :     '. . . Went off to the capital's
        High hill . . .'

*She suddenly smiles and her shoulders shake with slightly*
*sinister jollity as she looks from side to side, then continues to*
*sing.*

EUPHROSYNE :     '. . . to dry himself,
        Shake himself and look around . . .'

*Shot 445. Medium close-up of the two.* EUPHROSYNE *continues*
*to look to and fro with bright, rodent-like eyes, smiling slightly*
*as she sings.*

EUPHROSYNE :     ' To see if anyone was coming to look
             for him.'

*She jogs up and down, and sings louder.*

EUPHROSYNE :    ' The hunters whistle
        Searching out the black beaver.
        The hunters follow the scent.
        They will find the black beaver.'

*Shot 446. Close-up of* VLADIMIR, *his eyes closed.* EUPHROSYNE
*leans over him, her hand on his jewelled cap. A* CHOIR
*accompanies her song.*

EUPHROSYNE :     ' They want . . .'

*Shot 447. Close-up of* VLADIMIR's *face. He opens his eyes and*
*looks round anxiously.*

EUPHROSYNE *off* :    '. . . to catch and skin the beaver . . .'

*Shot 448. Resume on close-up of her leaning towards* VLADIMIR,
*who is staring up towards camera.*

EUPHROSYNE :     '. . . And with its fur then to adorn . . .'

*Shot 449. Resume on close-up of* VLADIMIR, *looking up anxi-*
*ously.* EUPHROSYNE's *hand caresses his shoulder on the right*
*of frame.*

EUPHROSYNE *off* :    '. . . A kingly mantle . . .'

*He raises his head.*

*Shot 450. Low angle medium close-up of the two of them.*
*Link on the motion as* VLADIMIR *sits up and gazes at*

180

Euphrosyne *in alarm. The latter, in profile, looks down at her son with a fanatical gleam in her eye, then raises her arms and sings at the top of her voice, accompanied by the* Choir, *off.*

Euphrosyne :         '. . . In order to array . . .'
*She turns towards camera as she sings.*
*Shot 451. Close-up of* Euphrosyne, *slightly low angle, as she continues to sing. She raises her arms again, gazing fanatically upwards.*

Euphrosyne :         '. . . Tsar . . .'
*Shot 452. Low angle medium close-up of the two of them,* Euphrosyne *with her arms upraised,* Vladimir *gazing up at her in alarm, his hand at his throat.*

Euphrosyne :         '. . . Vladimir ! . . .'
*On the last syllable of his name,* Vladimir *gives a cry of terror, claps his hand to his head and rushes off to the right.* Euphrosyne *lowers her arms. Loud music. She stretches out her hand and follows him.*

*Shot 453. The music continues loudly. Medium shot of* Euphrosyne. *The camera tracks and pans with her towards the right as she hurries across and sinks to her knees in medium close-up, three-quarter back view, before* Vladimir, *who is cowering in a wooden chair in the background. She advances*

*towards him on her knees. The music ends.*

EUPHROSYNE : I'd suffer . . .

*Shot 454. Reverse angle medium close-up of the two of them,
VLADIMIR in profile in the foreground, as EUPHROSYNE comes
up to him and lays a hand on his breast. He looks down at her,
terrified.*

EUPHROSYNE : . . . the pangs of your birth . . . *She gazes upwards,
her eyes staring madly* . . . a hundred times over . . . *She turns
towards him. He recoils, his hand on the arm of the chair* . . . for
you to ascend . . .

*Shot 455. High angle close-up of VLADIMIR as he rises from
the bottom of frame, lit from below, gazing desperately away
from EUPHROSYNE as her hand comes into shot and she lays
it on his shoulder.*

EUPHROSYNE : . . . the throne.

*Shot 456. Close-up of EUPHROSYNE as she comes into shot
from the right and gazes fanatically towards camera.*

EUPHROSYNE : To see you seated on the Tsar's throne! . . .

*Shot 457. Medium close-up of the two of them, VLADIMIR in
profile in the foreground. He stands petrified as she starts
forward and feverishly kisses his hand.*

EUPHROSYNE : Take the crown . . .

VLADIMIR *recoils in alarm as* EUPHROSYNE *looks sideways up
at him.*

*Shot 458. Close-up of VLADIMIR gazing towards camera,
EUPHROSYNE partly visible on the left.*

EUPHROSYNE : Take the collar!

VLADIMIR *looking off to the right* : I've always been frightened of
blood!

EUPHROSYNE *puts an arm around his shoulders and he moves
slightly to the right so that both their faces are in frame.*

EUPHROSYNE *softly* : You won't have to shed it. That will be Peter's
job!

*They both look off to the right, then suddenly whip round.*

*Shot 459. On the sound of the door groaning on its hinges,
cut to a long shot of the room. Link on the motion as EUPH-
ROSYNE and VLADIMIR look quickly round in the foreground.
PETER VOLYNETS appears in the background and, without
noticing them, looks slowly towards the left, his head bowed.*

182

*Shot 460. Medium shot of* PETER *from the position of the icon on the wall. He comes slowly into the centre of the shot from the right, glances towards* VLADIMIR *and* EUPHROSYNE, *off, then sinks slowly to his knees before the icon.*

*Shot 461. Medium close-up of* VLADIMIR *seated in his chair,* EUPHROSYNE *standing behind him. They both turn away from* PETER *and she bends forward as he speaks, looking down, then off to the right.*

VLADIMIR : Yes . . . but after . . . , to be haunted by remorse for the rest of my life . . . always seeing him wherever I go, enduring his silent reproaches . . .

*As he speaks, he leans forward in his chair and camera pans briefly right as* EUPHROSYNE *comes round behind the chair and leans forward to speak in* VLADIMIR'S *ear from the other side.*

EUPHROSYNE *looking towards camera*: Whatever else you need fear — it's not that. When the throne is yours, you will punish the regicide . . . VLADIMIR, *terrified, draws away from his mother. Camera pans left with him,* EUPHROSYNE *leans towards him again from the right* . . . and others, too . . . VLADIMIR *leaps from his chair in terror and disappears on the left of frame.* EUPHROSYNE *starts after him.*

*Shot 462. Long shot of the room, the table in the foreground with the candelabra on it.* VLADIMIR *runs towards camera and throws himself down across the table, his head in his hands. In the background* EUPHROSYNE *leans forward from the chair, looking after him.*

EUPHROSYNE : A sovereign should not stray from the path of righteousness . . . VLADIMIR *raises his head in alarm* . . . if he can help it . . . EUPHROSYNE *comes towards him. She continues sternly* . . . but he must be prepared . . . *She slaps her hand on the table and* VLADIMIR *scuttles away from camera like a frightened rabbit.*

*Shot 463. Reverse angle medium shot of* VLADIMIR *as he rushes forward round a pillar then throws himself down on a bench in the foreground.*

EUPHROSYNE *off*: . . . to tread . . .

*Shot 464. Close-up of* PETER *as he rises into shot, looking off right, listening attentively.*

EUPHROSYNE *continuing, off*: . . . the path of evil . . .

*Shot 465. Low angle medium close-up of* EUPHROSYNE *stand-*

*ing by the table.*

EUPHROSYNE : . . . if necessary.

> *Shot 466. Resume on* VLADIMIR *in medium close-up, looking away from camera towards* EUPHROSYNE, *off-screen. Music. He suddenly turns with a start and looks towards camera, leaning slowly forwards.*

> *Shot 467. Medium close-up of the door opening slowly.*

> *Shot 468. Resume on medium close-up of* EUPHROSYNE, *by the table. She also turns with a start and moves away from camera, towards* VLADIMIR.

> *Shot 469. Reverse angle medium shot as* EUPHROSYNE *comes round behind the pillar. She advances towards camera and crouches down by the bench, then leans forward, her face coming into close-up.* VLADIMIR'S *head rises into shot on the right. They both peer anxiously forward, their faces coming into extreme close-up.*

> *Shot 470. Close-up of the door closing again slowly.*

> *Shot 471. The music continues loudly. Resume on close-up of* EUPHROSYNE *and* VLADIMIR. *They recoil away from camera, eyes wide with alarm.*

> *Shot 472. Reverse angle long shot towards the door,* EUPHROSYNE *and* VLADIMIR *in close-up, backs to camera. In the background,* MALYUTA *approaches carrying an object which is covered with an embroidered cloth.* EUPHROSYNE *and* VLADIMIR *shrink back and disappear on opposite sides of the frame.* MALYUTA *comes into medium close-up, staring straight ahead. As the music continues he raises the covered object, surmounted by a jewel, so that it masks his face, then thrusts it forward till it fills the screen.*

> *Shot 473. Reverse angle medium shot, slightly from below, of* EUPHROSYNE *and* VLADIMIR *retreating back towards the pillar.* VLADIMIR *cowers behind his mother, who puts out a protective arm.* MALYUTA *appears in back view in the foreground and advances, his bulky black-clad figure masking them completely. He bows low in front of them.**

---

* Some historians claim that Malyuta, acting on Ivan's orders and aided by the Oprichniks, first murdered mother and son, then had their bodies hurled from the highest window of the Kremlin. *The Great Soviet Encyclopedia* observes on the subject: ' The princes and boyars stopped at nothing in

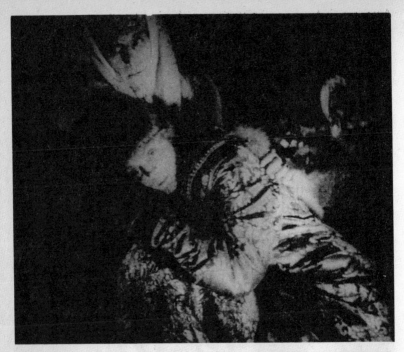

*Shot 474. Close-up of* EUPHROSYNE *and* VLADIMIR, *following* MALYUTA *with their eyes as he rises again, she suspiciously, he in alarm.*

*Shot 475. Reverse angle close-up of* MALYUTA *holding the object up in front of his face. He moves it aside and thrusts his face forward into extreme close-up, staring up at the couple.*

MALYUTA : Our great sovereign . . .

*Shot 476. Resume on close-up of* EUPHROSYNE *and* VLADIMIR, *listening. As* MALYUTA *continues, off, he thrusts the object into view from the right, offering it to* EUPHROSYNE.

MALYUTA *off* : . . . offers you a cup of wine. EUPHROSYNE *takes the covered cup, gazing suspiciously off at* MALYUTA, *while* VLADIMIR *watches anxiously over her shoulder.* Moreover our great sovereign . . .

*Shot 477. High angle close-up of* MALYUTA, *looking up at them with ironic obseqiousness.*

MALYUTA : . . . invites his cousin Vladimir Andreyevich . . .

*Shot 478. Close-up of the mother and son, still looking uneasy.*

MALYUTA *off* : . . . to the royal table.

*They exchange glances.*

*Shot 479. Medium close-up of* VLADIMIR *and* EUPHROSYNE. *They begin to turn away,* EUPHROSYNE *holding the covered goblet of wine, still staring suspiciously at* MALYUTA.

*Shot 480. Reverse angle medium shot with link on the motion as* EUPHROSYNE *and* VLADIMIR *turn away from* MALYUTA, *who straightens up behind them.* PETER VOLYNETS *is seen looking on, in the background on the left.* EUPHROSYNE *comes towards camera and pauses in medium close-up.*

EUPHROSYNE : The hand of God! VLADIMIR *comes up behind her. She moves right, towards the table, camera panning with her and cutting out* VLADIMIR. *She puts the goblet down on the table, then leans forwards and whispers triumphantly.* Our cause prospers! VLADIMIR *rushes in from the left and hugs her fearfully.* You will

---

their struggle against the centralised state. After the discovery, in 1567, of a massive plot by the boyars, headed by Prince Vladimir Staritsky, it emerged that the conspirators' plans went so far as to include the handing over of Ivan himself to the King of Poland '. Eisenstein's version, therefore, is partly imaginary.

accompany Peter . . .

*Shot 481. Low angle close-up of* PETER, *looking on.*

EUPHROSYNE : . . . to the banquet . . . *Music.*

*Shot 482. Close-up of the mother and son in profile.* EUPH-
ROSYNE *kisses* VLADIMIR *on the forehead and looks at him
for a moment while he continues to gaze at her in alarm. Then
she turns and walks away from camera, pushing him in front
of her, her hand on his shoulder.*

*Shot 483. Medium shot towards the door.* VLADIMIR *walks
nervously into frame from the left, looking back towards*
EUPHROSYNE, *off-screen.* PETER *follows him. The two of them
pause in the doorway as* MALYUTA *appears in back view from
the right and walks towards them.*

*Shot 484. Medium close-up of* EUPHROSYNE, *looking after
them.*

EUPHROSYNE *calling after* VLADIMIR : And don't forget to wear . . .

*Shot 485. Low angle medium shot of* VLADIMIR *and* PETER
*by the door,* MALYUTA *in back view in the foreground.*

EUPHROSYNE *off* : . . . your new kaftan.

VLADIMIR *backs nervously out through the doorway, followed
by* PETER.

MALYUTA *ironically* : I'll remind him ! *He follows them out.*

*Shot 486. Long shot of the room, the covered goblet on the
table in the foreground.* EUPHROSYNE *hurries towards it as she
speaks.*

EUPHROSYNE : The hand of God! . . . *She leans forward, her hand on the top of the goblet, as she continues triumphantly.* Our cause prospers! *She starts to remove the cloth from the goblet.*

*Shot 487. High angle close-up as* EUPHROSYNE *removes the cover to reveal the goblet which she used to poison* ANASTASIA. *It is empty.*

*Shot 488. Close-up of* EUPHROSYNE *looking up suspiciously, not recognising it.*

EUPHROSYNE : It's empty!

*Shot 489. There is a sudden crash of drums. Close-up of the goblet as we saw it on top of the balustrade in* ANASTASIA'S *room. Fade out.\**

*Shot 490.† Loud music as the* OPRICHNIKS *dance frenziedly in the* TSAR'S *banqueting room. Low angle medium shot of a group of* OPRICHNIKS, *clad in brilliant red robes. Two of them fling another dancer, clad in gold, into the air, while the others twirl frenziedly around. Above them, on the richly painted ceiling, a figure of God looks down from a cloud.*

*Shot 491. A longer shot of the same scene, revealing more of the fresco on the ceiling: angels with haloes looking downwards. In the foreground a row of* OPRICHNIKS, *clad in black, leap forward, flinging their hands in the air.*

*Shot 492. Another low angle shot. The line of black-clad* OPRICHNIKS *leaps forward in the background, while other dancers, clad in gold, twirl past in close-up, their robes flying.*

*Shot 493. Sound of the stamping of feet over the music. Low angle close-up of* OPRICHNIKS *in red, moving from side to side with sweeping motions of their arms.*

*Shot 494. The sound of stamping continues. Low angle medium close-up of the* OPRICHNIKS *in black, stamping their boots on the floor.*

*Shot 495. Low angle close-up of an* OPRICHNIK *in gold performing a wild Russian dance, others behind him, the figure of God on the ceiling in the background.*

*Shot 496. Low angle medium shot: the black-clad dancers*

---

\* End of the sixth reel (300 metres).

† From this sequence, the film is in colour (Sovalor). In fact, it was made from Agfa film seized from the Germans at the end of the war.

*part to make way for a* FIGURE, *disguised in female Russian peasant costume, wearing a painted female mask with long plaits and a gold crown. It advances towards camera, beneath the figure of God on the ceiling, and stretches out its arms.*

*Shot 497. Low angle medium close-up of the* FIGURE *with link on the motion as it twirls round, arms spread.*

*Shot 498. Low angle medium close-up of black-clad* OPRICH-NIKS *stamping their feet and waving their arms.*

*Shot 499. Low angle medium close-up of the* FIGURE *dancing. It twirls round, skirts flying, the* OPRICHNIKS *clapping their hands in the background, then bends to and fro with mincing female movements.*

*Shot 500. A closer shot of the* FIGURE *dancing, the painting of God on the ceiling above. The black-clad* OPRICHNIKS *circle round in front of it, stamping their feet.*

*Shot 501. Low angle close-up of the* FIGURE *mincing to and fro. One* OPRICHNIK, *clad in black, seizes it from behind, putting his arms round its chest, while another tries to grab hold of it from the front. Other dancers, in red, move past in the foreground from left to right. The foot-stamping continues.*

*Shot 502. Low angle medium close-up of* IVAN, *seated in a carved chair, draining a cup of wine. He throws his arm in the air, holding the cup, and shouts hoarsely.*

IVAN : Holla! Holla! *He tosses the cup away and leans forward. Behind him the red painted ceiling glows like the fires of hell in the candlelight, while servants pass, carrying dishes and pitchers of wine.* Faster! Faster!

*Shot 503. Close-up of* IVAN *leaning forward, his ravaged face lit redly by the flickering candles.*

IVAN : That's it! Faster! Faster! *He sits back again.*

*Shot 504. Low angle medium shot of the dancers prancing forward on bent legs, their arms in the air, the masked* FIGURE *amongst them. The ceiling glows red in the background.*

*Shot 505. A slightly closer shot of the same scene. The masked* FIGURE *comes towards camera and goes out of frame on the left. The dancers leap after it waving their arms, coming into close-up until the screen is a blur of gold and red shapes.*

*Shot 506. The frenzied music continues. Low angle medium shot of a line of black-clad* OPRICHNIKS, *dancing backwards* with arms outspread, their feet stamping thunderously on the floor, the red glow of the ceiling behind them.

*Shot 507. A closer shot of the same scene. The* OPRICHNIKS *clap their hands, then fling their arms wide again and dance back towards the right.*

*Shot 508. Low angle medium close-up of several* OPRICHNIKS *in black, dancing wildly with arms outspread and grinning as they advance towards the right.*

*Shot 509. Medium shot: the black-clad dancers have formed a square into which leaps another, dressed in red, and begins a wild cossack dance. He is joined by another in gold, who runs in from the left and begins to dance, his tunic flying. The other dancers close in around them, waving their hands. Slight re-framing as a third dancer in red appears on the right. Black-clad dancers run in from all directions, filling the screen.*

*Shot 510. Close-up of a black-clad* OPRICHNIK *at floor level, dancing with knees bent. Others, dressed in red, clap their hands behind him, in time to the music.*

*Shot 511. Medium shot of the dancers in the square, surrounded by the other* OPRICHNIKS.

*Shot 512. Low angle medium close-up of three black-clad dancers, grinning and waving their arms. In the background, the masked* FIGURE *is just visible beneath the red ceiling.*

*Shot 513. Low angle medium shot as the masked* FIGURE *comes flying into the square over the heads of the spectators, then begins to dance, holding up its skirts.*

*Shot 514. A slightly longer shot of the same scene with link on the motion as the* FIGURE *leaps into the air, kicking out its legs. In the background, the spectators wave and clap their hands frenziedly, in time to the music.*

*Shot 515. Long shot towards* IVAN'S *table at the top of some steps.* IVAN *looks on in the background while a drunken figure lies sprawled across the steps in the foreground. The masked* FIGURE *dances across frame from right to left, leaping over the drunken figure and throwing up its skirts. Hordes of* OPRICHNIKS *follow; first a group in black, then a group in red, the first of whom trips over the drunken figure and sprawls on the ground, followed by his companions.*

*Shot 516. A slightly closer shot of the same scene with link on*

*the motion as the red-clad* Oprichniks *sprawl on the ground,
waving their arms. A third group, clad in gold, comes in
behind and piles on top of the others, filling the screen with
struggling bodies.*

*Shot 517. As the music ends with a crash of drums, cut to
medium close-up of* Ivan *in his chair, leaning forward across*
Vladimir, *who is partly visible at bottom of frame, sprawled,
head down, across the table.* Ivan *leans back and flings his
arm in the air.*

Ivan *shouting* : Bravo ! Bravo !

*At* Ivan's *words,* Vladimir *raises his head with a start and
looks groggily around, completely drunk. He blinks and sighs
as* Ivan *leans forward, puts a fatherly arm around his shoulder,
and forces on him another cup of wine.*

*Shot 518. Close-up of the two of them as* Vladimir *drinks,
his face buried in the cup, while* Ivan *holds it.* Ivan *removes
the cup off-screen to the left, while* Vladimir *looks up, swal-
lows and blinks.* Ivan *leans forward again, his hand on*
Vladimir's *shoulder.*

Ivan : Ah, Brother Vladimir, you don't love me. *He lays his head
affectionately on* Vladimir's. You don't care that I am so alone,
that I'm just a poor, abandoned orphan . . .

*Shot 519. Medium shot of the two of them. In the back-
ground, servants hurry past with dishes and pitchers of wine,
under the blood-red ceiling. In the foreground sits* Alexey
Basmanov, *looking fat and debauched, listening.*

Ivan *to* Vladimir : . . . whom no one pities.

Basmanov *turns drunkenly towards them and smashes his fist
down on the table, overturning a plate.*

Basmanov *angrily, turning back towards camera* : It's not right
for the Tsar to fraternise with the landowners . . .

*Shot 520. Close-up of* Basmanov, *beetle-browed, his wrinkled
face lit by the glow of the candles.*

Basmanov *continuing* : . . . and above all not with the Staritskys !
*The music fades out.*

Ivan *off* : It is not for you, Alexey . . .

*Shot 521. Medium close-up of* Ivan, *leaning forward against
the red glow of the ceiling, his arm round* Vladimir, *who is
resting his head on the arm of the chair. The servants continue*

*to hurry past in the background. Three candles burn like fiery horns just above* IVAN'S *head, giving him a devilish appearance.*

IVAN : . . . to teach the Tsar his business. It is not for you to raise your hand . . .

*Shot 522. Close-up of* BASMANOV *facing camera,* IVAN *in the background.*

IVAN : . . . against the Tsar's relations.

BASMANOV *turns and gets up, leaning across the table towards* IVAN *and masking him with his bulky, black figure.*

BASMANOV : But it was you who taught me . . .

*Shot 523. Medium close-up of* IVAN, VLADIMIR *at his side.*

BASMANOV : . . . to weed them out.

IVAN *placing a hand on* VLADIMIR'S *head* : The Tsar's connections outshine all other connections. As the celestial tamarind . . . *He raises his other hand* . . . outshines homely oak.

BASMANOV *off* : Aren't we . . .

*Shot 524. Low angle close-up of* BASMANOV *against the red ceiling. He raises both arms in the air as he continues.*

BASMANOV : . . . the new forest growing about you?

IVAN *off* : I don't . . .

*Shot 525. High angle medium close-up of* IVAN *as he rises angrily to his feet and puts a hand on the back of his chair.*

IVAN : . . . hack down oaks to make room for wretched aspens. *The shadows of passing servants move across the ceiling behind him.* VLADIMIR *looks on, blinking stupidly from his place beside the chair.* Don't touch the Tsar's relations! IVAN *leans forward slightly as he continues.* The ties of blood . . .

*Shot 526. Close-up of* IVAN *leaning angrily towards* BASMANOV.

IVAN : . . . are sacred! *He points at* VLADIMIR.

BASMANOV *off* : Aren't we who are closest to you bound to you by other blood — blood which has been shed?

BASMANOV'S *head comes into frame on the left and he looks up at* IVAN.

IVAN *pushing* BASMANOV *aside* : You're no relation of mine . . .

*Shot 527. Shot of* BASMANOV *as he falls back on the bench.*

*Shot 528. Resume on* IVAN.

IVAN : You are my slaves . . . I raised you from the dust . . .

*Shot 529. High angle close-up of* BASMANOV *on the bench,*

*looking up at* IVAN, *the candelabra beside him.*

IVAN *off* : . . . to crush the boyar traitors.

   *Shot 530. Low angle close-up of* IVAN *glaring down at*
   BASMANOV.

IVAN : I express my will through you. *He draws back.*

   *Shot 531. Medium close-up of* IVAN *with link on the motion
   as he sinks back into his chair,* VLADIMIR *beside him.*

IVAN : Your function is to serve me, not to teach me how to behave.
VLADIMIR *attempts to look haughty but his head lolls drunkenly.*
IVAN *puts an arm round him again and leans forward.* Keep to
your place . . .

   *Shot 532. Low angle close-up of* BASMANOV *gazing up at* IVAN.

IVAN *off* : . . . Basmanovs !

   *Music.* BASMANOV *turns to the left as* MALYUTA *speaks off.*

MALYUTA *mockingly, off* : You are beginning to catch . . .

   *Shot 533. Medium close-up of* MALYUTA *leaning back in his
   chair, looking right, towards* BASMANOV.

MALYUTA : . . . the boyars' sickness . . . you are beginning to get
ideas about rank . . .

   *Shot 534. High angle close-up of* MALYUTA, *one eye half
   closed. His red beard glows in the candlelight as he looks at*
   BASMANOV, *off-screen.*

MALYUTA : Would you like to put yourself . . .

   *Shot 535. Low angle close-up of* BASMANOV.

MALYUTA *off* : . . . beside the Tsar ?

BASMANOV *angrily, rising to his feet and gazing upwards* : I've
sworn never to fraternise with the boyars . . . *He lays both hands
on his chest, fists clenched* . . . nor with the landowners. *With an
angry glance towards* IVAN, *off-screen, he moves towards camera
and off to the right, his face momentarily caught by the glow from
the ceiling.*

   *Shot 536. The music suddenly grows more frenzied. Close-up
   of* IVAN, *bent over* VLADIMIR, *one hand on his shoulder, the
   other holding his skull-cap. More servants pass in the background.* IVAN *follows* BASMANOV *suspiciously with his eyes,
   then replaces the cap on* VLADIMIR'S *head.*

   *Shot 537. Low angle medium shot of one of the tables, laden
   with silver vessels, a drunken figure sprawled across it on the
   left, the painted ceiling above. The masked* FIGURE *dances into*

*frame from the right and turns in the foreground, looking off, holding the mask up in front of its face.*

*Shot 538. Close-up of the* FIGURE. *The mask is removed to reveal the face of* FYODOR BASMANOV. *He leans forward, gazing jealously across at* IVAN, *off-screen to the right. (Still on page 187)*

IVAN *off* : I am alone . . .

*Shot 539. Close-up of* IVAN *leaning over* VLADIMIR, *his arm round his shoulder.*

IVAN : . . . a poor orphan. *He nods reflectively, then looks down at* VLADIMIR. No one loves or pities me ! . . . *He sits up slightly and looks across at* FYODOR. *His eyes narrow and he jerks his head at him as a signal to start his song. (Production still on page 187)*

*Shot 540. Close-up of* FYODOR; *he smiles at the* TSAR, *mask in hand.*

*Shot 541. Low angle medium close-up of* FYODOR *standing by the table, looking across at the* TSAR. *He replaces his mask and there is a crash of cymbals as he bangs his hand down on the table and moves towards camera.*

*Shot 542. Close-up of* IVAN *leaning over* VLADIMIR *again and caressing his shoulder as he listens to the song.*

FYODOR *singing* :       ' The guests have assembled . . .'

*Shot 543. Low angle medium close-up of* FYODOR *singing, mask in hand, a roguish expression on his face. He is surrounded by black-clad* OPRICHNIKS.

FYODOR :              ' In the courtyards of the boyars . . .'

*The* OPRICHNIKS *reply in chorus, throwing up their hands.*

CHORUS :              ' In the courtyards of the boyars . . .'

*Shot 544. A closer low angle shot of* FYODOR, *gesticulating with his mask as he continues to sing.*

FYODOR *singing* :       ' The axes skim the necks of the boyars . . .'

*He bows towards the left as the* OPRICHNIKS *reply in chorus.*

CHORUS :              ' The axes, the axes . . .'

*Shot 545. Low angle medium close-up of grinning* OPRICHNIKS *in the* CHORUS, *wagging their hands to and fro as they sing.*

CHORUS :              ' Come along ! Come along ! '

*Shot 546. Medium shot of* FYODOR *mincing to and fro, his mask in front of his face, one hand on his hip, as the* OPRICH-NIKS *sing, forming a sea of white faces and hands behind him*

CHORUS :                  ' What happens next? What happens next? '
*Shot 547. Low angle medium close-up of the same group (as in shot 545) waving their hands and singing.*
CHORUS :                  ' Come on, tell us more, '
*Shot 548. Low angle medium close-up of another group singing.*
CHORUS :                  ' Come on, tell us more.'
*Shot 549. Low angle close-up of an* OPRICHNIK *leaning forward and singing.*
OPRICHNIK *singing* :    ' Strike with the axes.'
*Shot 550. Close-up of a moustached* OPRICHNIK *bending down and whistling.*
*Shot 551. Very rapid low angle medium close-up of* OPRICH-NIKS *throwing back their heads and singing.*
CHORUS :                  ' Hi! '
*Shot 552. High angle medium shot of dancers in red and gold whirling in a frenzy,* FYODOR *in their midst.*
CHORUS :                  ' Hey, hey, hey, hey, hey, hey, hey, hey!'
*Shot 553. High angle, slightly closer shot of the same scene.*
CHORUS :                  ' Hey, hey, hey, hey, hey, hey, hey, hey!'
*554. Low angle medium close-up of* FYODOR *spreading his arms and singing, passing his mask from hand to hand as he does so, the* OPRICHNIKS *behind him.*
FYODOR *singing* :       ' The gates have split down the middle.'
*Two* OPRICHNIKS *appear behind him on either side and sing over his shoulder.*
CHORUS :                  ' Down the middle . . .'
*They whistle.*
FYODOR *waving his mask and singing* :
                         ' The golden goblets pass . . .'
*Shot 555. Low angle close-up of* FYODOR *with link on the motion as he passes his mask across to the left. A grinning* OPRICHNIK *looks over his shoulder.*
FYODOR :                 ' . . . from hand to hand . . .'
*He twists the mask to and fro, looking coyly away from it.*
CHORUS :                  ' From hand to hand . . .'
*As the* OPRICHNIKS *continue to sing,* FYODOR *passes the mask to and fro in front of his face, tilting it slightly towards him and looking coyly round at it.*

198

CHORUS :              ' Come along. Come along.
                       What happens next? What happens next?
                       Come on, tell us more,
                       Come on, tell us more!'

*Shot 556. Low angle close-up of one of the* OPRICHNIKS *leaning forward in front of some candles and singing through cupped hands.*

OPRICHNIK :           ' Strike with the axes! '

*Shot 557. Close-up of the moustached* OPRICHNIK *bending forward and whistling,* FYODOR'S *skirts whirling behind him.*

*Shot 558. Resume on the first* OPRICHNIK *(as shot 556). He throws up his hands and shouts.*

OPRICHNIK :           ' Hi! '

*Shot 559. High angle medium long shot of all the* OPRICHNIKS *dancing round in a circle with* FYODOR *whirling round on the floor in the middle.*

CHORUS :              ' Hey, hey, hey, hey, hey, hey, hey!'

*Shot 560. High angle medium shot of the same scene. The* OPRICHNIKS *dance round holding their hands out towards* FYODOR, *shaking them in time to their singing.*

CHORUS :              ' Hey, hey, hey, hey, hey, hey, hey!'

*Shot 561. High angle medium close-up of* FYODOR *whirling round on the floor in the opposite direction to the dancers. The song ends.*

*Shot 562. Medium close-up of* IVAN *looking down at* VLADIMIR *who is leaning back drunkenly, his head resting on the arm of the chair.*

VLADIMIR : Oh, you are wrong, Tsar of all the Russias . . . IVAN *leans over* VLADIMIR *and looks down at him as he continues, drunkenly* . . . you have friends . . .

IVAN : I haven't one . . .

VLADIMIR : Yes, you have!

IVAN : Don't lie.

VLADIMIR *sitting up and turning to face* IVAN : I'm not lying.

IVAN : Then who is my friend?

VLADIMIR : Well, me for one.

IVAN : I don't believe you!

VLADIMIR *crossing himself unsteadily* : I swear it!

IVAN *leaning forward and grasping his wrist* : Don't swear it. Prove it by your actions!

VLADIMIR *pursing his lips and speaking in the* TSAR'S *ear*: I will prove it!

> *They turn and look off to the right as they hear* FYODOR'S *voice.*
>
> *Shot 563. Music. Medium close-up of* FYODOR, *mask in hand, taking up the song again in the middle of the* OPRICH-NIKS. *As he sings, he presses his cheek lovingly against the mask while the* OPRICHNIKS *lean slowly forward from either side.*

FYODOR *singing*:  ' And when the guests are parting
　　　　　　　　　　Having drunk their fill . . .'

CHORUS:　　　　　' Drunk their fill . . .'

> *They spring back again.*
>
> *Shot 564. Low angle close-up of* FYODOR, *mask in hand. He gazes jealously across at the* TSAR, *then begins to sing again as the* OPRICHNIKS *lean forward around him.*

FYODOR *singing*:  ' They set fire to the castle.'

> *He turns towards camera and gestures with his mask.*

CHORUS:　　　　　　' Set fire to the castle . . .'

> FYODOR *puts the mask up in front of his face again.*
>
> *Shot 565. Resume on medium close-up of* FYODOR. *He steps back as the* OPRICHNIKS *close in and circle round him, waving their hands in the air.*

CHORUS:　　　　　' Come along. Come along.
　　　　　　　　　　What happens next? What happens next?
　　　　　　　　　　Come on, tell us more,
　　　　　　　　　　Come on, tell us more! '

> *Shot 566. Low angle close-up of the* OPRICHNIK *by the candles, shouting.*

OPRICHNIK *shouting*: ' Strike with the axes! '

> *Shot 567. High angle close-up of the moustached* OPRICHNIK *whistling.*
>
> *Shot 568. Medium close-up from floor level of an* OPRICHNIK *in red, dancing frenziedly with knees bent, others behind him, the tables in the background.*

CHORUS:　　　　　　' Hi! . . . Hey, hey, hey, hey, hey,
　　　　　　　　　　　　　　　　　　　　hey! . . .'

> *Shot 569. High angle medium shot of* FYODOR, *masked,*

*leaping up and down in the midst of the frenziedly whirling dancers.*

*Shot 570. A slightly longer shot of the same scene. The screen is a mass of whirling, multi-coloured shapes.*

Chorus :   '. . . Hey, hey, hey, hey!'

*Shot 571. Crash of cymbals. High angle medium shot of the* Oprichniks, *leaping forward, waving their arms in the air.*

*Shot 572. Low angle medium long shot of one of the tables. Tinged with red, the ceiling above is painted with the faces of saints.* Fyodor *comes running in from the right and leaps up onto the table, pursued by the* Oprichniks.

*Shot 573. Low angle medium close-up of* Fyodor *on the table, with link on the motion as he turns to face camera, tears off his mask and throws it away, spreading his arms wide and shouting. Black-clad* Oprichniks *appear at the bottom of frame as they clamber up around him.*

*Shot 574. Resume on low angle medium long shot of* Fyodor *standing on the table. The music rises to a crescendo as* Oprichniks, *clad in red and gold, rush into frame in the foreground, yelling madly, and pile up around him, tearing off his female clothes.*

*Shot 575. Low angle medium shot of* Fyodor *leaping up and down on the table, supported by two black-clad* Oprichniks. *The yelling continues as the last of his female garments is passed back over the heads of the* Oprichniks *and out of frame to the right.*

*Shot 576. Low angle medium close-up of* Fyodor *leaping up and down, wearing an embroidered tunic and a necklace of beads. Suddenly he stops. The shouting ceases and the music dies away as he gazes suspiciously off to the right.* Oprichniks *on either side of him turn to follow his gaze.*

*Shot 577. Medium long shot of what he sees. By the doorway,* Peter Volynets *sits alone on a bench, his head bowed, dressed in black, while servants carrying empty trays hurry out past him.*

*Shot 578. Low angle close-up of* Fyodor *looking off to the right, an* Oprichnik *looking over his shoulder on either side.*

Fyodor : What is Archbishop Pimen's man . . .

*Shot 579. Medium shot of* Peter, *in profile, sitting motionless by the door.* A Servant *hurries in behind him with a loaded tray.*

FYODOR : . . . doing amongst the servants?*

*Shot 580. Resume on low angle close-up of* FYODOR. *The* OPRICHNIK *on the right turns to him.*

OPRICHNIK : Pimen assigned him to the service of Vladimir Andreyevich.

FYODOR *removes his necklace of beads and bends down out of frame.*

*Shot 581. Close-up of* FYODOR *as he leans across the table and gazes off towards* PETER. IVAN *and* VLADIMIR *are seen in soft focus in the background. (Still on page 188)*

*Shot 582. Medium shot of* PETER, *seated. (Still on page 188)*

*Shot 583. As shot 581.* FYODOR *turns away from camera, looking across at* IVAN.

*Shot 584. Close-up of* IVAN *sitting up and looking off right, towards* PETER. *Then he turns and looks off left.*

*Shot 585. Close-up of* MALYUTA *raising his head as the* TSAR *looks at him, then turning to look towards* PETER. *He leans forward suspiciously.*

*Shot 586. Medium long shot of* PETER *slowly getting up and going out through the doorway.*

*Shot 587. Medium close-up of* IVAN *watching* PETER *go,* VLADIMIR *sitting blinking beside him. He turns back towards* MALYUTA.

---

* H. Valloton, the Swiss historian, comments apropos Peter (or Piotr): ' In the summer of 1569 a certain Peter, a vagabond born in the Ukraine who had been released from the Novgorod prisons, came to Moscow to denounce a conspiracy between the archbishop and leading citizens of Novgorod. He claimed they had decided to hand over the town to Lithuania and that they had signed an agreement to this effect with King Sigismund Augustus which they had hidden behind the icon of the Virgin in the Saint Sophia Cathedral. In fact, a document was found bearing the signature of Archbishop Pimen and numerous magistrates and was declared authentic. Some of Ivan's intimates — Basmanov amongst them — must have taken part in this plot, the purpose of which was to cede Novgorod and Pskov to Lithuania, thereby procuring Poland's support for dethroning Ivan IV and substituting his first cousin Vladimir. It is possible that such a plot existed . . .' But the historian remains sceptical. His views do not disagree with those of *The Great Soviet Encyclopedia* quoted earlier. It is this plot which is evoked in the second scene of the third part of the scenario (which was never filmed).

*Shot 588. Medium close-up of* MALYUTA. *Servants pass with pitchers of wine in the background. He registers the* TSAR'S *glance, rises slowly and goes off left.*

*Shot 589. Resume on medium close-up of* IVAN *and* VLADIMIR. *The* TSAR *turns back towards* VLADIMIR *and gives him a play-ful and none too gentle push.*

IVAN : You lie . . . You won't prove anything!

VLADIMIR : I will . . . *Stretching up towards* IVAN *and beating his palm inanely on his chest* . . . I will prove it to you!

*Shot 590. Low angle medium close-up of candles burning under the blood-red ceiling.*

*Shot 591. Resume on* IVAN *and* VLADIMIR. *The latter, still drunk, leans confidentially towards the* TSAR *and speaks in his ear.*

VLADIMIR : You sit here celebrating . . . and you don't even know some people want you out of the way.

IVAN *jocularly* : Is that so?

VLADIMIR *nodding drunkenly* : I swear it!

IVAN *with mock amazement* : And who do they want in my place?

VLADIMIR *opens his mouth wide, then shuts it and screws his face up in an inane expression. He gives the* TSAR *a jocular push, then shakes his head to and fro, waving his hand.*

VLADIMIR : You'd never guess!

IVAN *gazes at him suspiciously. Music.*

*Shot 592. Long shot of the table, slight high angle, with* IVAN *and* VLADIMIR *seated in the background. Black-clad* OPRICH-NIKS *circle round them and come towards camera, carrying black swans with silver coronets on platters above their heads.*

*Shot 593. A closer shot of the same scene. The* OPRICHNIKS *pass in front of the camera from right to left while* VLADIMIR *gazes up at them, watched by* IVAN. *(Still on page 188)*

*Shot 594. Medium shot of the two of them. The swans pass behind them from left to right while* VLADIMIR *gazes up at them in stupefaction, still watched closely by* IVAN.

*Shot 595. Low angle medium close-up of a swan's head with its silver coronet against the ceiling. Another passes in the background.*

*Shot 596. Close-up of the drunken* VLADIMIR. *He looks round, beaming inanely at the spectacle.*

*Shot 597. Low angle close-up of the crowned head of a swan, a jewel in its eye, against the red ceiling.*

*Shot 598. Low angle medium shot of* IVAN *and* VLADIMIR, *the swan in the foreground on the left.* VLADIMIR *has risen to his feet, gazing up at the swan with his arm outstretched in childish wonder. (Still on page 188) He stretches forward and tries to touch the crowned head but misses and falls full-length across the table.*

*Shot 599. Close-up of* VLADIMIR *lying across the table. Behind him,* IVAN *sits back in his chair, then leans forward over him as he begins to speak.*

VLADIMIR : I said to her : who'd want to be Tsar? *He looks up.*

*Shot 600. Close-up of* IVAN's *face in profile as he leans forward with great interest.*

VLADIMIR : Plots . . . executions . . .

*Shot 601. Close-up of* VLADIMIR. *He looks towards camera as he speaks, slurring his words.*

VLADIMIR : . . . As for me . . . I'm just a peaceful man; all I ask of life is to . . . *He taps a goblet beside him* . . . drink and live in peace . . . *He looks up at* IVAN *and laughs.*

*Shot 602. Resume on close-up of* IVAN's *face.*

IVAN *thoughtfully*: Indeed, who'd want to be Tsar? . . . The task . . .

*Shot 603. Close-up of* VLADIMIR *looking up at* IVAN, *listening.*

IVAN *off* : . . . is a heavy one !

VLADIMIR : That's exactly what I said . . . Why do I want to be Tsar? *He sits up, his head moving out of frame.* But she insists . . .

*Shot 604. Another close-up of* VLADIMIR *looking towards camera,* IVAN's *arm on the chair behind him.*

VLADIMIR : Take it . . . take the crown . . . Take it . . .

*Shot 605. Resume on close-up of* IVAN *in profile.*

VLADIMIR *continues, off* : Take the collar . . .

IVAN *reflectively*: Take the crown . . . *He looks towards camera.* . . . take it? *He suddenly bends towards the right.*

*Shot 606. Close-up of the two with link on the motion as* IVAN *bends down and seizes* VLADIMIR *by the shoulders from behind.* VLADIMIR's *head lolls at the impact and he blinks.*

IVAN *urgently*: Take it ! . . . *Leaning forward over* VLADIMIR's *shoulder and almost shouting.* Take it ! Why not? Take it cousin !

IVAN *leaps to his feet. There is a crash of cymbals.*

*Shot 607. Low angle medium close-up of* IVAN *with link on the motion as he leaps to his feet in front of his chair and claps his hands in the air. There is a crash of drums.*

IVAN *raising an arm and shouting*: Bring the Tsar's regalia!*

*Shot 608. Medium shot of two gold-bloused* OPRICHNIKS *running up.*

*Shot 609. Medium shot of* IVAN, *slightly low angle. He stands over* VLADIMIR *as* OPRICHNIKS, *dressed in red, hurry past camera from left to right, to carry out his orders. Loud music.*

*Shot 610. Medium close-up, slightly low angle, of two* OPRICHNIKS, *clad in gold, who turn and hurry away from camera.*

*Shot 611. Resume on low angle medium close-up of* IVAN. *Glaring down at the table, he makes two sweeping motions with his arm.*

*Shot 612. Medium shot of the table,* IVAN *and* VLADIMIR *in the background. As the* TSAR *makes another sweeping movement with his arm, an* OPRICHNIK *on the left whips away the table-cloth, sending goblets and dishes flying, while three more come forward on the right to pick up the table.*

*Shot 613. Medium close-up of several* OPRICHNIKS *as they carry one of the tables past camera, from right to left, revealing another being carried out of the hall in the background.*

*Shot 614. Low angle medium shot towards* IVAN, *who descends from his chair, leaving* VLADIMIR *seated with his hands outstretched towards the vanished table. The loud music continues as* IVAN *moves towards camera and bends forward, looking off towards the left. Behind him,* VLADIMIR *casts vainly around for the table.*

*Shot 615. Medium shot following the direction of* IVAN's *gaze.* OPRICHNIKS *hurry to and fro in front of the camera while behind him others bring forward the* TSAR's *throne. Finally, a red carpet is brought on from the right, and unrolled from the foot of the throne.*

*Shot 616. Close-up of* IVAN *watching, looking off left. He turns slowly away from camera. End of the music.*

---

* End of the seventh reel (300 metres).

*Shot 617. Medium shot of the table where* VLADIMIR *is still seated as* IVAN *goes towards him, from the left. He helps him to his feet and propels him back towards the left,* VLADIMIR *staggering as he goes. Music.*

*Shot 618. Low angle medium shot of* IVAN *as he helps* VLADIMIR *towards the throne, which is in the foreground on the left. Above them hovers the figure of God, painted on the ceiling, his glowing halo standing out against a blue background.* IVAN *plants* VLADIMIR *in front of the throne and begins to withdraw, leaving him swaying slightly.*

*Shot 619. Low angle medium close-up of* VLADIMIR *gazing down at the proceedings with a mixture of fear and amazement. He claps a hand to his cheek and shoots a glance towards* IVAN, *off-screen to the right.*

*Shot 620. Low angle medium shot of* VLADIMIR, *his hand to his cheek, watching in wonderment as the* TSAR's *regalia is brought on from the left. Two* OPRICHNIKS *are leaning over the back of the throne, watching him from behind, whilst two more, clad in gold, appear with the sceptre and orb and position themselves behind* VLADIMIR. *He turns to watch them, his hand still pressed to his cheek. Then two more* OPRICHNIKS, *clad in red, bring forward the royal robe and finally* FYODOR *appears from the left, bearing the* TSAR's *crown on an embroidered cloth.*

*Shot 621. A closer low angle shot of* VLADIMIR, *now wearing the royal robe. In front of him, two* OPRICHNIKS *clad in red bow low, backs to camera, offering the heavy imperial collar. Two black-clad* OPRICHNIKS, *standing on either side of* VLADIMIR, *take the collar and place it round his neck. The other* OPRICHNIKS *withdraw on either side of frame.*

*Shot 622. Low angle close-up of* VLADIMIR *as the two black-clad* OPRICHNIKS *lower the* TSAR's *cross on a chain down over his head and place it round his neck.*

*Shot 623. Low angle medium close-up. The two* OPRICHNIKS *sit* VLADIMIR *down on the throne where he remains swaying slightly, looking owlishly from side to side, his hands stretched out to receive the orb and sceptre. He hiccoughs. Two gold-clad* OPRICHNIKS *come forward on either side of him and place the orb and sceptre in his hands. He sits looking from one to the other.*

*Shot 624. Medium shot of* VLADIMIR *seated on the throne, towards the bottom of frame, the red ceiling above.* IVAN *comes forward in profile on the right and makes a sign towards* FYODOR, *who enters from the left, bearing the crown, as a* CHOIR *comes in with the music. Standing just behind the throne,* IVAN *exchanges a glance with* FYODOR *as he takes the crown from him. (Still on page 188)*

*Shot 625. Low angle medium close-up of* IVAN *and* FYODOR *standing over* VLADIMIR. *He sits looking bewildered as* IVAN *lowers the crown slowly onto his head, gazing at it intently as he does so. (Still on page 188)* IVAN *presses the crown firmly down on* VLADIMIR'S *head so that it almost comes down over his eyes, then glances at* FYODOR, *who grins at him and withdraws to the right, bowing.* FYODOR *moves to follow him.*

*Shot 626. Medium long shot of the throne, slightly low angle, with steps leading down in front of it, covered in the red carpet.* OPRICHNIKS *stand watching in the background as* IVAN *comes down the steps, bowing low, followed by* FYODOR. *As the latter goes out of frame to the right,* IVAN *stands at the bottom of the steps and turns to face* VLADIMIR. *He kneels down on the red carpet and bows his head, one hand on the steps.* FYODOR *reappears on the right and imitates him, followed by the watching* OPRICHNIKS. *(Still on page 188)*

*Shot 627. High angle medium shot of* OPRICHNIKS *on their knees, bowing low.*

*Shot 628. High angle medium close-up of* IVAN *on the red carpet, his head bowed to the ground. He looks up for a moment and gazes off to the left, then drops his head again.*

*Shot 629. Low angle medium close-up of* VLADIMIR, *sitting on the throne, looking bewildered. Gradually he gains confidence; he looks from the sceptre to the orb and a foolish smile creeps over his face. He assumes a regal posture, planting his elbows firmly on the arms of the throne.*

*Shot 630. High angle medium shot of the* OPRICHNIKS, *raising their hands in the air and then prostrating themselves. (Still on page 188)*

*Shot 631. Close-up of* IVAN, *raising his head slowly, and gazing up at* VLADIMIR.

207

*Shot 632. Low angle medium close-up of* VLADIMIR. *He looks from side to side, smiling inanely, and settles himself more comfortably on the throne.*

*Shot 633. High angle close-up of* IVAN *gazing up at him, watching his reactions closely.*

*Shot 634. Resume on low angle medium close-up of* VLADIMIR. *The smile fades from his face and his expression hardens.*

*Shot 635. High angle medium close-up of* IVAN, *kneeling on the steps, looking up sideways at* VLADIMIR. *A bell tolls, off.* IVAN *suddenly leans back.*

*Shot 636. Low angle close-up of* FYODOR *with link on the motion as* IVAN *leans abruptly back and grips him by the shoulder, glaring off towards* VLADIMIR.*

IVAN *turning to* FYODOR : He likes it . . . *There is a roll of drums.* IVAN *looks back towards* VLADIMIR *and leaps up, moving partly out of frame* . . . this lackey of the Poles !

*Shot 637. Close-up of* IVAN *glaring across at* VLADIMIR. *He looks up and listens as the bell tolls again, off.*

*Shot 638. Low angle close-up of* FYODOR, *also listening, as* IVAN *sinks down beside him and the bell tolls again.*

*Shot 639. Medium close-up of the two of them:* IVAN *with his head raised, listening to the tolling of the bell,* FYODOR *watching him. Suddenly the* TSAR *gets up and moves away from camera while* FYODOR *goes off to the right.* IVAN *turns to face camera in medium shot and raises a hand.*

IVAN : The farce is over. *Behind him, the prostrate* OPRICHNIKS *raise their heads.* IVAN *turns to face them.* Enough of this ungodly revelry ! *He walks away towards the left.*

*Shot 640. Low angle medium shot of candles burning in two candelabras under the red ceiling.* IVAN *appears from the right and turns to face camera, raising an arm as he speaks.*

IVAN : Brothers, let's address ourselves to the Almighty !

*Shot 641. Low angle medium shot: the bell continues to toll as* OPRICHNIKS *in black cowls and cassocks file past from left to right, carrying candles. The ceiling glows a fiery red above them.*

---

\* The whole scene is obviously a parody of Ivan's coronation at the beginning of the first part. The tragic ambiance of the cathedral scene which follows is intended to counterbalance it.

*Shot 642. Low angle shot of* Ivan *coming forward beside the candelabra. He stops in close-up, holding up a candle.*

Ivan *grimly, gazing off left, towards* Vladimir : Let us think upon our last hour! *He moves off left.*

*A* Choir *begins to sing quietly, off.*

Choir : ' Awake, my soul,

Awake . . .'

*Shot 643. Low angle medium close-up of* Vladimir *drowsing on the throne.* Oprichniks *in monk's habits file past behind him.*

*Shot 644. High angle medium shot of* Oprichniks *dressed in gold, kneeling as others in black cowls and cassocks file between them with candles, coming towards the left.*

*Shot 645. Low angle medium shot of* Vladimir *drowsing on the throne; the figure of God glows in the candlelight on the ceiling above. Ivan approaches from the right, bearing a candle, as the* Choir *continues to sing, off. He thrusts the candle at* Vladimir. *(Production still on page 221)*

*Shot 646. Low angle medium close-up of* Vladimir *on the throne, his head lolling sideways.* Ivan *bends towards him on the right.*

Ivan : Lead us to the cathedral!

Vladimir *wakes with a start. He looks helplessly from the candle to the sceptre and orb in his hands.* Fyodor *and another* Oprichnik *come in from the left and take them from him, then go off again.* Ivan *hands* Vladimir *the candle. He takes it in one hand, looks at it, then transfers it to the other, and, taking a deep breath, rises unsteadily from the throne, as* Ivan *bows low beside him.*

*Shot 647. Low angle medium shot with link on the motion as* Vladimir *rises unsteadily to his feet and totters forward, holding out the candle. He goes out of frame to the right and black-cowled* Oprichniks *file after him with candles.*

*Shot 648. Medium long shot of* Vladimir *as he descends the steps in front of the throne and walks slowly and unsteadily along the red carpet and off to the right. (Still on page 221) Black-cowled* Oprichniks *follow him from the left while others stand ranged against the wall in the background.*

*Shot 649. Low angle medium close-up of* Ivan *by the throne.*

*The rosy halo of the figure of God glows above him on the ceiling as he leans forward, watching* VLADIMIR *go.* FYODOR, *wearing a black cowl, comes in from the left and leans over the back of the throne, also watching* VLADIMIR. IVAN *turns momentarily towards him. A bell tolls. (Still on page 221)*
*Shot 650. Medium shot of* VLADIMIR, *moving from the left towards the doorway, candle in hand. The bell tolls again as he bends down to look through the doorway and starts back in alarm.*
*Shot 651. Resume on low angle medium close-up of* IVAN *and* FYODOR *watching* VLADIMIR, *off-screen to the right. They start back and* IVAN *rises to his feet.*
*Shot 652. Close-up of* VLADIMIR *in profile, turned towards the doorway, a painted woman's face on the wall behind him. He peers towards the door again, hiccoughs and closes his eyes, then turns back to face camera while the bell tolls again. He suddenly opens his eyes wide in terror, and a shadow falls across his face as the* CHOIR *starts to sing again. Then a blue light falls across his face as he stares down towards camera, his face frozen with fear. The woman's face gazes down from the wall behind.*

*Shot 653. High angle long shot of the interior of the cathedral. A shaft of pale light, coming from the left, casts dark blue shadows everywhere.* PETER VOLYNETS *emerges from behind a column in the middle of shot and runs towards the left, disappearing behind another column. Then he runs out again and across to another pillar in right foreground, where he pauses, looking up towards camera. The* CHOIR *continues to sing, off.*

*Shot 654. Low angle close-up of* VLADIMIR, *his face bathed in blue light, staring in terror. Candlelight falls on his face again and he shudders, looking nervously from side to side, then turning round to look behind him.*
*Shot 655. Low angle medium shot of* IVAN *standing by the throne,* FYODOR *on the left. The* TSAR *takes a step forward and bows mockingly as he addresses* VLADIMIR.
IVAN : A Tsar does not draw back . . .
*Shot 656. Low angle close-up of* IVAN *as he straightens up and*

*continues firmly.*

IVAN : . . . The Tsar is always first to enter! *He raises a finger in
a mocking salute.*

> *Shot 657. Resume on low angle medium close-up of* IVAN *with
> link on the motion as he brings his arm down and bows low to*
> VLADIMIR. FYODOR, *behind him on the left, and the cowled*
> OPRICHNIKS *in the background do likewise.* IVAN *and* FYODOR
> *raise their heads.*

> *Shot 658. High angle medium shot of the black-cowled*
> OPRICHNIKS *bowing low to* VLADIMIR.

> *Shot 659. Low angle medium close-up of* VLADIMIR *standing in
> front of the doorway. He stretches out a hand in terrified
> supplication. Black-cowled* OPRICHNIKS *move past him on
> either side.*

> *Shot 660. Resume on high angle medium shot of the*
> OPRICHNIKS *as they bow once more.*

> *Shot 661. High angle close-up of* FYODOR'S *mask lying for-
> gotten on a step.*

> *Shot 662. Resume on low angle medium close-up of* VLADIMIR.
> *He drops his hand and looks anxiously from side to side, re-
> treating backwards as the black-cowled* OPRICHNIKS *close in
> around him, masking him from view. The music stops and the*
> CHOIR *begins to sing again softly.*

> *Shot 663.\* Medium shot of the snow-covered courtyard where
> the* KOLYCHEVS *were executed earlier. It is dark.* VLADIMIR
> *advances slowly from the left, his royal mantle glittering,
> candle in hand. He pauses in the centre of shot and looks
> nervously back, then moves on again and out of frame to the
> right. Black-cowled* OPRICHNIKS *follow from the left with
> candles.*

> *Shot 664. Long shot of the courtyard, slight high angle.*
> VLADIMIR *is in the centre of shot moving away from camera,
> towards the archway with the figure of Christ above it, in the
> background. (Still on page 221) He looks back again as the
> procession of* OPRICHNIKS *follows him from the left.*

> *Shot 665. Low angle medium close-up of the archway as*
> VLADIMIR *moves towards it from the left, three-quarters back*

---

\* As from this shot, the following sequence is seen in blue and white only,
on colour film.

*to camera. As the* CHOIR *continues to sing off, he bends down and looks through the archway, his shadow on the wall behind him. Then he looks back at the* OPRICHNIKS *again.*

*Shot 666. Medium long shot of the archway, slight high angle.* VLADIMIR *moves to the right of it, facing camera; his hand claws nervously at his collar and he glances up at the figure of Christ. As the* OPRICHNIKS *close in from all sides, in the foreground, he bends and goes through the low archway. The* OPRICHNIKS *follow, holding up their candles, filling the lower half of the screen.*

*Shot 667. Close-up of the crown on* VLADIMIR'S *head, inside the cathedral. As the singing ends,* VLADIMIR *turns to face camera, the upper part of his face coming into view. Music. He looks nervously from side to side, then turns towards the right.*

*Shot 668. Low angle medium close-up of* VLADIMIR *crouching at the top of the steps leading up into the cathedral. Link on the motion as he turns away from camera and, getting up, moves on into the cathedral. The* OPRICHNIKS *follow him up the steps, in the foreground.*

*Shot 669. Medium shot, slightly low angle, of* VLADIMIR *advancing between the columns of the cathedral, candle in hand, gazing nervously upwards. Camera tracks with him from left to right as the* OPRICHNIKS *follow, their shadows moving across the frescoed wall. The music gets louder as* VLADIMIR *disappears behind a column, then reappears on the other side; he pauses to look nervously at the* OPRICHNIKS, *then moves off to the right. The black-cowled figures follow him in the background.*

*Shot 670. Long shot of the cathedral interior from beneath an archway. Camera tracks briefly to the right as* VLADIMIR *advances at the head of a long procession of black-cowled* OPRICHNIKS.

*Shot 671. Close-up of* PETER VOLYNETS *as he appears from behind a column. (Still on page 221) He peers forward, watching* VLADIMIR, *then goes out of frame to the right.*

*Shot 672. Medium shot of the procession of* OPRICHNIKS *moving towards camera, between the columns. A* CHOIR *begins to chant loudly.*

*Shot 673. High angle long shot as* VLADIMIR *advances into a shaft of light, throwing a vast shadow across the stone floor. He pauses and then moves along it to the right, coming diagonally towards camera.*

*Shot 674. Low angle medium shot of* VLADIMIR *coming slowly towards camera. The vast shadows of the* OPRICHNIKS *move slowly across a fresco representing the Last Judgement, on the wall behind him. (Still on page 222)*

*Shot 675. Low angle medium shot of the* OPRICHNIKS' *shadows moving across another part of the wall.* MALYUTA *approaches from the darkness, in the centre of shot, and leans forward, looking suspiciously round.*

*Shot 676. Low angle medium close-up of* VLADIMIR. *The shadows of the* OPRICHNIKS *move across the frescoed wall behind him. He looks nervously off to the right, then turns round, looking behind him.*

*Shot 677. Close-up of* MALYUTA *moving forward, watching something through narrowed eyes.*

*Shot 678. Resume on low angle medium close-up of* VLADIMIR *as he turns and gazes up at the fresco. God sits in judgement, gazing sternly down.*

*Shot 679. Close-up of* PETER *armed with a knife.*

*Shot 680. Medium shot: he suddenly goes out of frame. End of the singing.\**

---

\* End of the eighth reel (300 metres).

*Shot 681. High angle long shot of* VLADIMIR *standing, back to camera, looking up at the fresco on the wall. There is a crash of cymbals as* PETER *runs up behind him from left foreground and plants his knife in his back. Roll of drums.* VLADIMIR *spins round, his arms in the air, letting out a pathetic cry.*

VLADIMIR *crying out* : A-a-ah! . . .

*Shot 682. Low angle close-up of* VLADIMIR'S *hand holding his candle between thumb and forefinger. The candle slips from his grasp. Music. (Still on page 222)*

*Shot 683. Resume on long shot of the scene.* PETER *has disappeared into the shadows.* VLADIMIR *falls forward onto the cathedral floor, his arms outstretched. A figure races across from left to right behind him. The* OPRICHNIKS *move forward on the left, their shadows moving across the wall, while* MALYUTA *stands tensely in the background.*

*Shot 684. Low angle medium close-up of* FYODOR, *candle in hand, tearing off his monk's cowl.*

*Shot 685. Medium close-up of* MALYUTA, *crouching forward. He rushes towards camera, filling the screen.*

*Shot 686. Medium shot of* PETER, *backing towards the frescoed wall, his knife raised. Shadows race across the wall as* MALYUTA *and* FYODOR *rush in from the left and seize him. Music. They bring him struggling towards camera.*

*Shot 687. Low angle close-up of the three of them, struggling.* MALYUTA *seizes the knife. End of the music. There is a hoarse cry, off.\**

EUPHROSYNE *off* : Ivan!

*Shot 688. Long shot towards the other end of the cathedral.* EUPHROSYNE *comes running and shouting past the ranks of black-cowled* OPRICHNIKS.

EUPHROSYNE : Ivan is no more! *She stops in medium shot and shouts triumphantly, arms outspread.* Good people, look!

*Shot 689. Low angle close-up of* EUPHROSYNE. *She throws an arm up, holding her black shawl, and stares madly down at the body, off-screen.*

---

\* For this incident, Eisenstein possibly adapted the historical event in which Ivan himself stabbed the old Prince Chelyadin to death during a banquet, after having dressed him in the costume and regalia of the Tsar.

EUPHROSYNE : Ivan is no more !

*Shot 690. Long shot of the cathedral, VLADIMIR's body sprawled face downwards in the foreground. EUPHROSYNE hurries forwards and puts her foot on the body as she speaks. (Still on page 222)*

EUPHROSYNE *triumphantly shouting again* : The brute is dead! *She throws back her shawl and spreads both arms, speaking almost in a whisper.* Russia shall flourish . . .

*Shot 691. Low angle medium close-up of her. She raises her arms higher.*

EUPHROSYNE : . . . under a boyar Tsar ! . . . Vladimir ! *She lowers her arms slowly to her breast.*

*Shot 692. Close-up of her, slightly low angle. She looks slowly towards the left as the shadows of OPRICHNIKS pass on the wall behind. Funereal music begins softly.*

*Shot 693. Low angle medium close-up of three black-cowled OPRICHNIKS watching her, candles in hand. They move aside and the ranks of OPRICHNIKS part behind them to show IVAN, in his black monk's habit, advancing slowly from the far end of the cathedral, staff in hand. The music continues as he comes into medium shot between the ranks of OPRICHNIKS.*

*Shot 694. Medium shot of EUPHROSYNE, the body at her feet, staring in amazement as IVAN comes slowly towards her, from the ranks of OPRICHNIKS in the background. He draws level with her on the left and stands motionless, gazing at her with his head raised. She cautiously takes a step towards him and touches the cross hanging around his neck, as if to see whether he is real, then recoils.*

*Shot 695. Medium close-up of her, backing away from IVAN, staring off at him in disbelief. She stumbles against the body, almost loses her balance and stares down at it.*

*Shot 696. Close-up from above of VLADIMIR lying face downwards, the crown askew on his head.*

*Shot 697. Low angle medium close-up: IVAN stands on the left, his head thrown back, holding his staff. On the right, EUPHROSYNE gazes down at the body. (Still on page 222) The music continues as she steps forwards in front of IVAN and sinks to her knees, so that only her head is in shot, eyes wildly staring, muttering to herself in bewilderment. IVAN steps slowly past her in the background without looking down.*

*Shot 698. Medium close-up of* EUPHROSYNE *kneeling beside* VLADIMIR'S *body, the ranks of* OPRICHNIKS *stretching away on either side in the background. She leans slowly forward and turns over the body.*

*Shot 699. Close-up of* EUPHROSYNE *supporting the dead* VLADIMIR, *whose face stares, glassy-eyed, at the camera. She tilts his face up towards her.*

*Shot 700. Resume on medium close-up:* EUPHROSYNE *recognises her son and flings herself back with a desperate cry. (Still on page 222)*

EUPHROSYNE : No . . . Ah ! . . . Ah ! . . .

*Shot 701. Medium close-up of* PETER, *who also gives a desperate cry and struggles to break free of* MALYUTA *and* FYODOR. *They grip him savagely and* FYODOR *rips his shirt from his chest in the struggle.*

PETER *shouting desperately* : Torture me ! . . . Execute me ! . . . You'll never make me speak !

*Shot 702. Low angle close-up of* IVAN *leaning on his staff. He pricks up his ears as* PETER *continues off.*

PETER *off* : I won't give anyone away.

*The music starts again as* IVAN *turns slowly in* PETER'S *direction.*

*Shot 703. Medium shot of* MALYUTA, PETER *and* FYODOR,

standing on right of frame, beneath the fresco of the Last
Judgement on the wall. IVAN's vast shadow moves across the
wall as he comes in from the left, then walks slowly towards
them, leaning on his staff.
Shot 704. Close-up of MALYUTA, PETER and FYODOR. They
look up as the TSAR approaches, and PETER bends backwards.
MALYUTA forces his head down savagely.

IVAN off: Why . . .
Shot 705. Low angle medium close-up of the three of them,
IVAN standing over them on the left.

IVAN: . . . are you holding him?
MALYUTA releases PETER and goes off left; FYODOR grips
PETER from behind as IVAN leans towards him. (Still on page
222)
Shot 706. Close-up of PETER looking sideways at IVAN. Link on
the motion as the latter bends towards him from the left and
tilts his head up, taking him by the chin.

IVAN sarcastically: It was not the Tsar he killed . . . He jerks his
thumb at VLADIMIR's body, off-screen . . . only the fool!
Shot 707. Low angle medium close-up of the three of them,
IVAN pointing over his shoulder. He waves a finger at FYODOR.

IVAN: Let him go. FYODOR relaxes his hold and as IVAN straightens
up, PETER pulls the torn shirt back across his bare chest. He cowers
back fearfully as IVAN transfers his staff to the other hand and
speaks, gazing off to the right. And it was not only a fool he killed
. . . but the Tsar's worst enemy! He raises a hand.
Shot 708. Medium shot of IVAN, standing with his hand raised,
FYODOR and PETER a few feet away on the right of frame.

IVAN: My grateful thanks! He bows low to PETER, (Still on page
222) then straightens up and transfers his staff from his right hand
to his left. The music ends.
Shot 709. Low angle close-up of IVAN.

IVAN grimly: As for her . . . He turns abruptly and looks off left.
Shot 710. High angle medium shot of PETER as he backs
hurriedly towards the wall from the left, then creeps slowly
along it as EUPHROSYNE's voice is heard.

EUPHROSYNE singing, off: 'They want to catch . . .'
Shot 711. Close-up from above of VLADIMIR's lifeless face, his
eyes staring.

EUPHROSYNE *off* : '. . . and skin the beaver . . .'

> *Shot 712. High angle medium close-up of* EUPHROSYNE *sitting by* VLADIMIR'S *body, his head cradled on her lap; haggard-eyed, she continues to sing, gazing upwards.*

EUPHROSYNE : '. . . And with its fur then to adorn

>> A kingly mantle for . . . for . . . for Tsar Vladi-
>> mir . . .'

> *As she sits singing, the bottom of the* TSAR'S *cassock appears behind her as he walks in from the right, preceded by his shadow. He makes a sign with his hand and* FYODOR *enters from the right, bends down and seizes* VLADIMIR'S *body by the feet, and drags it off.* EUPHROSYNE *hardly notices as* VLADI-MIR'S *head is dragged from her lap. She turns slightly, then continues singing, cradling the crown in her hands.*

> *Shot 713. Slightly low angle close-up of* IVAN *in profile, gazing down at her off-screen.*

IVAN *raising a crooked hand* : As for her . . .

EUPHROSYNE *singing, off* : '. . . and skin the beaver . . .'

> IVAN *glances towards camera, raising one eyebrow slightly, then drops his hand in a gesture of finality.*

> *Shot 714. Resume on high angle close-up of* EUPHROSYNE *sitting motionless, with a glazed expression, holding up the crown.* IVAN'S *cassock is seen behind her, on the right.* MALYUTA *enters from the right and bends down over her.*

> *Shot 715. Close-up of* MALYUTA'S *hands taking the crown from* EUPHROSYNE.

> *Shot 716. Resume on high angle medium close-up with link on the motion as* MALYUTA *takes the crown and walks off with it, to the left, only the bottom half of him visible.* EUPHROSYNE *sits motionless, her hands still raised to hold the crown, and begins to sing again.*

EUPHROSYNE *singing* : ' A black beaver was bathing . . .'

> IVAN *comes forward and the bottom half of his cassock passes in front of her as he walks off left.* EUPHROSYNE *lowers her hand slowly and the cassocks of the* OPRICHNIKS *file past behind and in front of her as they follow* IVAN. *The* CHOIR *begins to sing softly off.*

> *Shot 717. Long shot of the cathedral. A long line of* OPRICH-NIKS, *carrying candles, follows* IVAN *as he moves slowly past*

*camera from right to left, his face solemn.*

*Shot 718. High angle long shot of* IVAN *at the head of the long procession of* OPRICHNIKS. *The* CHOIR *sings loudly as he advances towards the altar, off-screen to the left. A row of candles burning in front of it is seen in the foreground.* IVAN *halts in the centre of shot and gazes up at the altar, crossing himself as the* OPRICHNIKS *come up behind him.*

CHOIR *singing, off* : ' I swear before God to accomplish, in Russia, my royal mission . . .' IVAN *bows his head and kneels. The* OPRICHNIKS *follow suit* '. . . to purge the Motherland . . .'

*Shot 719. High angle long shot of the two lines of* OPRICHNIKS, *stretching away down the cathedral, as they sink to their knees.*

CHOIR : '. . .of her savage enemies . . .'

*Shot 720. Close-up of* PETER, *his face hidden in his hands. He slowly clenches the fingers of his right hand to reveal an eye, staring off towards the left. (Still on page 222)*

CHOIR *off* : '. . . to shed with my own hands the blood of the guilty . . .'

*Shot 721. High angle medium shot of* IVAN *kneeling, head bowed, before the lighted candles. The* OPRICHNIKS *kneel behind him.*

CHOIR : '. . . without mercy, either to myself or to others . . .'

IVAN *raises his head (Still on page 223) and covers his eyes with his hands.*

*Shot 722. Close-up of* IVAN, *slightly low angle. His head is thrown back, one hand pressed over his eyes, the other holding his staff.*

IVAN *murmuring* : '. . . for the sake of the great land of Russia.' *Fade out.*


*Shot 723.\* Fade in on low angle medium close-up of* IVAN *seated on his carved chair in the banqueting hall, leaning forward with his head bowed. Candles burn on either side; the painted ceiling glows red above him. He slowly raises his head.*

IVAN : A Tsar must always weigh and assess. Mercy and gentleness

---

\* From this shot the picture returns to full colour.

for the good. Cruelty and torment for the wicked.

*Shot 724. Low angle close-up of him as he leans back slightly, gazing downwards towards the right.*

IVAN: A Tsar who hesitates in this will never make a Tsar! *A shadow falls across his face. Triumphant music. He turns to the left.* Today . . .

*Shot 725. Low angle medium close-up of* IVAN *seated. As he speaks loudly a shadow falls across the ceiling leaving only the rosy halo of the painted figure of God glowing directly above him.*

IVAN: . . . in Moscow, we have struck down the enemies of Russian unity . . .

*The* OPRICHNIKS *rise to their feet behind* IVAN, *who rises also. Shot 726. Low angle close-up with link on the motion as* IVAN *rises to his feet and flings an arm in the air.*

IVAN: My hands are free! *He lowers his arm and looks round to the right. As he continues to speak the* OPRICHNIKS *draw their swords and raise them in the air behind him.* From now on the sword of justice shall flash against those . . . *He turns to the left.*

*Shot 727. Medium shot of* IVAN *standing in front of his chair, one foot on the seat. Behind him the* OPRICHNIKS *stand with swords upraised, their blades gleaming in the candlelight. Link on the motion as* IVAN *turns towards the left and raises his hand, fingers spread. (Still on page 223)*

IVAN: . . . who dare to oppose from without the greatness of Russian might. *He sits down on his chair, his two hands resting on the arms, and gazes firmly towards camera.*

*Shot 728. Medium close-up of* IVAN, *seated, gazing towards camera.*

IVAN: We will not let Russia be abused!

*The music comes to a climax. Fade out.*

*Fade in and dissolve on a series of credits of cast and technicians. The music finishes as the words 'The End' appear on the screen.*

# A NOTE ON PART III

Eisenstein died while he was working on the shooting script of this third episode. Some 800 meters had been filmed, consisting mainly of scenes from the first episode which had been discarded during editing in anticipation of the projected Part III. As usual he also made numerous sketches in order to outline his intentions to those working with him. All that is definitely established is the scenario, which is more of a continuity with dialogue than a technical shooting script. This has been scrupulously adhered to, apart from the typographical layout. Eisenstein often starts a new paragraph, even cutting words in the middle, and we cannot be certain that all these fragments of sentences were in fact meant to correspond to different shots. The first two parts of the film do nothing to confirm this.

So far as historical sources are concerned, it should be pointed out that the author has drawn considerably on the abundant correspondence between Ivan and Kurbsky. Although enemies since the prince's defection (see Part I) the two men wrote to each other frequently and at length.

The first scene of Part III is situated at the Castle of Wolmar where Kurbsky is planning the revolt of Pskov and Novgorod. (The ferocious destruction of Novgorod is represented in the film by the scene in which a priest reads out all the names of the dead, which was based on historical fact.) It ends, not with Ivan's death, but with that of his friend Malyuta, wounded in the course of the long war in the Baltic Provinces. Their arrival at the sea and the victory on which the film ends are an historic transposition. Ivan lost the wars of the Baltic Provinces, and it was Peter the Great who realised his ambition of reaching the shores of the Baltic (Treaty of Nystadt, 1721). It must be added, moreover, that Ivan, who was a wily diplomat, had curious and somewhat uneasy dealings with Queen Elizabeth I, and at one time sought the hand of her niece (who according to historians was extremely ugly).

# IVAN THE TERRIBLE

## Part III

### Ivan's Struggles*

*In the Castle of Wolmar, heavy grey stone vaults transfix each other, frozen for eternity in a stony embrace, like mortal enemies. They support the heavy stone device, representing an heraldic animal, which dominates the Castle. A whisper floats up from below. It is the voice of* Prince Kurbsky *as he crouches over a parchment.*

Kurbsky *off*: You are right, Ivan, you are undeniably right! Nothing can be achieved without spilling blood. No regime can be established without spilling blood . . . Kurbsky *sits upright in a sudden access of rage.* Ravening beast! . . . At last even the gaping tombs call out for God's vengeance. The stones cry out. The heavenly trumpets resound . . . on behalf of the saints you have sacrificed . . . *A pause, then giving an order*: Write! . . . No, wait!

*The young Italian scribe* Ambrosio *stops writing and glances*

---

*There is no definitive title for this third part. According to articles that Eisenstein had written, he was thinking of calling it by the title used here.

227

*interrogatively at* KURBSKY. KURBSKY *speaks thoughtfully.*

KURBSKY : You are right, Ivan. If I'd sat on your throne I'd have done just the same. *Grinding his teeth.* But why should you and not I be covered with glory in tracing out the path of a great cause? . . . *He groans.* As for me, I lick the dust before the majesty of your splendour.

KURBSKY *sits on the trunk which contains the parchments. His voice is a hollow croak.*

KURBSKY : Why aren't these the hands which are building the great cause? *In a despairing cry.* Write . . . ' Murderer, monster, emissary of hell! ' *He does not believe his own cruel words, but shouts furiously.* Write! . . . ' You plunge Moscow into the shadows. You submerge her in a sea of blood! You pollute the Russian soil! . . .' *Shouting.* A lie! *Then adding in a whisper.* Ivan, you are great . . . *He goes up to* AMBROSIO *and hugs his slender shoulders.* AMBROSIO *feels the heat of his breath. It is not to the latter but to himself, not to himself but to the whole world, that he wants to unravel his thoughts, that he says despairingly* : You must understand him, Ambrosio. His task is not an easy one; he bears an overwhelming weight. All alone, abandoned by his friends! *He is carried away by his own words.* He shines transcendantly through all the blood he spills . . . He soars like God above a sea of blood : out of this blood he is fashioning something which will endure. Out of this blood he is founding a new cause : he is creating the Russian State.

AMBROSIO, *astonished, raises his head and asks* KURBSKY : If the Tsar of Moscow is so great why aren't you, Prince Kurbsky, at his side? . . .

*The question is scarcely audible but, in the soul of the traitor prince, the words roll like thunder, as if the vaults of the Castle of Wolmar were crumbling in his heart.*

KURBSKY : Why? I don't even know myself!

KURBSKY *suddenly hurls himself down on the couch. His blond curls sink into the cushions. The vaults loom heavily. They transfix each other like enemies in mortal combat . . . They are frozen throughout eternity in a stony embrace.*

*Under the vaults, the sound of hurried footsteps.*

AMBROSIO *shouting* : Prince! . . . KURBSKY *lies motionless.* Prince! KURBSKY *raises a heavy eyelid, his gaze is troubled, his curls tangled.*

AMBROSIO *still crying out* : A courier from Moscow has come for you.

> KURBSKY *leaps up, quick as an arrow, and throws himself on* AMBROSIO.

KURBSKY : Is it possible that the Tsar has pardoned me? That he is summoning me to Moscow? . . .

> *Rigid as a bar of steel, he squeezes* AMBROSIO *in nervous anticipation. A Polish cross glitters on his chest. His face sets in a frozen mask. His features turn pale for it is not the envoy of the Tsar who enters but the* BOYAR PENINSKY, *the envoy of* EUPHROSYNE STARITSKY. KURBSKY *hurls himself like a wild beast on the boyar.*

KURBSKY *crying out* : You? *Insulting him in Polish.* Dog's blood! *Mixing Russian and Polish insults.* Dog of hell! Devil's excrement!

> PENINSKY *trembles.* KURBSKY *shouts louder and louder.*

KURBSKY : Why are you shilly-shallying? You want to ruin me? You want to shame me in the eyes of Sigismund? What has held up the revolt? It's time to stir up the towns. What is Pskov waiting for? . . . And Novgorod? . . . It's time to tear apart Ivan's Russia!

PENINSKY *stammering* : The towns are ready. Pskov is ready. Novgorod is ready. All that is lacking is the courage. Everyone is frightened of the Tsar. Everyone fears retribution.

KURBSKY : This will be the signal : the moment the Tsar dares raise his hand to the free towns, march on Novgorod . . . sound the alarm throughout the whole of Russia, light the fires of revolt in all the corners of Russia . . . Fall back on Lithuania! *Calling.* Heinrich Staden!

> *A German knight appears before him: a sensual mouth, faded, flaxen hair. Rusty armour. He looks like a moulting eagle. A face swollen like an alcoholic's. Pouches under the eyes which are grey-blue, steely, cruel and empty. The cold grey of his eyes seems to reflect forever the frozen North Sea.* HEINRICH STADEN *has wide shoulders. He is powerfully built. His arms are long, his hands claw-like. His fists are covered with red hair and freckles. (Still on page 224)*

KURBSKY : You must infiltrate the ranks of the oprichniks . . . You'll pull the wool over the eyes of the whole brigade of devils. And send us information about the Tsar's armies.

229

KURBSKY *takes a purse filled with gold from a casket and hands it to* STADEN, *then rushes to* AMBROSIO, *shouting.*

KURBSKY : Write to Sigismund : ' The hour has come to strike ! '

*Inside* IVAN's *library: a door opens into the subterranean chamber.* MALYUTA *hurries in.* PETER VOLYNETS *follows. The shelves are full of books: Cicero, Titus, Livy, Suetonius.* FYODOR BASMANOV *and* IVAN's *confessor,* EUSTACE, *are standing.* EUSTACE *flicks absently through the pages of Aristophanes.* IVAN's *voice is heard, dictating.*

IVAN *off* : ' Aren't you ashamed, Kurbsky, to call scoundrels martyrs without asking yourself for what reason this one or that one has been punished? ' . . . *He continues, very sombrely.* ' And how can one help comparing you, Kurbsky, to Judas? '

*A pause. The* SCRIBE *stops writing. Without looking at anyone,* IVAN *crosses to his chair. His dull eyes appear fixed on some invisible spot.* PETER *throws himself to his knees before* IVAN. MALYUTA *whispers in* IVAN's *ear.*

MALYUTA : He wants to speak . . .

IVAN, *from his chair, glances at* PETER. *His eyes become attentive. It is evident that* IVAN *has been awaiting this moment, both from the triumphant look that* FYODOR *gives* IVAN, *and* IVAN's *satisfied look in reply.* PETER, *however, weeps at the* TSAR's *feet and returns to him a sum of money.*

PETER : I am not worthy to keep it. I have sworn no oath. I have concealed the truth from you, Tsar . . . Punish me, Tsar, I am unworthy . . .

*As tenderly as a loving father,* IVAN *consoles him and gives him water, then listens attentively.*

PETER : I shall conceal nothing about the crime. There was not one murderer but three . . . as an icon of the Blessed Virgin is often a triptych. Three hands were involved in this assassination . . . IVAN *leans towards* PETER *who continues speaking.* A foreign hand incited treachery. Another preached it. The third placed the knife in my hand . . . IVAN *leans further forward.* The first hand was Kurbsky's . . .

IVAN *groans in his distress and raises his eyes to heaven.*

IVAN : Andrew . . . Andrew ! . . . What else could you have wanted? Could it be my crown that you coveted?

230

PETER *continuing*: The second hand is Pimen's!

*IVAN sits bolt upright in his chair.*

IVAN: Pimen! He presided over the tribunal which condemned Philip to death!

PETER *continuing*: The third hand was Philip's. He was in league with Pimen . . . he carried out the suggestions of Pimen. It was he who, in the cathedral, convinced me by his impassioned arguments.

*IVAN continues to sit stupefied. His head falls forward on the table.*

IVAN *groaning*: Philip . . . Philip! . . . My last, my only friend . . .

PETER *continuing*: That's not all. Both the towns of Pskov and Novgorod were with Pimen in this plot.

*MALYUTA pricks up his ears. FYODOR draws closer. EUSTACE crosses himself.*

PETER: Pskov and Novgorod having combined with Pimen, the military chiefs and boyars are breaking with Moscow to join the Livonians.

EUSTACE: That's a lie.

*He shouts this out in a frenzy. The TSAR glances towards EUSTACE. A glitter of suspicion appears in the TSAR's eye.*

PETER *replying*: The proof is a sworn statement: the agreement between Pimen and Kurbsky with Poland and Livonia is concealed in the cathedral of Saint Sophia, behind the icon of the Blessed Virgin . . . a triptych!

*Struck to the heart by the treachery of his friends, IVAN, seated, leans forward on the table. In a scarcely audible whisper he addresses EUSTACE.*

IVAN: What should I do, father?

*With unexpected force and ferocity, the tiny priest replies.*

EUSTACE: Show no mercy. Novgorod must be chastised by fire and the sword.

*PETER gazes in stupefaction as he hears these direful words pronounced by a man who looks so mild and good-natured. But still more direful words follow as EUSTACE shouts like a man possessed.*

EUSTACE: Like Judas Maccabeus, like Joshua against the heathens, the Tsar must summon a crusade against Novgorod, the new Babylon! . . . So that the earth may tremble. So that the whole of

231

Russia may shudder as she sees the great sovereign punish the traitors!

*Tears of passionate conviction shine in* EUSTACE's *eyes.* FYODOR *grips his sword.* PETER *is enthralled. Only* MALYUTA *looks on incredulously as* IVAN *hugs his confessor.*

IVAN: We must organise the Novgorod campaign . . . *A smile comes to his lips.* But without a sound, without the beating of drums . . . We will march humbly and silently . . . So that no one . . . man, beast nor bird . . . can carry word to the rebel town that the Tsar, in all his wrath, is surging forward like an unleashed tempest . . . *He continues.* All links with Novgorod must be severed.

MALYUTA's *expression shows that he understands.*

IVAN: The flank-guards will go into action against the Livonians . . . FYODOR *hurries off to execute the order. The* TSAR *looks at* EUSTACE. You will stay in Moscow.

EUSTACE *looks surprised whilst* IVAN *winks maliciously.*

IVAN: Happy is he who stands apart from the council of the wicked. *More gravely still.* It is not mete that a just man be present where sins are committed. Otherwise how could a confessor hear these sins later at confession?

EUSTACE *follows the* TSAR *with a wide-eyed glance. His shining eyes fade out.*

*Fade in to a snow-covered plain. It is daytime. Skis glide silently past across the snow-covered plain. The skis glide across the snow. Detachments of oprichnik infantry advance on skis across the snow. The cavalry advances behind them. The* TSAR *rides amongst the knights.*
*Behind are left the snow-covered ruins of houses. Dead bodies lie in the snow. The skis glide across the snow . . . Novgorod sentries line the defences. The skiers approach silently. The bows rise. The arrows cleave the sky. The Novgorod sentries fall on the snow.*

IVAN *off*: So that no one . . . man, beast, nor bird . . . can bear word to the rebel town that the Tsar, in his wrath, is surging forward like an unleashed tempest . . .

*The* OPRICHNIKS *advance on the snow . . .*
*Bodies, pierced with arrows or hacked to pieces, lie stretched out on the snow. Slaughtered cattle lie around. A dog, dashing*

*away in terror, is struck by an arrow. Yelping hoarsely, the*
*dog buries its muzzle in the snow. The* TSAR'S *army glides*
*across the snow in the silence. A new face is seen among the*
OPRICHNIKS; *the German* OPRICHNIK, STADEN, *advances*

*across the snow and looks attentively about him. Arrows strike*
*down birds in flight.*

IVAN *off* : So that no one . . . man, beast, nor bird . . . can bear
word to the rebel town that the Tsar, in his wrath, is surging forward
like an unleashed tempest . . .

*The skis glide across the snow . . . The* TSAR *looks grim.*
PHILIP'S *treason weighs heavily on him. He calls* MALYUTA
*and hands him a message.*

IVAN : Go quickly to the Tver Monastery.

IVAN *looks grim against the snow-covered plain. Well in front,*
*the advance guards press forward. Suddenly the advance*
*guards see that a man has out-distanced them and is hastening*
*down a gully. The advance guards increase their pace. The*
*man runs. They pursue him . . . They pursue him in silence*
*because they are forbidden to call aloud. The bows rise. Three*
*arrows bring down the fugitive. The oprichniks advance on*
*their skis . . . The fugitive turns over on the snow, takes a*
*piece of paper from his cap and raises it to his mouth. He*
*tears off a bit in his teeth. One of the advance guards reaches*
*him and tears away the paper.* FYODOR BASMANOV *arrives, but*

*can find nothing: the fugitive is dead. The German* OPRICHNIK, STADEN, *comes up, looks attentively about him . . . The* OPRICHNIKS *advance on their skis. The skis glide across the snow. The* TSAR *looks morose.*

*Behind him stands* MALYUTA, *round-shouldered and dejected. An advance guard, on his skis, goes up to the* TSAR. FYODOR *hands the paper to the* TSAR, *murmuring.*

FYODOR: A report for Novgorod from Moscow to announce that the Tsar marches on the town. The signature has been torn off . . .

*The* TSAR *knits his brow, crumples the paper in his fist and throws it away, then gives the order to press the pace.*

*Novgorod is close: the rebel town rises up before the* TSAR. *Behind the* TSAR, *the snowy plains. The Moscow messenger lies covered with snow. Three arrows lie buried in his body . . . Novgorod at dawn. A great hall in* PIMEN'S *house. The vast apartment is feebly lit.* PIMEN *is surrounded by the* BOYARS *and captains of Novgorod. Amongst them stands the* BOYAR PENINSKY *who had visited* KURBSKY. PIMEN *of Novgorod is hardly recognisable. He seems to burn with a strange fire under his priestly robes; his impassive, waxy face shines with triumph,*

*his bony body, like the withered content of a reliquary, trembles excitedly. He has achieved his life's ambition. He has lived long enough to see his cause victorious. He rejoices in anticipation of the victory to come and speaks passionately.*

PIMEN: The hour has struck! Blessed by the emblem of the holy cross, we go into battle. We will rouse up Pskov and Novgorod. Pskov and Novgorod will bring in other towns. A message from Kurbsky has arrived: all is ready for the invasion. We don't want union with Moscow. We want to throw off the Moscow yoke and to ally ourselves with Livonia! *He goes up to one of his faithful supporters.* I have reliable agents in Moscow. If the Tsar marches on Novgorod, the news will fly from town to town, from border to border, like a flame, like a bird on the wing, like a tempest: Pskov and Novgorod will receive the Tsar armed and ready . . . *He sits down.* I await a messenger from Moscow from one minute to the next. Sent by a trusted man, a man who enjoys the Tsar's confidence. His name is . . .

*He opens his mouth to pronounce the name but stays silent . . . he cannot believe his eyes: in front of him, in the recess of the door, stands* IVAN. *Behind him* MALYUTA, *then the* BASMANOVS, *then the* OPRICHNIKS. *The* BOYARS *of Novgorod stand paralysed.*

IVAN: Arrest them!

*In a corner inside the cathedral, the wrathful face of Jehova stares out of the fresco of the Last Judgment. The heavenly Tsar carries out the Last Judgment, summons the just to Him and hurls the sinners into the flames of Gehenna. A* MONK *reads aloud in front of the choir.*

MONK: Remember, O Lord, Thy servants who died before their hour had sounded, from Adam to the present day.

*About the heavenly Tsar circles the fire: the celestial hierarchies are depicted. The flaming swords are directed downwards by the winged oprichniks of the heavenly Tsar — downwards where the sinners burn in eternal fire.*

MONK *off*: Remember, O Lord, Thy servant Vladimir Prince Staritsky . . . *The silhouette of the* MONK *stands out in the darkness.* Remember, Lord, Sister Eudoxia, known in this world as Euphrosyne Staritsky, who was drowned in the River Shaxna . . .

*The* MONK *has come to the end of one parchment. He unrolls a new list of the dead.*

MONK : Remember, Lord, the souls of Thy servants of Novgorod . . . *There follows a lugubrious list of names. The list continues interminably.* Remember, Lord, Pimen, High Lord of Novgorod, known in this world as Procopy Cherny (the Black). Kazarin and his two sons. Ishuk. Bogdan. Iohannis. Iohanna. Ignaty. Grigory. Fyodor. Istom . . . Prince Vasily . . .

TSAR IVAN *lies stretched out in the darkness under the fresco of the Last Judgment, in the corner where the flames of the eternal fire insatiably devour the sinners.* MALYUTA *stands behind him, in the background. Then the* BASMANOVS, *father and son. The German* OPRICHNIK, STADEN, *stands in a shadow. Not all the names of the executed are known, which is why, from time to time, the enumeration is interrupted by the words* : ' Their names are known to Thee, O Lord . . .'
*The* MONK'S *voice resounds above* IVAN.

MONK *off* : . . . Bakhmet. Iohannis. Bogdan. Michael. Tryphon. Artemys. Twenty members of the House of Ivanov : their names are known to Thee, O Lord . . .

TSAR IVAN *lies prostrate in the dust. He is dominated by the representation of the Last Judgement: the celestial judge sits bethroned above the clouds. Sparks shoot out of the eyes of Jehova and his grim face is full of rage . . . The sinners burn in everlasting flame at his feet. But the remorse which burns, tortures and devours the spirit of the earthly* TSAR, *the* TSAR *of Moscow, is even more terrifying than the everlasting flames. He ponders his responsibility. Sweat flows down his forehead. Tears flow from between his closed eyelids. The* TSAR *has lost weight, he looks ailing, he has aged twenty years . . .*

MONK *still reading* : Prince Peter. Nicephorus, his wife and his two sons. Simeon with his wife and his three daughters. Chizh with his wife, his son and daughter. Sumorok. Okhlop, Nechay . . .

FYODOR BASMANOV *goes up to* MALYUTA *and speaks to him.*
FYODOR : The total of those executed at Novgorod amounts to one thousand five hundred and five.

IVAN'S *lips whisper, as though he were seeking to excuse the terrible deed.*
IVAN : It's not wickedness. Not anger. Not cruelty. It is to punish

236

treason. Treason against the common cause.

*He awaits a reply from Jehovah. But the walls remain mute.
The words of the MONK ring out clearly.*

MONK : Anna, Alexis, Irene, Agatha. Xenia. Her two sons. Isaac.
The two daughters of Zachary. Glyceria. Eudoxia. Mary. The
fifteen women killed at Novgorod whose names are known to Thee,
O Lord . . .

ALEXEY BASMANOV *tells* MALYUTA : One hundred and seventy
monasteries have been destroyed . . .

*And* IVAN *hastens to explain the bloodthirsty action.*

IVAN : It's not for me. Not from self-interest. It's for the Motherland. It's not cruelty. That is how war is . . .

*He looks beseechingly to the eyes of the Eternal. The eyes of
the Eternal do not lower their gaze. Painted on the wall, they
look into the distance . . . The words of the MONK ring out
clearly.*

MONK : Dokuchay. Nicephorus. Callinicus. Parthenius. Prince
Boris. Prince Vladimir. Andrew. Prince Nikita. Three clerks. Five
ordinary men. Their names are known to Thee, O Lord.

IVAN *in anguish* : You say nothing, Celestial Tsar?

*He waits. There is no reply. Angrily, as though hurling a
challenge, the earthly* TSAR *repeats menacingly to the Celestial
Tsar.*

IVAN : You say nothing, Celestial Tsar?

*The earthly* TSAR, *with a sudden, violent gesture, hurls his
bejewelled sceptre at the Celestial Tsar. The sceptre smashes
against the flat wall. The pieces scatter. The precious stones
fly upwards. As vainly as* IVAN's *prayers. And the earthly*
TSAR *crumbles, crushed by the implacability of the Celestial
Tsar.*

IVAN : You don't reply to the earthly Tsar.

*Muttering, exhausted,* IVAN *throws himself against the wall.
The angry, painted Jehovah sits mutely on his throne above
the stars. The celestial hierarchies about him remain silent.
The sinners burning in everlasting flames remain silent.*

MONK *off* : Alexis and his wife. Vasily and his wife. Andrew and
his wife. His son Lazarus. Bogdan and his wife. Nezhdan and his
wife. Baloban and his wife . . .

FYODOR *gazes in anguished pity at the* TSAR. *He whispers in*

237

*the* TSAR'S *ear.*

FYODOR : It's hard to be a Tsar . . .

> IVAN *groans and writhes on the ground. The fire consumes
> his soul.*

MONK *off* : Molchan. Vsyachin. Gryasnov. Ivan. Polivov. Obernibesov. A visiting scribe. Nelyub . . .

> *A manservant goes up to* ALEXEY BASMANOV. *It is* DEMYAN,
> *who used to serve the* STARITSKYS.

DEMYAN : Where shall we deliver the golden icon frames from the Church of St Theodore-Stratilatos at Novgorod? To the Mint or . . . ?

BASMANOV : To the Mint. To the Treasury.

> BASMANOV *glances sideways at his son* FYODOR *whose tear-
> filled eyes never leave* IVAN. *He hears nothing . . .*

MONK *off* : The German Rop. The Lithuanian Maxim. The fisherman Korepan. The cook Moliva. The fisherman Yozh. Seventeen people in Bolshoye Ivanov. Three people in Gorodische. Their names are known to Thee, O Lord . . .

BASMANOV *adds between his teeth to* DEMYAN : You will deliver one third of the consignment to the Basmanov country estate : see that no one knows, as usual.

> *Close by a cheerful voice rings out.*

STADEN : I will buy the whole consignment. *The German comes up.* I shall pay in sables which I have . . . acquired at Novgorod !

> FYODOR *turns brusquely round and regards him fixedly.*

FYODOR : You cheat the treasury? You betray the Tsar?

DEMYAN *trying to justify himself*: Alexey Danilovich always does so.

FYODOR *turning* : I am going to tell the Tsar !

> DEMYAN *presses up against the wall in terror.* BASMANOV
> *seizes his son by the arm.* STADEN *turns pale and hisses between
> his teeth.*

STADEN : If you betray me, you will also betray your father !

> *They eye each other like two animals weighing each other up.
> They breathe each other's breath.* DEMYAN *trembles as he
> watches from a distance. A dull succession of blows interrupts
> them. They look in the direction of the sound.* TSAR IVAN
> *bangs his forehead against the flagstones in a rapid sequence
> of genuflexions. His eyes swim with blood. The blood blinds
> him. The blood enters his ears and deafens him. He sees*

238

*nothing. He straightens up, staggers, throws out his arms. He breathes deeply and looks for a support.*

IVAN : A priest, a priest . . .

*He murmurs the words through cracked lips then gets up. FYODOR lowers his gaze and turns and disappears behind a column. BASMANOV reaches after his son, his arms in the air. STADEN grins sarcastically . . . IVAN staggers down the cathedral.*

DEMYAN : As sure as God is holy, he's going to repeat everything to the Tsar !

*DEMYAN, his teeth chattering and repeatedly crossing himself, plunges into the darkness of the cathedral, whilst the camera returns to the TSAR who passes blindly in front of BASMANOV and STADEN. His face like stone, BASMANOV gazes after FYODOR. There is no fear, only sadness in his eyes. Sadness because his son is forever lost to him. STADEN gives the old man an encouraging tap on the back . . .*

IVAN *groaning* : I want to confess . . .

*Staggering, stumbling, dragging one foot after the other, he plunges through the darkness of the cathedral. He advances towards the choir, passing the indifferent MONK, and the golden door of the sanctuary, as he makes for a small door with an angel above it. The door creaks open.*

EUSTACE : Who calls on the Lord?

*EUSTACE's voice echoes clearly across from the altar.*

IVAN : The unworthy slave Ivan . . .

MONK *off* : Remember, O Lord, the souls of one thousand five hundred and five of Thy servants . . .

*A very long pause. MALYUTA stands silent, head bowed. FYODOR stands further off. They are overwhelmed by the TSAR's hard destiny . . . BASMANOV gazes motionless at his son. The MONK unrolls a new list of the dead.*

MONK : Remember, O Lord, the souls of Thy servants . . . Pimen, Patriarch of Novgorod, known to his world as Prokopy Cherny . . .

*EUSTACE leans towards the TSAR and listens. The voice of IVAN sounds from beneath his stole. His breathing is irregular. His soul is wracked by lamentation.*

IVAN : It is agonising to build a state at such a price . . .

*Blood mixed with sweat flows down his forehead. He mutters some names. The confessor's cross hangs by him.*

IVAN *continuing*: The cursed, treacherous line of the Kolychevs cruelly punished . . . EUSTACE's *cross trembles.* IVAN *continues.* Philip, the Metropolitan Bishop of Moscow, strangled in the Monastery of Tver . . .

EUSTACE *changes colour; anxiety clouds the angelic purity of his look.*

EUSTACE *whispering*: Philip? . . .

*The cross beside* IVAN *has dropped still lower.*

IVAN *continuing*: The brothers of the unworthy Philip, Andrew, Vasily, Benedict . . .

EUSTACE *demands in tones of mortal terror*: And . . . Timothy?

IVAN *raises his eyes. The question takes him aback.*

IVAN: We are looking for him.

EUSTACE *in a strangled voice*: And Michael?

IVAN *becomes suspicious; he knits his brow and pronounces each word with great distinctness.*

IVAN: We will catch him.

EUSTACE *draws aside, breathing heavily as* IVAN *continues.*

IVAN: Only the youngest can't be found.

IVAN *seizes* EUSTACE *by his cross. He drags the cross down until he is face to face with his confessor.*

IVAN: Can it be that you too belong to this accursed line? Would you not be the youngest of the Kolychevs who disappeared without trace? . . . *He goes up closer still to his confessor.* Would you not be the last born, concealed by Philip Kolychev right here in the lion's mouth? *His eyes bore into* EUSTACE. Would it not be you who sent the message to Novgorod?

*His hands reach up the chain of the cross to his confessor's throat . . . Already* EUSTACE *has sunk to his knees.* TSAR IVAN *hovers over him like a vulture.*

IVAN: Speak . . . Speak . . .

*The chain tightens about* EUSTACE's *neck. He suffocates. His voice comes in a rattle.*

EUSTACE: I shall tell all . . . *He turns towards the* TSAR's *ear and whispers, panting.* Kurbsky is waiting a signal . . . All the frontier guards are in the pay of the Livonian ambassador . . . Your own boyars will deliver you up to the enemy . . .

IVAN *furiously thrusts* EUSTACE *away. In a rage he covers his face with his hands.* EUSTACE *continues from the floor.*

EUSTACE : The conspirators include the Chancellor Mikita Funikov, Prince Afanasy Vazemsky, the commanders of the Livonian outposts, the princes Lobanov, Bychkov, Khokholkov, Rostovosky . . .

*IVAN advances on EUSTACE as one about to crush the head of a hedgehog.*

IVAN : Continue. Who else is caught up in the toils of these calumnies?

*More dead than alive, the confessor crouches on the floor. MALYUTA surges up out of the darkness. EUSTACE cowers.*

IVAN : Arrest him! Interrogate him! Make him talk! . . .

*MALYUTA seizes hold of EUSTACE. IVAN uncovers his face. His eyes shine with a new strength and purpose. He shouts at the top of his voice.*

IVAN : Fyodor!

*FYODOR BASMANOV runs forward. With a savage gaiety, IVAN gives orders.*

IVAN : Scribe, come here. *The SCRIBE comes running.* Write . . . to Kurbsky. *He adds, pronouncing with great distinctness :* You will sign the message . . . in the name of . . . Eustace!


*In Sigismund's Palace,* KURBSKY *is heard shouting.*

KURBSKY *off* : We've captured Ivan.

*KURBSKY enters and unfolds a message secretly arrived from Moscow. The representatives of the coalition against Moscow bend eagerly over the message. KURBSKY shows them the text and explains.*

KURBSKY : The Livonian frontier guards are all in our pay. The road to Moscow is wide open.

*SIGISMUND smiles wanly. His gout has worsened with the years, twisting his foot and paralysing his right arm. He cannot make any sign with his hand. But the king's smile suffices. All cry out enthusiastically.*

ALL : Hurrah!

*For no one suspects that the message is the one IVAN dictated in the preceding scene. Nor that the message is falsely signed with EUSTACE's name. But suddenly SIGISMUND is seized by doubts. Without speaking, grimacing with pain, he turns to one of his courtiers. And the COURTIER expresses the king's*

241

*thought.*

COURTIER : But England . . . ?

> SIGISMUND *indicates another* COURTIER *with his left hand and the latter rapidly formulates the king's question.*

SECOND COURTIER : Is there an alliance between Ivan of Moscow and Queen Elizabeth?

> *A merry, round-faced* JESTER *sums up the general trend of thought.*

JESTER : The king wants to know whether Redhead Bess will kick us in the . . .

> *The* JESTER *slaps his own rump, jumps on the table and places his heavy posterior on the big map laid out on the table. Seated thus on the province of Muscovy, somewhere between Lithuania and Livonia (as between two stools) the* JESTER *gives a cunning smile. Then shaking his head so that the bells of his bonnet tinkle, he takes his lute and starts to sing a ballad to Redhead Bess.*

JESTER *singing* : ' The king lost his way in the white, white fog.
                Drifted on to the British shore.
                A man set out to the royal domain.
                He took part in the wisest parleys . . .'
*The mandolines play. Dissolve.*

*In the recess of a Tudor window, in Windsor Castle, a curly-haired* PAGE *sits singing.*

PAGE : ' God alone in His heavenly heights
Knows whom Bess receives at night.
To whom she gives honey . . .
To whom she gives wax . . .
To whom she gives a sting.
And to each in turn He says :
" Redhead Bess . . ." '

*In a corner room in Windsor Castle* QUEEN ELIZABETH *of
England is holding a secret audience. Time has left its imprint
on the features of the Virgin* QUEEN. *Her clothes are ever more
sumptuous. She has powdered her face ever whiter. And this
makes her hair appear more flaming red than ever. The
favourite of the day, half hidden by the gilded lace of his
richly decorated costume, is younger than ever. The* QUEEN,
*silhouetted against her throne, resembles a gold-clad sentry
zealously on guard. The favourite of the day stands in the
semi-darkness behind her. It is not yet Essex. At this time
Essex is still almost a child. Perhaps it is Christopher Hutton or
Edward Verney. But, more probably, it is the youthful* CHARLES
BLOUNT — ' curly-headed adolescent of good figure, tender
visage, blushing scarlet when Her Majesty's glance settles on
him benevolently'. In front of the* QUEEN, *the secret*
AMBASSADOR. *His clothes are severe and it is only his round
face that enables us to recognise the man who, under the
guise of* JESTER, *interprets the wishes of the imperial German
princes at* SIGISMUND'S *court. His face is now tired and sweaty.
The* GERMAN AMBASSADOR'S *voice is hoarse and he coughs
breathlessly.*

PAGE *off* : ' Night and day a man holds forth.
A thousand marvels promises.
The man sings until he is hoarse.
Queen Bess keeps her own counsel . . .'

*It is apparent that the audience has gone on for a long time.
The knees of the* GERMAN AMBASSADOR *are sagging with tired-
ness. He contemplates with superstitious horror the statuesque
immobility of the* QUEEN, *capable of standing motionless
throughout long hours of interminable audiences. Half-fainting,
the* GERMAN AMBASSADOR *addresses the* QUEEN *for the tenth
time.*

GERMAN AMBASSADOR : The coalition against Ivan requires that England should leave its hands free. As far as Germany is concerned, the Queen must undertake to provide no obstacle to the attack on Moscow. The coalition requires that England should help the Germans. *He wipes his brow.*

PAGE *singing* : ' God alone in his heavenly heights
    Knows who is bought and who is sold
    By Redhead Bess . . .'

 ELIZABETH *gazes glassy-eyed into the distance.*

PAGE : ' To whom she gives honey . . .
   To whom she gives wax . . .
   To whom she gives a sting.
   And to each in his turn
   Redhead Bess . . .'

*The young* BLOUNT *stands beside the royal throne. An agonising pause. The mandolines strike up loudly. At last the* QUEEN *gives the long-awaited consent.*

ELIZABETH : The English regiments will go to Russia.

*As is true of all* ELIZABETH'S *decisions, this allows a double interpretation: if one wishes one can accord a contrary sense to that which the* GERMAN AMBASSADOR *wants to hear. But the exhausted* AMBASSADOR *is no longer capable of assessing the possible implications of the* QUEEN'S *reply. Delighted by these words he hurriedly leaves by a small secret door which slams behind him . . . and, unexpectedly, there bursts forth a* CHORUS *of ostlers in the courtyard, beyond the reception room of Windsor Castle.*

CHORUS : ' Raise up the icy draught, for Bess.
   Drink up, roisterers ! Beat on, ocean ! '

GERMAN AMBASSADOR : Oof !

CHORUS : ' For Good Queen Bess,
   For the devil's own Bess,
   For Redhead Bess . . .'

*The* GERMAN AMBASSADOR'S *strength ebbs. His knees sag. Friendly hands save him from falling . . . He groans.*

GERMAN AMBASSADOR : She is as artful and cunning as a demon.*
 *The* GERMAN AMBASSADOR'S *glance alights on the man who*

---

*Untranslatable pun : Bess, in Russian, means ' demon '.

has come to his aid: OSIP NEPEYA, *the ambassador from Moscow.*

CHORUS: ' Good old Bess,
        Wise old Bess.
        Bess the brazen,
        Bess the great,
        Bess the Queen of England.'

*Drunk with his success, the* GERMAN AMBASSADOR *gets up arrogantly and goes off with a mocking smile* ...

ELIZABETH *off*: Ha! Ha! Ha!

*The soldierly laugh of* QUEEN BESS *echoes through the door.* NEPEYA *looks anxiously at the door. But within, the motionless sphinx has come suddenly to life:* ELIZABETH, *with youthful verve, is just ending a phrase addressed to the young* BLOUNT.

ELIZABETH: As always the German is ready to pay with the skin of an unkilled bear. This time it's the Russian bear! ...

BLOUNT *surprised*: But your reply, your Majesty?

*In answer, the* QUEEN *herself begins to sing maliciously.*

ELIZABETH: ' God alone in His heavenly heights

Knows who is bought and who is sold
    By Redhead Bess . . .'
*She interrupts her song and exclaims to* BLOUNT.
ELIZABETH : Here's your first lesson in diplomacy.
*The* PAGE *sings in the window recess.*
PAGE : ' To whom she gives a sting,
    To whom she gives wax
    To whom she gives honey . . .'
*The* QUEEN *takes* BLOUNT'S *tender chin in her long fingers.*
ELIZABETH : ' And to each in turn . . .'
*The* QUEEN *taps* BLOUNT'S *cheek.*
PAGE *off* : ' Redhead Bess . . .'
*The* QUEEN *throws herself in an armchair and laughs un-controllably.*
BLOUNT *kissing the* QUEEN'S *hand* : Of all the merry wives of
Windsor, Bess, there isn't one your equal.
*The* QUEEN *laughs . . . and it is hard to know what she is
laughing at—the* GERMAN AMBASSADOR, *her own thoughts, or
her favourite's words which, towards the end of her reign, will
be enshrined in the title of an immortal comedy . . . But it is
more probable that the* QUEEN *is laughing for a quite different
reason. The* QUEEN *looks at* BLOUNT. BLOUNT'S *tender visage
turns scarlet. The sound of the mandolines comes from far off.
And, as if it were departing on tip-toe, the song of the* CHORUS
*fades away.*
CHORUS : ' Our Queen Bess . . .
    Redhead Bess . . .
    Bess the brazen . . .
    Bess the Queen of England . . .'
*The scene fades out. The mandolines strike up loudly. Suddenly
kettledrums ring out. Once. Twice. Thrice.*

*On the Livonian frontier, at an outpost near Rotten Marsh,
it is twilight. A patrol. A man on a tree. Another on a horse
under the tree. The guard house. Inside, the commandant,
Prince* LOBANOV-ROSTOVSKY. *Suddenly a group of* OPRICH-
NIKS *enters.* MALYUTA *is at their head. The commandant is
arrested. In the darkness the Strelitz regiments continue to
advance.*

246

*Twilight. A patrol. A man on a tree. Another under the tree on horseback. And the same thing happens as before, with the difference that here the commandant is Prince* BYCHKOV-ROSTOVSKY. *And that the* OPRICHNIKS *who arrest him are led by* ALEXEY BASMANOV.

*The Strelitz regiments advance through the darkness.*

*At an outpost near the Bitch's Bridge the same scene repeats itself. But the commandant who is seized is Prince* KHOK-HOLKOV-ROSTOVSKY, *and the* OPRICHNIKS *are headed by* FYODOR BASMANOV.

*The Strelitz regiments advance through the darkness.*

*Fade out.*

*Fade in to the* TSAR's *hall in the village of Alexandrov. It is All-Souls'-Day. The* TSAR *and the* OPRICHNIKS *wear monks' habits. Above the* TSAR *and the* OPRICHNIKS *is a fresco of forty martyred saints painted against a background of sky. They direct their gaze downwards. Their golden halos shine brightly.* FYODOR *sings. He is standing beside the lectern; the psalm book has been turned upside down; he is taking part in* IVAN's *favourite game. He sings the profane hymn to the executed in a high falsetto. The* CHOIR *sings the second part.*

FYODOR : ' Peace to their souls, Jesus,
        Now with the saints,
        Peace to the souls of the boyars, of the commandants,
        Of the traitors who hand over the Tsar's frontiers,
        In return for gold, silver and flattery . . .'

*Six pairs of brimming goblets clang dully together; the noise is like the tolling of bells.*

FYODOR : '. . . In order to build up fortunes . . .' *The goblets clang together . . .* ' and give joy to the devil.'

*Once again the goblets come together. Then twice more.*

FYODOR : '. . . Eternal repose to those who have sold the kingdom for a few pieces of silver.' *Still more clanging of goblets.* ' Who have opened the frontier to the Germans.'

*All the goblets come together.*

FYODOR : '. . . And who today dwell in heaven.'

OPRICHNIK CHOIR : ' They no longer know illness, grief, sighs, but rejoice in the life eternal . . .'

*They dance accompanied by the* CHOIR *and by the rapid clanging of the goblets.*

CHOIR : '. . . The weeping over their tombs turns to joyous singing . . . Have pity on me, Lord, have pity ! . . .'

FYODOR BASMANOV *sings louder than anyone; nevertheless he pointedly avoids the gaze both of his father and of the German* STADEN. BASMANOV's *gaze does not wander from his son.*

TSAR IVAN *sits in the middle of the table. A celestial, paradisal town is painted on the wall behind him. But the* TSAR *gazes absently, morosely, reflectively before him . . . The wild singing continues.*

CHORUS : ' Peace to their souls, Jesus,
      To the souls of the boyars, the commandants,
      The traitors
      Who burn in the flames
      Of hell,
      Who stew in pots
      Like shrimps . . .'

*Dully six pairs of goblets clang against each other, ringing out like bells.*

CHORUS : '. . . Those who have had their heads cut off . . .'
*Two goblets clang together.*

CHORUS : '. . . Those who died on the scaffold . . .'
*Two more goblets clang together.*

CHORUS : '. . . Those who rot on gibbets . . .'
*Two more goblets clang together.*

CHORUS : '. . . Those whose carrion made Moscow stink . . .'
*All the goblets clang together.*

FYODOR : '. . . Those who are going to present themselves before God . . .'

CHORUS : '. . . No longer shall they know sickness,
      Nor grief, nor lamentation,
      But taste life eternal . . .'

*The* OPRICHNIKS *dance, accompanied by the* CHORUS . . .

CHORUS : '. . . The weeping over their tombs turns to joyous singing . . .'

*. . . and by the rapid clanging of the goblets.*

*As the song gets wilder, the* TSAR's *expression becomes*

248

*grimmer. The more outrageous the words, the gloomier he becomes.*

*And suddenly the* TSAR *interrupts the song and says.*

IVAN : The cause of the oprichniks is not a subject for laughter.

*Everyone stops. The silence is scarcely broken by the clink of a solitary goblet.*

IVAN : But there are some amongst us who have traded the cause of the oprichniks for gold . . .

*The* OPRICHNIKS *huddle close together.*

IVAN *continuing* : There are some who betray the Tsar's confidence, who barter the oprichniks' holy oath . . . who turn it into coin . . .

*The emotion increases with the gathering surge of the indictment. Each* OPRICHNIK, *sitting, pale with fear, asks himself whether it is he who is being accused.* FYODOR *gazes fixedly at* STADEN. STADEN *betrays his uneasiness. He grips his sword tightly and murmurs between his teeth.*

STADEN : Have mercy, Herr Gott.

IVAN *continuing remorselessly* : There is amongst you one who is both venerable and who enjoys the highest confidence . . .

IVAN *looks before him, but the* OPRICHNIKS *gaze first at each other then, little by little, they all look in the same direction.*

IVAN : And this wretch has betrayed my confidence. He has betrayed the Tsar. Till the end of time he has dishonoured the cause of the oprichniks by his greed . . .

*All eyes come to rest on the same place. All eyes gaze at* ALEXEY BASMANOV. BASMANOV *does not see the glances fixed on him. He looks stonily down at his goblet. The* TSAR *also looks at* BASMANOV, *then turns away.* BASMANOV *gets up suddenly.* FYODOR *turns.* BASMANOV *looks at his son.*

BASMANOV *murmuring* : Can it be . . . my son?

FYODOR *says nothing and does not look at his father.* BASMANOV *turns to the* TSAR *with the intention of justifying himself, but suddenly he perceives that there is a tray by the* TSAR'S *elbow. There are grapes on the tray. The* TSAR *takes a grape and puts it in his mouth. But the tray is held by the former serf of the Staritskys,* BASMANOV'S *one-time assistant,* DEMYAN TESHATA. DEMYAN *smiles cunningly.* BASMANOV *stops short and sighs.*

BASMANOV: It's not my son . . . Thank God!

*Quietly he leaves the table, stops in the middle of the hall and bows his head. For the first time the son looks at his father. His features are grief-stricken. His father does not observe this fact; he stays where he is standing, head lowered. The Tsar's glance passes interrogatively across those present.*

IVAN: Who is worthy enough to cut off so wise a head?

*Every gaze remains lowered. Only MALYUTA looks at IVAN. IVAN's scrutiny passes sadly across the faces of the OPRICHNIKS.*

IVAN: You do not hold to your oath.

*His eyes rest on FYODOR whose head is lowered . . . FYODOR feels the TSAR's gaze on him. Despite himself he raises his head to look the TSAR right in the eyes. The TSAR subjects FYODOR to a bitter test: with a scarcely perceptible movement, he nods his head . . . FYDOR leaves the table, goes up to his father and leads him off. In passing he glances at STADEN who realises that his own life is worth no more than that of BASMANOV, and that that life is coming to an end. Under FYODOR's gaze STADEN loses his composure. FYODOR turns*

*and takes out his father. They leave. DEMYAN follows them, his eyes smiling . . .*

IVAN *spits out between his teeth*: The traitor must be thrown to the dogs.

*Darkness. The BASMANOVS stand in the dark. Father and son. They are silent, then the father speaks.*

BASMANOV: Don't be distressed. I was tempted. I am guilty. I've been caught. So much the worse for me. Let it be a lesson to you.

250

Let me kiss you before I die!

*He hugs his son and suddenly whispers passionately in his ear.*

BASMANOV *very quietly*: I have piled up whole mountains of gold. I was keeping it all for my son . . . FYODOR *looks perturbed as his father continues.* For you alone I weighed down my soul with sin. I betrayed my oath. Not for me, but for you. I was suffering because I had lost you. I only sacrificed myself for you.

FYODOR *terrified*: But was it not a sin? A betrayal? Isn't that why you are going to die by my own hand?

BASMANOV *with passion*: Death doesn't scare me. So long as our line continues . . . in order that my great nephews, my great great nephews, my grandsons and great grandsons may enrich themselves and multiply, so that through them I shall live forever. Guard the Basmanov treasure carefully to that end, so that my sons, grandsons, great grand-nephews will rival the descendants of the Tsar. So that my gold after my death may raise me to the level of Ivan. Who knows which of us will prevail? Who knows which line will last the longer? Which tree will outgrow the other in the centuries to come?

> FYODOR *listens to these seditious, tempting words. They do not leave him unmoved. The father sadly but eagerly stares into the eyes of his son, a last, lingering look before he dies. He hears the echo of his own blood, pulsing in that of his son, but he also perceives the hesitation . . . As if the terrible oath of the oprichniks were echoing in the air, preventing him from making the decision . . . And the father takes his son's white neck in his powerful hands, the hands of a BASMANOV.*

BASMANOV: I shall strangle you . . . I shall curse you as I am dying if you don't break the terrible oath!

> FYODOR'S *hand gropes at the breast of his father. His eyes gaze into the far distance of the years to come. He repeats dully through bloodless lips the oprichnik oath which he is betraying.*

FYODOR: 'Renounce kith and kin, forget father and mother . . .'

> *His fingers grope towards the cross that his father wears about his neck.*

BASMANOV: Swear that you will preserve everything from going to Ivan's descendants. Swear that you will keep everything for the descendants of the Basmanovs!

> FYODOR'S *eyes grow dim as he suffocates under the pressure of*

251

*his father's hands.*

FYODOR *muttering*: I swear!

*He kisses the cross on his father's chest. With this inhuman kiss the* BASMANOVS *take leave of each other.*

BASMANOV: I am freed from a great weight.

FYODOR *firmly*: The Tsar is waiting, we must make an end.

BASMANOV: I am going to pray. Finish me off as I pray . . . the same way that we executed the traitor Turuntay-Pronsky . . . Give me the blow that I taught you at Kazan.

*He turns, bares his neck, lowers his head, stretches it forward, murmurs a prayer.* FYODOR'S *sword flashes in the darkness and with one stroke severs the grey head of* ALEXEY BASMANOV.

*In the Great Hall the door is closed. On this door the German* STADEN *has fixed his haggard gaze. The hilt of the German* OPRICHNIK'S *sword trembles in his hand. Ivan, in a state of mounting tension, gazes tormentedly at the door. At last the door opens and* FYODOR *reappears: his head is bowed, his hair sticks to his forehead. He raises his head.* IVAN *looks him straight in the eye. But already the gaze of* FYODOR *is impure; it cannot withstand that of* IVAN. *The* TSAR'S *lips twitch as he speaks hollowly.*

IVAN: You showed no pity to your father, Fyodor. Why should you pity or defend me?

FYODOR *grasps that the* TSAR *has divined the secret talk between him and his father . . . he tries to frame a reply: too late. A curt order is rapped out.*

IVAN: Arrest him!

*Like a madman* FYODOR *tries to throw himself on the* TSAR. *With a single bound,* STADEN *intervenes and thrusts his dagger through* FYODOR'S *breast.*

*The curved silhouette of* IVAN *sinks back into his chair.*

IVAN: That is the end of the Basmanovs.

FYODOR *lies motionless. His glassy gaze stares upwards at the halos of the forty martyrs, who look down at the dying man.*

*A single tear rolls down the grey beard of* TSAR IVAN. *It remains suspended on the point of his beard like a raindrop on a funeral wreath.*

IVAN: Have pity on me, O Lord, have pity . . .

*A bell rings feebly. The ringing stops. Suddenly the eye of the dying man brightens.* FYODOR, *at the end of his strength, raises himself on an elbow. With his last atom of strength he tries to tear himself from the grip of death, in order to accomplish his last supreme duty.*

FYODOR : Do not trust the German, O Tsar ! . . .

*His curly head falls back. He is dead.* FYODOR *lies on the floor, a fallen angel in his black robe, which unfolds like a pair of wings upon the flagstones. The* TSAR *raises his heavy eyelids; his gaze stops on the German,* STADEN.

IVAN : How promptly the foreign guest comes to the defence of the Tsar against his own oprichniks !

*The heavy hand of* MALYUTA *falls on* STADEN's *shoulder. His teeth chattering,* STADEN *tries to free himself, but the hand which grasps him is heavy, and the hold does not loosen. Suddenly we hear a sound behind the door. Everyone turns around as a* MESSENGER *comes rushing in.*

MESSENGER : The Livonians are coming !

*They all rise, forgetting everything else.* IVAN's *eyes shine as he mutters between his teeth with savage joy.*

IVAN : You are caught, Prince Andrew Mikhailovich !

MALYUTA : We've got Kurbsky !

IVAN *shouting* : Forward !

*They shed their black robes, revealing the shining gold of their kaftans beneath. The swords, drawn from their sheaths, glitter.*

ALL *shouting* : On to Livonia !

MALYUTA *calling out* : To the Baltic sea ! *(Still on page 224)*

*The Russian countryside. It is daytime. Already the dazzling Russian cavalry is galloping towards the frontier. The song follows the galloping cavalry.*

CHOIR : ' Oceanic sea,
    Blue sea, blue sea,
    Beloved sea . . .'

*The banners of the* TSAR *shine brightly in the burning sun. The* OPRICHNIKS *gallop on their horses, the gold of their kaftans glittering.*

CHOIR : ' The Muscovite army rises
    Like a threatening cloud

253

It goes towards the seas
To conquer its birthright.'
*Each rider loudly beats the small drum fastened to his saddle,
and the noise urges the horses onward.*

CHOIR : ' Oceanic seas,
Conquered with spears
So that the ships
Can sail everywhere . . .'

*TSAR IVAN and MALYUTA gallop onward at the head of the
regiments. The riders hug their mounts closely, so that each
man and his horse seems to be cast in molten lead.*

CHOIR : ' Oceanic sea,
Blue sea, blue sea,
Russian Sea ! '


*The tent of KURBSKY at night. The tent is sumptuously
decorated. Tapers burn in candelabras. Flat plates and dishes
lie scattered about, along with cannon balls, kegs of powder,
fine weapons and rich armour. Military maps are strewn on a
low table, mixed up with playing cards and dice, as though
mingling the folly of games of chance with games of strategy.
The cards and the dice are appropriate in the context of this
mad march on Moscow.*

*The GERMAN AMBASSADOR who was in England at the audi-
ence with QUEEN ELIZABETH comes running into KURBSKY's
tent. The folly of the march on Moscow becomes even more
apparent.*

GERMAN AMBASSADOR : The Muscovite has caught us in a trap :
Redhead Bess is on his side !

KURBSKY *furious* : The red-headed witch has deceived us? We must
retreat immediately.

GERMAN AMBASSADOR *shouting* : We must attack ! We must fly
to Moscow as swift as the lightning. The road is open; we have
bribed the frontier posts.

KURBSKY *pathetically, going down on one knee* : Hail to the Most
High. *He raises his arms and cries out.* My beloved fatherland :
take the son who adores you into your arms; he is sending enemy
regiments against his own country. To Moscow !

*The trumpeters raise the trumpets to their lips. They do not even have time to blow; the dull roar of cannon fire rents the silence. More cannon fire. KURBSKY is aghast.*

*The trumpeters lower their trumpets. We hear the sound of artillery fire in the distance. A MESSENGER runs in.*

MESSENGER: We were fired upon at the frontier post at Rotten Marsh!

KURBSKY *furious*: You lie!

*Another MESSENGER runs in.*

SECOND MESSENGER: We were fired on at the frontier post at Crooked Stream!

*KURBSKY's rage increases as he yells.*

KURBSKY: A lie!

*A THIRD MESSENGER runs in and falls to the ground.*

THIRD MESSENGER: A vast Russian army lies by the Bitch's Bridge!

*The GERMAN AMBASSADOR rushes out of the tent. KURBSKY, foaming at the mouth and too overcome with rage to speak, hurls himself on the MESSENGER who is lying before him, pulls him to his feet and shakes him furiously.*

*From the crest of a hill Russian gunners fire incendiary shells at the tent. The brothers FOMA and YEROMA CHOKHOV command a battery. Bearded, in their uniforms, they are a fine-looking pair. We recognise some old cannons among the new ones: The ' Nightingale ' cannon, the ' Lion ' and the ' Bold '. They are an imposing pair, the two bearded CHOKHOV brothers, FOMA and YEROMA. And, as always, their eyes shine, full of youth and zest, as they make jokes as they used to at Kazan.*

FOMA: We're old men, the two of us . . .

YEROMA: But behind our cannons we're as young as ever!

FOMA: Foma aims the ' Nightingale '!

YEROMA: And Yeroma aims the ' Bold '!

*The gunners laugh. The cannons fire their salvos.*

*In his rage, KURBSKY hurls the MESSENGER back onto a pile of plates. Suddenly, a cannon ball carries away the roof of the tent. We see the camp in flames. KURBSKY only barely succeeds in escaping from the tent. An incendiary shell lands inside the tent. MALYUTA bursts in, astride his horse, accompanied by*

PETER VOLYNETS. *The tent is empty. We hear the hissing of a cannon ball.* MALYUTA's *horse tramples the playing-cards and the maps under his large hoof, and we see from both that the game is up.*

*The tent is empty; only a rich suit of armour shines in a corner.* PETER VOLYNETS *raises its visor with his pike and sees that it is empty.*

PETER : He has fled!

*He lowers his pike. The gilded armour topples and falls to the ground, clanging like an empty bucket. The armour rolls to* MALYUTA's *feet.*

MALYUTA : Don't dawdle, Volynets! *He spurs on his horse.* We must catch him!

*The tent bursts into flames. The smoke rises in a black column to the sky.* MALYUTA *has gone.* VOLYNETS *has a hard time catching up with him.* TSAR IVAN *gallops forward with the cavalry across a backdrop of flames. His hair flies in the wind. His nostrils are dilated and his eyes shine.*

IVAN : We will mercilessly drive the Germans out of our land, as did our glorious ancestor, Alexander Nevsky.

*The* TSAR *looks twenty years younger as he gallops past the flames with his cavalry.*

*The Castle of Wolmar. It is night. Darkness. We hear the sound of firing.* SERVANTS *pass, carrying torches and crying out.*

SERVANTS : The Russian is coming!

*They leap over a large bed, running for their lives. On the bed,* KURBSKY *awakens. He sits up, horrified, and flees, half-naked.*

*The Russian cavalry gallops along the road to Wolmar.*

TSAR IVAN *enters the Castle of Wolmar.* MALYUTA *and* PETER VOLYNETS *are with him.* IVAN *cries out joyously.*

IVAN : The German cities are not prepared for warrior combat. They prefer to bow their haughty heads!

*Even more joyously,* IVAN *dictates the end of another letter to* KURBSKY.

IVAN : Where in Wolmar did you think, Kurbsky, that you would be able to find repose? Now, for your greater misfortune, God has led us there and, with His help, we have chased you out.

> *Livonian* PEASANTS *enter the room, dragging the German* OPRICHNIK, HEINRICH STADEN, *behind them; he tries to resist. The* PEASANTS *throw themselves down on their knees before* IVAN.

IVAN : What is it?

PEASANTS : He pillaged our belongings; he set fire to our salt-meats.

> STADEN *tries to justify himself.* IVAN *goes up to him, furious.*

IVAN : We have not come as conquerors, but to recover our ancestral lands. *To the* PEASANTS. Who are you?

PEASANTS : We are tenant farmers of the Order of Livonia.

> *They stretch out their calloused hands to the* TSAR.

IVAN *giving an order* : Distribute seed to them. Let them plough the earth which is ours forever. Let them plough the Russian soil!

> *The* PEASANTS *rush up to* IVAN *and surround him. This is too much for* STADEN *who spits out a curse and jumps out of the window. The* PEASANTS *run after him to catch him. The sound of their flails rings out in the air . . . And* IVAN *dictates to the* SCRIBE *the rest of his letter to* KURBSKY.

IVAN : 'Written on our native Livonian soil, in the city of Wolmar, year 7086 (1577).'

> *On the road to Weissenstein. The cannons advance.* FOMA, YEROMA *and* MALYUTA *gallop ahead. The Russian cavalry rides onward. The 'Wolf', the 'Lion' and the 'Basilisk' cannons are dragged up a crest and set up there.* FOMA *and* YEROMA, *bearded and impressive in their uniforms, call out to each other.*

FOMA : See how Foma aims the ' Lion ' !

YEROMA : And Yeroma the ' Basilisk ' !

> *The ' Basilisk ' gives a great* Boom, *fired by* YEROMA.

> *The Castle of Weissenstein at dawn: in the great Gothic hall the sound of artillery fire is heard in the distance. The sound of the cannons grows closer. An enormous chandelier trembles; it is made out of antlers, with a golden Madonna in the centre.* KASPAR VON OLDENBOCK *stands before a table. (It was*

KASPAR *who, many years ago, went as ambassador to the young* IVAN. *We remember him from the prologue.)*

*Now,* OLDENBOCK *has aged and is deadly pale. He is surrounded by knights, a chaplain, army officers, anxious ladies and, some distance away,* PRINCE KURBSKY.

OLDENBOCK : It is impossible to fight against the barbarian. He leads Tartar as well as Russian regiments. Our own slaves, the Estonians, the Latvians and the Lithuanians are fighting on his side. The workers of Wolmar have given up their livestock to him. They gave him grain at Wenden. Everywhere, they await the Muscovite barbarian to recognise him as their legitimate sovereign. *Lowering his voice, he adds* : Our own garrison went over to the Russian side during the night.

KURBSKY : Death to the deserters.

*There is general movement. Everyone gets up.* KURBSKY, *even paler than* OLDENBOCK, *cries out.*

KURBSKY : We must flee ! We must flee ! There is no army stronger than the Russian army.

*A sarcastic voice calls out.*

VOICE *off* : The deserter prince knows this well since the battle of Revel !

*Near the table, we see the unfortunate fat* GERMAN *who went as ambassador to* QUEEN ELIZABETH. KURBSKY *leaps up and is about to throw himself on him when . . . we hear the deafening sound of nearby cannon fire.* KURBSKY *recognises the cannon and raises his head.*

KURBSKY : That's the ' Nightingale '. *Second round of cannon fire.* The ' Lion '! *Shouting.* The ' Wolf '. The ' Singer '. The ' Bold '! Ivan's favourite cannons. *In a paroxysm of rage, he yells* : That means the Terrible is near ! *Another round of cannon fire.* ' Basilisk '!

*We do not know if this last exclamation is a reference to the cannon or to the* TSAR. *General confusion. Some people fall on their knees. The ladies, on their knees, begin to pray, invoking Christ and the Madonna.* KURBSKY *cries out hysterically.*

KURBSKY : We must flee while there is still time !

OLDENBOCK : Honour forbids us escape through flight. *Explaining to the* GERMAN AMBASSADOR. Our former slaves would hang us. *He goes up to a small concealed door and opens it.* He who has no

258

honour can flee . . .

> *A pause. All look at* KURBSKY. *We hear the dull roar of cannon fire.* KURBSKY *runs to the door. The clanking of his spurs fades away in the distance.*

VOICES : What about us?

> OLDENBOCK *makes a sign to the musicians. The orchestra strikes up and starts to play deafeningly in an effort to drown the increasingly loud sound of cannon fire.*

> KURBSKY *comes rushing out of a small gate. A* SERVANT *is holding his horse.*

KURBSKY : Only one horse? What about you?

SERVANT : My master knew that only one horse would be required.

> KURBSKY *strikes the* SERVANT *with his riding crop and disappears, jumping over some bushes. The* SERVANT *goes back into the castle by the small gate and operates a lever which conceals the entrance with stones.*

> *The knights and officers, frantic because all is lost, rush over to the ladies. Beer runs in rivers. Everyone starts dancing wildly. We hear the sound of cannon fire and of battering rams. The orchestra plays on. The people in the hall shudder and come to a standstill, listening. During this pause, we hear the dull thudding of the battering-ram as well as the roar of cannon. The hysterical dancing starts again.*

> OLDENBOCK, *followed by the* GERMAN JESTER-AMBASSADOR, *goes over to the secret door.*

OLDENBOCK : And we . . . we shall go and pray to the Almighty.

> *Accompanied by the* GERMAN AMBASSADOR, *he goes down a stone staircase leading to the cellars. They enter an underground chapel. Sound of the battering-rams in the distance.*

> *Dancing in the great hall. The battering rams strike. Dancing. The Russian trumpets call on the Russian troops to storm the castle.*

> IVAN *sends three captains to lead the army in its assault.*

> *Furious,* MALYUTA *bites his fingernails, horribly jealous. The trumpets sound. The Russian captain leads the assault.*

> *In the cellars; we hear the muffled sound of the Russian troops storming the castle . . .* OLDENBOCK *lights a fuse with a torch.*

*The castle is being stormed.*
*The dancing continues.*
*An explosion. A wall collapses.*
*The dance comes to a stop.*

OLDENBOCK *looks delighted. The* GERMAN *trembles.*
*The dance starts up again, more wildly than ever. The trumpets ring out. The trampling of horses can be heard. The dance continues.*
*The battering rams crash against the wall. Two* RUSSIANS, *whom we first encountered at the seige of Kazan, rhythmically operate the battering rams. The noise of the dancing and the music are heard. One* RUSSIAN *speaks to the other.*
RUSSIAN: We would have really caught it from the Tsar if we'd defended the castle like that!
*A footstep is heard.* OLDENBOCK *lights the second fuse*
*The army mounts the assault.*
*The dance continues. The battering rams crash.*
OLDENBOCK, *tense and watchful, listens. There is an explosion. The hall collapses. The army falls back. A wing of the army swings back on its axis.*
OLDENBOCK, *satisfied, falls to his knees before the altar.*
*The army retreats.*

*It falls back to where* IVAN *is standing. He is furious.*
IVAN *shouting*: Forward!
   *In his rage he wrenches the royal standard from* PETER
VOLYNETS *and hurls himself into the middle of his troops.*
MALYUTA *rises to block his way like a wall of stone.*
MALYUTA: Your job is to construct the State, not to rip your guts
out on a powder keg. *He falls to his knees.* I shall go myself. I've
waited for this honour for twenty years. Give me the standard!
   IVAN *reflects: the army, demoralised by the explosions, has
flocked together like sheep. He must make a decision; he hands
the standard to* MALYUTA.
IVAN: You are the last, the only one who remains to me.
   *He kisses him on the forehead and makes the sign of the cross.
Then he despatches him to the castle walls. The* TSAR'S *caress
gives* MALYUTA *wings and he lets out a great cry. The cry is
echoed by the trumpets. The* TSAR'S *standard floats on the
breeze. The army hurtles to the assault.*

   OLDENBOCK *leaps up, not believing his eyes or his ears.*
OLDENBOCK: The Russian army is returning to the attack?
   *He pulls aside the altar cloth: the altar is composed of powder
kegs. The fuse writhes on the ground like a black serpent.*

   MALYUTA *races towards the castle walls and passes from battering ram to battering ram. He does not climb over obstacles, he
flies.* PETER VOLYNETS *cannot keep up with him. The trumpets
blow. The army mounts the assault.*
   OLDENBOCK *lights the third and last fuse . . . The fuse burns.*
   MALYUTA *flies from battering ram to battering ram, urging on
the army which follows him.*
   *Suddenly a cry of despair rings out from the cellar: the*
GERMAN AMBASSADOR *has grasped what is going on. He throws
himself on* OLDENBOCK. *In mortal terror he grabs at the fuse
to extinguish it.* OLDENBOCK *grasps him in a grip of iron and
prevents him reaching the fuse. The flame runs up the fuse.*
   MALYUTA *hoists himself on the wall.* IVAN *ecstatically watches
his favourite.* VOLYNETS *cannot keep up with* MALYUTA. *He
hurries forward, staggers, lets himself be outdistanced, falls.*
   *The* GERMAN AMBASSADOR *frees himself with a cry and pushes*
OLDENBOCK *aside. He catches the fuse in his teeth, tears it*

*away and rolls on the ground with it, extinguishing it with his body.*

MALYUTA *reaches the top of the wall and cries out.*

MALYUTA: Prince Andrew Mikhaïlovich, can you hear me?

KURBSKY *gallops along beside a marsh. The sound of a gunshot. He falls from his horse and runs along the marsh like a hare.*

MALYUTA *raises high the standard.*

OLDENBOCK *takes a torch and raises his arm. The* GERMAN AMBASSADOR *sees him and throws himself on* OLDENBOCK *with a cry.*

MALYUTA *triumphantly sets up the standard on the wall.*

OLDENBOCK *strangles the* GERMAN AMBASSADOR. OLDENBOCK *hurls the torch over the* GERMAN AMBASSADOR *onto the powder kegs.*

*A third explosion—the last—rings out and the tower blows up: stones and beams fall about* MALYUTA. *The gold of the royal standard, which escapes damage, gleams in the debris.* IVAN *frantically raps out orders. He hurries with his soldiers to rejoin* MALYUTA *who, with superhuman strength, is holding up an arch. He holds the standard in his free hand and cries out for reinforcements. The* TSAR *hurries on with the army. The wall starts to crumble about* MALYUTA, *who continues to support it with one arm, brandishing the standard with the other. He calls for reinforcements with a deep groan . . . The army dashes to the assault.* PETER VOLYNETS *reaches* MALYUTA *on the ruins of the tower. The wall moves forward. It crumbles.*

MALYUTA *continues to support the wall with his arm, his knees. He hands the standard to* PETER VOLYNETS. PETER *takes it and tries to help* MALYUTA.

MALYUTA *shouting*: Don't waste time, Volynets! *The wall crumbles.* You will lose yourself and the banner! *Summoning his remaining strength, he adds*: Fly upwards, plant the standard in the sky!

*The wall falls forward with a groan and crumbles on* MALYUTA, *whose bones crack. The veins swell in his bull-like neck. His eyes bulge from their sockets. Blood flows from under his finger-*

*nails. He shouts out in agony.*

MALYUTA *shouting*: Be off, you devil's whelp! *His voice cracks.*
Love Ivan with all your might. There's no one left to protect him!

*Tears blind* VOLYNETS' *eyes as he raises the standard and
dashes up the ruin of the tower. The standard glitters in the
blue sky like a star.*

MALYUTA *looks up then collapses with the remains of the wall,
the stones and beams about him.*

VOLYNETS *has hoisted the standard.* MALYUTA *rolls down to
the ground.* IVAN *runs up and leans over him. All around
sounds the roar of the assault.* MALYUTA *looks at the standard
floating above the castle like a second sun in the sky.*

MALYUTA *mumbling*: I only regret one thing . . . I shall never see
the sea.

*IVAN stretches to his full height.*

IVAN: You will see it.

*He raises* MALYUTA *up on to a stretcher. The forests burn. The
Russians advance. The Livonians flee. All hope lost,* KURBSKY
*flees across the marsh towards the muddy wastes.*

IVAN *and* MALYUTA *are on a hilltop.*

IVAN: Do you smell it?

*Both distend their nostrils.*

IVAN: . . . the smell of salt?

*A new cavalry charge. The Russians cut the Livonians to bits.
The horsemen flee. Back on the hill,* IVAN *and* MALYUTA.

IVAN: Do you hear?

*Above the music of the battle can be heard the regular beating
of the waves.*

MALYUTA: I hear . . .

*Standards fall at* IVAN's *feet. The cannons roar.* FOMA *stands by
the cannons.* YEROMA *leads the cavalry charge. Above the
galloping hooves, the shouting and the trumpets, can be heard
the regular beating of the waves and thunder of the sea which
is no longer far away . . . Already* IVAN *and* MALYUTA *have
reached the dunes.* MALYUTA *is at the end of his strength.
Everything grows quiet.* MALYUTA's *eyes have shut. And* IVAN
*murmurs softly to him.*

IVAN: Do you see it?

*Far off is a narrow strip of the Baltic. The water is covered with foam.* MALYUTA *raises himself, opens his eyes wide and cries out.*

MALYUTA : I see it!

*And he dies.*

*The waves roar in reply as they rise up, come crashing down and rise once again. The trumpets echo their roar.*

*Spellbound,* IVAN *goes down to the waves, and the sea grows calm. Then gently the waves advance to lick the feet of the ruler of all the Russias.*

IVAN : Henceforth and till the sounding of the last trump, the sea will submit to the Russian State.

FOMA *looks on.* YEROMA *looks on. The old men look on. The young men look on. The Russian army looks on. And in acknowledgment of the* TSAR's *words, the Russian army raises a great cry. The trumpets ring out. The sea roars. The waves rise up.*

IVAN : We have reached the sea, and here we will stay!

*The end of the film passes across the screen and the* CHOIR *is heard singing, off.*

Choir : ' Oceanic sea,
    Blue sea,
    Blue sea,
    Russian Sea.'